Politics, pauperism and power in late nineteenth-century Ireland

Manchester University Press

Politics, pauperism and power in late nineteenth-century Ireland

VIRGINIA CROSSMAN

Manchester University Press
Manchester and New York

distributed exclusively in the USA by Palgrave

362.5809415
C 95p

Published by Manchester University Press
Oxford Road, Manchester M13 9NR, UK
and Room 400, 175 Fifth Avenue, New York, NY 10010, USA
www.manchesteruniversitypress.co.uk

Distributed exclusively in the USA by
Palgrave, 175 Fifth Avenue, New York,
NY 10010, USA

Distributed exclusively in Canada by
UBC Press, University of British Columbia, 2029 West Mall,
Vancouver, BC, Canada V6T 1Z2

British Library Cataloguing-in-Publication Data
A catalogue record for this book is available from the British Library

Library of Congress Cataloging-in-Publication Data applied for

ISBN 0 7190 7377 4 *hardback*
EAN 978 0 7190 7377 9

First published 2006

15 14 13 12 11 10 09 08 07 06   10 9 8 7 6 5 4 3 2 1

Typeset in Palatino
by Action Publishing Technology Ltd, Gloucester
Printed in Great Britain
by CPI, Bath

Contents

Acknowledgements

This project would never have been brought to completion without the support of colleagues in the history departments of Staffordshire, Keele and Oxford Brookes Universities. I am grateful to them all but most particularly to my former colleagues at Staffordshire. The decimation of a fine History department through managerial short-sightedness remains a source of deep regret. I am also grateful to the School of Humanities and Social Sciences at Staffordshire for allowing me sabbatical leave first in 1998 to undertake research in Ireland, and again in 2001. This second period of leave was extended by a research leave award from the AHRB.

In conducting the research for this study, I received assistance from the staff of the Bodleian Library Oxford, the British Library, Cork Archives Institute, the National Archives, London, the National Archives of Ireland, the National Library of Ireland, the Public Record Office of Northern Ireland, the Scottish Record Office and Wexford County Library, and I am grateful for permission to reproduce material from the collections under their care.

I have discussed the Irish poor law with friends, family and colleagues and have gained from their insights. I am also grateful to the anonymous readers at Manchester University Press, whose comments on the text have helped me to clarify my ideas and sharpen my conclusions.

Introduction

The poor laws were a fundamental component of nineteenth-century government throughout the United Kingdom. Ratepayer, pauper, poor law guardian or functionary, almost everyone had an interest in the poor law system. Administration of the system occupied politicians and officials at both local and national levels, and provides crucial insights into perceptions of poverty and welfare and of social rights and duties. But whereas historians have subjected the operation of the poor laws in England to intense scrutiny, comparatively little attention has focused on the Irish poor laws. Studies of the new English poor law of 1834 have ranged from early assessments of the character, impact and development of the workhouse system to more recent explorations of the different welfare regimes operating in the English regions.[1] Discourses and practices of poor law administration have been analysed as central elements of governance and social policy. Workhouses have been studied as institutions of moral regulation and reformation, and as sites of social and sexual degradation.[2] The political background to the introduction and operation of the new poor law has been extensively debated and the impact of political change on the theory and practice of welfare assessed.[3] Research on the Irish poor law is strikingly limited in comparison. With the exception of Helen Burke's study of the South Dublin Union which provides a useful overview of the development of the poor law system from 1838 until 1872 together with an analysis of relief practices within a major urban union, and William L. Feingold's work on the 'nationalisation' of Irish poor law boards,[4] almost all the published works on the Irish poor law focus on the years of the Great Famine (1845–50). Many of these are local studies that examine the provision of poor relief to famine victims in a particular union but make little attempt to place this within a wider context.[5] Our knowledge of a system that lasted from 1838 until 1925 is thus largely based on information about how it operated during an exceptional five-year period shortly after its introduction. This neglect has impoverished our understanding of a central element of nineteenth-century Irish history.

One of the main reasons why the Irish poor law has been overlooked as a topic for historical research lies in the apparent paucity of surviving sources. Unlike the situation in Britain where material detailing the activities of boards of guardians is supplemented by the records of the central authorities responsible for its administration, in Ireland surviving boards of guardians' records are patchy and largely limited to minute books, while the archives of the Irish Poor Law Commissioners and Local Government Board were destroyed when the Dublin Customs House was burned in 1921. However, much material does survive in local record offices, in private papers, in newspaper reports and, perhaps most significantly for the purposes of this study, in the Chief Secretary's Office Registered Papers. Buried within the latter are files of correspondence between the Chief Secretary's Office – the hub of government administration in Ireland – and the Local Government Board. Since the Chief Secretary required information on any local government matter regarded as having political significance, these files provide a unique insight into the proceedings of the Local Government Board, and the conduct of poor law administration and poor law politics.

Prior to 1898, Irish poor law boards were the only local bodies in rural areas to include an elected element. All ratepayers holding property valued at £4 or over, including women, were entitled to vote in poor law elections. Candidates for election had to meet a slightly higher property qualification. This varied from around £30 to £6 according to the rateable value of the district. Elected guardians served alongside local magistrates acting ex-officio. In the later decades of the nineteenth century, poor law elections were increasingly contested as part of the national campaign for Irish self-government. With the growing success of candidates standing for election as representatives both of the tenantry and the national movement, the dominance of poor law boards by landowners began to be eroded. As William L. Feingold demonstrated in his pioneering study of Irish poor law boards, up until the late 1870s landlords or their agents occupied the positions of chairman, vice-chairman and deputy vice-chairman on the vast majority of poor law boards. By 1886 this was no longer the case.[6] The resulting transfer in power that took place in many unions from landowners to land-holders was to produce a far more politicised and polarised poor law system.

This book explores the significance of this process for Irish politics and for the poor. One of the consequences of the change in the political complexion of boards of guardians was that some boards began to apply their own interpretations of entitlement and to redefine terms such as 'destitute' and 'able-bodied'. In so doing they were challenging the authority of central government to regulate the poor law system and the legitimacy of the poor law itself. Nationalist guardians were able to exploit the fact that under the poor law decisions were made at local level. The central authorities could prevent guardians from acting in ways that were directly contrary to poor law regulations, but they could not prevent them from granting relief to whomsoever they saw fit. By providing a different kind of welfare system from that provided by landlord-controlled boards, nationalist guardians could demonstrate their responsiveness to local concerns as well as providing local people with a taste of the practical benefits of a home rule government.

Mindful of Lynn Hollen Lees's injunction that the 'changing story of the poor laws in Britain must be told against a back-drop of ideas about poverty, work, gender, and the state, as well as about individual responsibility',[7] this study assesses ideolog-ical as well as political and administrative developments. In Ireland, as in England, the growing influence of popular repre-sentatives encouraged a shift in emphasis within the relief system away from deterrence and punishment towards assis-tance and treatment. Relationships between different interest groups – professionals and amateurs, welfare providers and welfare recipients, the respectable and the non-respectable –

reflected this shift. Through an analysis of the terms and conduct of these relationships, the following chapters explore issues of power and identity, reassess the terms of social and political citizenship operating in post-Famine Ireland, and re-evaluate the role of nationalism, class and gender in shaping Irish politics and society.

The book is organised thematically. The first chapter provides a general survey of the poor law system in the nineteenth century. The five chapters that follow examine different aspects of the system from the politicisation of poor law boards and poor law services to the role of women in poor law administration. Analysis concentrates on the 1880s and 1890s, thus encompassing the period identified by Feingold as seeing the 'nationalisation' of Irish poor law boards (1872–1886) and its aftermath. One effect of focusing on the process and consequences of politicisation is to place nationalist guardians centre stage, whilst unionist guardians in Ulster and elsewhere are largely relegated to the wings. This imbalance is partially corrected in the final chapter that addresses gender issues by way of a case study of the Clogher Board of Guardians in County Tyrone. The work ends in 1899 when poor law administration was absorbed into the new system of democratic local government established by the Local Government Act of 1898.

Notes

1 M.A. Crowther, *The Workhouse System 1834–1929: The History of an English Social Institution* (London, Methuen, 1981); Steven King, *Poverty and Welfare in England 1700–1850: A Regional Perspective* (Manchester, Manchester University Press, 2000).
2 Felix Driver, *Power and Pauperism: The Workhouse System 1834–1884* (Cambridge, Cambridge University Press, 1993); Seth Koven, *Slumming: Sexual and Social Politics in Victorian London* (Princeton, Princeton University Press, 2004).
3 See, for example, Peter Mandler, 'The Making of the New Poor Law Redivivus', *Past and Present*, 117 (1987), 131–57; Anthony Brundage, David Englander and Peter Mandler, 'Debate: The Making of the New Poor Law Redivivus', *Past and Present*, 127 (1990), 183–201; Lynn Hollen Lees, *The Solidarities of Strangers: The English Poor Laws and the People, 1700–1948* (Cambridge, Cambridge

University Press, 1998); Alan Kidd, *State, Society and the Poor in Nineteenth-century England* (Basingstoke, Macmillan, 1999).

4 Helen Burke, *The People and the Poor Laws in Nineteenth-Century Ireland* (Littlehampton, Women's Education Bureau, 1987); William L. Feingold, *The Revolt of the Tenantry: The Transformation of Local Government in Ireland 1872–1886* (Boston Mass., Northeastern University Press, 1984).

5 Some of the more valuable local studies include, Ciarán Ó Murchadha, *Sable Wings over the Land: Ennis, County Clare, and Its Wider Community During the Great Famine* (Ennis, Clasp Press, 1998); Christine Kinealy and Gerard Mac Atasney, *The Hidden Famine: Poverty, Hunger and Sectarianism in Belfast 1840–50* (London, Pluto Press, 2000); Michelle O'Mahony, *Famine in Cork City: Famine Life at Cork Union Workhouse* (Cork, Mercier Pres, 2005).

6 Feingold, *Revolt of the Tenantry*, pp. 173–80.

7 Lees, *The Solidarities of Strangers*, p. 349.

1

The poor law system in nineteenth-century Ireland

In the preface to his history of the Irish poor law, the architect of the system, Sir George Nicholls, reminded his readers that the Irish poor law was 'in its origin no more than a branch of the English law', and that while the Irish system had over time developed its own distinctive character, it remained the case that the 'the English and the Irish [poor] laws are similar in principle and identical in their objects. The aim sought to be obtained by each is, to relieve the community from the demoralisation as well as from the danger consequent on the prevalence of extensive and unmitigated destitution'.[1] As Nicholls's remarks indicate, the Irish poor law cannot be understood in isolation. It drew on the same ideas as the English system, followed similar practices and operated within a similar administrative framework. In exploring what those ideas and practices were and how that framework was constructed, my aim here is to provide not a history of the Irish poor laws, but an ideological and administrative context for the chapters that follow. Discussion begins with an analysis of the poor law system as it evolved in Ireland and moves on to examine the role of central government in overseeing the system's operation.

Poverty and pauperism

The rationale of the new English poor law of 1834 and thus of the Irish poor law derived from the perceived distinction between poverty and pauperism. Poverty was presented as an inevitable and in some ways beneficial aspect of civil society, and one that it was neither possible nor necessary to eliminate. Pauperism on the other hand derived from the choices of individuals and represented a threat to society by disrupting social and economic relationships based on the free operation of the labour market. Poverty required relief, pauperism required deterrence. This distinction built on the older idea of the deserving and undeserving poor. The deserving poor were unable to support themselves while the non-deserving chose not to work. It also linked into the concept of respectability. The respectable classes were economically independent, unless afflicted by sickness or disability in which case they fell into the category of the deserving poor. The non-respectable depended on relief, or on money obtained from immoral activities such as crime or prostitution. These concepts shaped social and political relationships throughout the United Kingdom. The deserving and respectable qualified for social, and increasingly for political, citizenship, while the undeserving and non-respectable were marginalised and excluded. Interpretations of poverty and entitlement did not remain static, however. As poor law boards became more representative of the population, so definitions of entitlement became more elastic. Applicants for relief were increasingly judged according to reputation and conduct, as well as income. Exploring the wider implications of these shifts in perception and interpretation provides one of the central themes of this study.

Poverty and poor relief were subjects of investigation and debate throughout the British Isles during the late eighteenth and early nineteenth centuries. Discussion of an Irish poor law reflected this wider debate and proposals for reform were heavily influenced by perceptions of the existing systems of poor relief in England and Scotland. While tax-based relief systems, such as that in England, attracted criticism on the grounds that the relief provided was both expensive and demoralising to the poor, the existence of poor laws was, as Joanna Innes has noted, widely believed to have helped to save England from revolution. In this political climate, state provision for the Irish poor could be advanced as a means of reducing poverty and disorder, and promoting economic and social development and political stability, so long as it followed the English model.[2]

The Irish Poor Relief Act 1838

By the 1830s, pressure was growing for the introduction of some form of national system of poor relief in Ireland. The extent of poverty was not only a pressing issue in itself, but it was also impacting on Britain. The influx of Irish migrants into British cities was thought to be depressing wages and lowering the standard of living of the British working class, whilst also threatening the health of the local population. But if all agreed that something needed to be done, there was far less agreement on what form intervention should take. In 1833 the Whig government established a royal commission on the condition of the poorer classes in Ireland, chaired by the Archbishop of Dublin, Richard Whately. After an investigation lasting three years, the commission concluded that the English workhouse system was fundamentally unsuited to Ireland. The circumstances of the two countries, the commissioners noted, 'differ widely; and legislation, we submit, should have reference to circumstances as well as to principles'.[3] Believing that one of the fundamental causes of poverty in Ireland was lack of employment, they recommended the introduction of large-scale public works, state-sponsored emigration and local provision for the sick, elderly and lunatic poor. Ministers summarily rejected these recommendations, regarding them as too complex and too expensive. In seeking to devise a means of relieving poverty rather than destitution, the commission was felt to have set itself too ambitious an assignment. They had, Russell complained, focused too much on the question of improving 'the general welfare of the country' rather than confining themselves 'entirely as to the question of the destitute classes, which was more practically put into their hands'.[4] Furthermore, they appeared to have ignored the lessons of the English poor law. For, as one of the assistant commissioners to the inquiry argued, 'if anything has been proved more decisively than another by the operation of the Poor Law Amendment Act in England, it is that the workhouse is an all-sufficient test of destitution, and that it is the only test; that it succeeds as a mode of relief, and that all other modes fail'.[5]

The decision to send the English Poor Law Commissioner, George Nicholls, to report on the feasibility of establishing the workhouse system in Ireland, reflected the government's determination to concentrate its attention on destitution rather than poverty, and its preference for an established over an untried system. Where the Whately Commission argued for state-sponsored measures to address both under-development and destitution, Nicholls maintained that economic improvement could only take place once provision for the relief of the destitute was in place. A poor law, he maintained, was necessary

> as a first step toward bringing about improvement in the habits and social conditions of the people. Without such improvement, peace, good order, and security cannot exist in Ireland; and without these, it is vain to look for that accumulation of wealth, and influx of capital, which are necessary for developing its resources, agricultural and commercial, and for providing profitable employment for the population.[6]

Nicholls concluded that the workhouse system could be successfully and advantageously adapted to Irish conditions. Limiting relief to the workhouse would provide an effective test of destitution, while the introduction of poor rates would enable property to be made liable for the relief of destitution. Such a measure, he argued, 'would serve to connect the interests of landlords and tenants, and so become a means of benefiting both, and promoting the general peace and prosperity of the country'.[7] The belief that Irish property should be made to support Irish poverty was a key factor in Russell's support for the poor law and was to unite liberal Whigs and humanist Tories behind the Irish Poor Relief Bill. Introducing the measure in February 1837, Russell presented it as a means of promoting civilization, improvement and social concord, 'showing a disposition in the state and in the community at large to attend to the welfare of all classes'. It would, he later predicted, help to unite the various classes in Ireland, 'the landlord with the peasant, the man of capital with the man who depends wholly upon his labour'.[8]

Nicholls proposed that the Irish poor law 'should assimilate in all respects as nearly as possible to that established in England, varying only in those instances, in which the different circumstances of the two countries require it'.[9] Such instances were relatively small in number, but the resultant variations

were to have a significant impact on the way the system operated. The structural framework followed the English model in
that Ireland was to be divided into unions each provided with a
workhouse in which people could seek relief. Administration of
the union was to be entrusted to boards of guardians drawn
from local ratepayers. But to take account of the greater extent of
poverty and destitution, and to prevent guardians from being
overwhelmed by demands for relief, the Irish act contained no
provision for outdoor relief. Relief could only be offered in the
workhouse and since there was to be no right to relief, guardians
were under no obligation to provide other forms of relief if the
workhouse was full. There was no law of settlement in Ireland.
This meant that whereas in England guardians were only
obliged to relieve the local poor and could forcibly remove any
applicant unable to establish 'residency' in the union to their
place of birth, in Ireland guardians were obliged to grant relief
to any destitute person, whether or not they were resident in the
union, as long as there was space in the workhouse. Clergymen,
who could and did act as poor law guardians in England, were
barred from doing so in Ireland where religious divisions were
deeper. And, to reflect the relative inexperience of Irish administrators, the Poor Law Commissioners were given greater
powers of supervision over the Irish system than they had over
the English. Most significantly, they were empowered to
dissolve any board of guardians that was failing to discharge its
duties and place the management of the union in the hands of
paid officers.[10]

   To further the aim of assimilation, Nicholls had recommended that the English Poor Law Commission should
implement the Irish act. This would promote unity of practice
and principle and would avoid the 'angry comment' that might
be excited were an Irish Commission to look to England for
experienced officials.[11] This view prevailed within cabinet
despite the pleas of the lord lieutenant, Lord Mulgrave, for an
independent central authority in Ireland. Even if the members
were English, he argued, this 'would not I believe at all excite
that morbid national feeling which would be roused by the
name of subjection to the English Board'.[12] In the event, administrative uniformity outweighed the potential insult to national
feeling. Informing MPs that the Irish act would operate under

the superintendence of the English Board in London, 'with a view to insure regularity', Russell explained that the English Commissioners had very considerable experience in the operation of the existing poor law and were therefore 'properly prepared to superintend its execution in Ireland'.[13]

Following the passage of the act in 1838, and despite warnings from the Irish under-secretary, Thomas Drummond, that he would be 'anything but popular here', Nicholls was sent to Ireland to put the act into operation.[14] Under his supervision the Irish act was implemented with notable speed if uneven efficiency. (Complaints about badly sited and poorly constructed workhouses rumbled on into the mid-1840s.) By the time of Nicholls's return to England in 1842, the whole of Ireland had been divided into 130 unions, and workhouses had been opened or were under construction in all of them.[15] In England, by contrast, 18 unions were still without workhouses twenty years after the passage of the 1834 act.[16] Despite vocal criticism of the new legislation from many landowners and some active resistance to the collection of poor rate, the erection of Irish workhouses proceeded without widespread opposition, and there was nothing to compare to the anti-Poor Law protests that disturbed parts of England well into the 1840s.[17]

The relief system established in Ireland was harsher than that in England, adhering much more closely to the principles of the New Poor Law than the English system ever did in practice. This is perhaps most apparent in relation to outdoor relief. The New English Poor Law allowed for the granting of outdoor relief to the impotent poor, while envisaging that the able-bodied would be relieved only in the workhouse. In practice, however, this strict division proved impossible to maintain. Outdoor relief remained the primary form of relief in England. The workhouse, Alan Kidd observes, 'only ever accommodated a minority of paupers'.[18] In Ireland, where there was no outdoor relief, the workhouse test operated as intended deterring all but the truly desperate from applying for relief. During the early years of the system the turnover in workhouses was high and few held anything like their full capacity. This situation was to change dramatically during the Great Famine when workhouses were filled to more than double their intended capacity.

Under the pressure of extreme distress, the rigid and inflexible nature of the workhouse system was starkly exposed. If effective famine relief was to be provided under the poor law, it was clear that reform was essential. The Poor Relief Extension Act of 1847 recognised the right to relief of the impotent poor and empowered guardians to relieve such people either within or outside the workhouse. Outdoor relief could also be granted to the able-bodied on a temporary basis if the workhouse was full. At the same time, a separate Irish Poor Law Commission was created with powers to dissolve or alter any union without the consent of guardians, and to appoint inspectors to assist in the execution of the poor laws.[19] The creation of an independent poor law commission for Ireland, Christine Kinealy suggests, 'gave official recognition to what was, in fact, already a reality'. The English commissioners had taken little direct interest in Irish affairs, 'and the two Boards had rarely communicated with each other'.[20] The poor law underwent further amendment in 1862 when workhouse hospitals were opened to sick people who were not destitute, and provision was made for the board-ing-out of orphan and deserted children up to the age of five.[21]

Poor relief in post-Famine Ireland

The immediate post-Famine period saw a return to low levels of workhouse occupancy and of relief distribution generally. Less than 1 per cent of the total Irish population was receiving relief in the 1860s, compared to around 4 per cent in England.[22] The Irish poor, we must assume, relied on other means such as charity and emigration to survive. While most Irish boards of guardians now granted some outdoor relief, the proportion was much lower than that in England. At the beginning of the 1870s, for example, 24 per cent of those receiving poor relief in Ireland were receiving outdoor relief, compared to 85 per cent in England.[23] From the 1870s the number and proportion of Irish paupers receiving outdoor relief significantly increased. The average daily number receiving outdoor relief in Ireland rose from 6,263 in the early 1860s to 56,619 in the mid-1890s.[24] Guardians in Leinster led the way in the granting of outdoor relief but by the end of the nineteenth century their colleagues in Munster and Connaught had overtaken them. Between 1878 and

1896, the percentage of paupers in receipt of outdoor as opposed to indoor relief in Leinster at the commencement of the year rose from 47 to 57 per cent. Munster and Connaught experienced even more marked increases with the percentage of recipients rising from 40 to 64 per cent in Munster and from 37 to 61 per cent in Connaught. In Ulster, by contrast, the increase was from 28 to 45 per cent.[25]

W.L. Feingold interpreted the steep rise in the levels of expenditure on outdoor relief in Munster and Connaught as providing 'yet another view of the growing politicisation of the boards of guardians'. For, at a time when boards of guardians in Munster and Connaught were coming under the control of elected, tenant guardians, those in Ulster remained largely landlord-dominated. Landlord-controlled boards across the country generally adhered more closely to New Poor Law principles, and were thus less generous with outdoor relief than those controlled by tenants were. But as Feingold himself acknowledged, the expansion of outdoor relief was not related to politics alone.[26] Some boards of guardians did present the granting of outdoor relief as part of the wider nationalist agenda. The Cork Board, for example, passed a resolution in 1887 declaring that they would maintain their outdoor relief list, 'until the Irish people were allowed to manage their own affairs'.[27] But advocacy of a more liberal approach to outdoor relief was not confined to nationalists. Social reformer and Unionist Isabella Tod, for example, campaigned for a relaxation of the regulations governing outdoor relief to enable more women to be relieved outside the workhouse. Irish guardians, unlike those in England, had no power to grant outdoor relief to widows with only one child or to deserted wives. Yet such groups, Tod argued, contained 'respectable people, wholly unused to ordinary pauper ways [and] it is evident that nothing can be more short-sighted than to give them only the choice between the workhouse and no help at all'.[28]

Outdoor relief was popular with many guardians and ratepayers because it was perceived to be economical and because guardians could use their discretion in awarding it. Applicants regarded as deserving could be granted outdoor relief, while those regarded as undeserving could be condemned to the workhouse. In the late 1870s outdoor relief

was being granted in the Cavan Union on the production of a
memorial signed by local ratepayers. Guardians defended this
practice on the grounds that the ratepayers 'have to pay the
money'. It was, however, criticised by one of the union's relieving officers as inappropriate and ineffectual. Many of the
recipients were unsuitable, and the small amounts granted were
'only a kind of penal servitude ... simple starvation – for they
cannot live on it'.[29] This remained a feature of outdoor relief and
was one reason why the poor law authorities disapproved of it.
In his half-yearly report for 1895, the auditor of Youghal Board
of Guardians, Courtney Croker, drew the attention of the
guardians to 'the large number of persons who receive 1s per
week. If such persons were really destitute', he observed, 'such
a grant would be wholly inadequate, but they are not destitute
and therefore the grant of so small a sum only has a demoralising effect on the recipient and unduly increases the burden on
the rate-payers'.[30]

Throughout the post-Famine period, the poor law authorities
sought to discourage the use of outdoor relief, and to remind
guardians, in the words of a circular issued in 1887, that experience in England and Ireland had 'proved conclusively that the
direct tendency of any system of outdoor relief is to demoralise
the people and absorb the property of the country'.[31] They were,
however, fighting a losing battle. Advocates of outdoor relief
could convincingly claim to represent popular opinion. As a
correspondent to the *Tyrone Constitution* explained in January
1899, outdoor relief was not only cheaper, it was

> a relief that is naturally more in favour with old and frail people,
> who, no longer able to work, have a reasonable distaste for life in
> the workhouse. The more the workhouse is rather the poorhouse
> [and] is confined to the care of the sick and otherwise perfectly
> helpless as well as indigent, the more it will accord with modern
> sentiment.[32]

The Vice-Regal Commission on Poor Law Reform which
reported in 1906, found that outdoor relief was

> often, and we think we may say generally, given to persons who,
> though poor, are by no means destitute of resources and means of
> livelihood ... Instead of being the sole support of the destitute, it
> has become merely an item in the receipts of the poor person ...

This is not at all what was intended by the Poor-law, but the system seems to be popular, and it appears to have taken root.[33]

The expansion of outdoor relief in Ireland reflected the desire of poor law guardians to discriminate more effectually between applicants for relief, as well as the influence of ratepayers. It also illustrates the extent to which boards of guardians were able to adjust the relief system in line with popular perceptions and priorities. Relief practices were thus the product of social, political and ideological developments, and need to be located and understood within these contexts.

During the second half of the nineteenth century poor law guardians acquired a variety of new powers and responsibilities. Looking back over the history of the poor law system in 1899, the authors of *A Guide to Irish Local Government* described how, from being

the mere guardians of the workhouse [poor law boards] became the public sewer-makers, the custodians of burial grounds and wells, the constructors of waterworks, the proprietors of dwellings for labourers, the executors of compulsory vaccination laws, and the laws relating to the sanitation of dwellings and public nuisances, and the repositories of a number of other powers down to the muzzling of dogs and the slaughtering of diseased animals.[34]

As central government assumed greater responsibility for public health and social welfare, poor law boards became the administering authority for an increasingly diverse body of legislation. Administration of local dispensaries was transferred from grand juries to poor law boards in 1851, and the latter were designated rural sanitary authorities under the Public Health Acts of 1874 and 1878. During the 1880s they became responsible for improving the rural housing stock. Under the provisions of the labourers acts, which form the subject of Chapter 5, boards of guardians were empowered to undertake improvement schemes in districts where existing accommodation for agricultural labourers was inadequate. Promotion of improvement schemes and other local works, together with expanding relief lists, pushed annual poor law expenditure up from around £0.5 million in 1859 to over £1 million in 1876 and to around £1.5 million in 1895.[35]

The Local Government Board for Ireland

By the early 1870s, poor law boards constituted one of the most important branches of Irish local government, a fact that received statutory recognition in 1872 when the Irish Poor Law Commission was abolished and its powers vested in the newly constituted Local Government Board for Ireland.[36] In creating one central authority to supervise the administration of all forms of local government, ministers were once again seeking to assimilate Irish and English administrative practice. As the Marquess of Hartington explained to the Commons in July 1872, the object of the Local Government Board (Ireland) Bill was 'simply to apply to Ireland, so far as was practicable, the policy of the Act passed last year placing the administration of the Poor Law, of the Local Government Acts, and of the Sanitary Acts, under the Local Government Board'. No further explanation was judged to be necessary.[37] Since the Irish Poor Law Commission was already responsible for much public health legislation, the creation of the Local Government Board was a far less radical step in Ireland than in England where responsibility for local administration had been shared between four different departments.[38] Nevertheless, the remit of the new Board was more extensive and its powers, as the *Freeman's Journal* noted, were 'far greater ... than were ever possessed by the Poor Law Commission in its most palmy days'.[39] Thus while it is true that the new board was in terms of personnel and outlook, 'the poor law commission under a new name', its establishment was a significant development and was seen to be so by contemporaries. Welcoming the concentration of supervisory powers regarding sanitary matters and the streamlining of administrative procedures, the *Freeman's Journal* anticipated the measure being 'the instrument of a vast deal of good'.[40]

The Irish Local Government Board comprised the president, who was the chief secretary for Ireland, the vice-president, and three commissioners, one of whom was the Irish under-secretary acting ex-officio. Since the Chief Secretary was frequently either absent from Ireland or occupied with other duties, the vice-president acted as effective head of the Board. Relations between the three permanent members of the Board and their two ex-officio colleagues were generally good, if only because the latter rarely interfered in the activities and decisions of the former. There were times, however, when political and departmental priorities diverged leaving the Board uncomfortably isolated within the Irish administration. This is perhaps most evident during the period of A.J. Balfour's chief secretaryship (1887–91). In May 1889, Balfour sought to clarify the arrangement of business between the Local Government Board and the Chief Secretary's Office. He had, he assured, the vice-president, Sir Henry Robinson,

> no desire to alter a system which appears to have worked fairly well for many years past and which I understand you approve of, i.e. the Under-Secretary, though a member of your Board, should not be obliged to see or to deal with papers concerned with Local Government and with Local Government alone, but that he should be consulted on all questions which may touch on the dominion of politics or general administration.

The difficulty, as Balfour acknowledged, lay in deciding 'what is political or administrative; what is concerned with politics or with general administration; and what is finally a matter for the Local Government Board'. This, he concluded,

> must purely depend on the general condition of the country ... At the present moment I am certainly of [the] opinion that all questions connected with the dissolution of Boards of Guardians or the amalgamation of Unions cannot be regarded as wholly alien to the political aspects of Irish Government of which the Under-Secretary is to take cognizance. But I think it not impossible that the time may come when Local Government Board matters can be considered apart from all other administrative questions in Ireland as they are now in England.[41]

If, as we shall see, Balfour's reassurances did little to ease relations between his office and the Board, this was because there was no agreement between them on what should, and should not, be regarded as 'political'.[42]

The Irish poor law system relied on the English system not only for its inspiration and rationale but also, until 1880, for its senior officials. Four assistant commissioners had been sent from England to assist Nicholls in establishing the system. Two of these, Edward Twistleton and Alfred Power, joined the Irish Poor Law Commission on its establishment in 1847; Twistleton as chief commissioner and Power as assistant commissioner. Following Twistleton's resignation in 1849, Power was appointed chief commissioner. He went on to serve as the first vice-president of the Local Government Board from 1872 until his retirement in 1880. Power's successor was an Irishman whose roots lay in the Protestant Ascendancy. Henry Robinson came from an old Dublin family and married the daughter of the 10th Viscount Valentia. He had extensive experience of poor law administration, having been a poor law inspector in Ireland for almost thirty years before being appointed assistant under-secretary and clerk to the Privy Council in 1876. He returned to the Local Government Board as vice-president in 1880 and remained there until his retirement early in 1891. Robinson's son, Henry Augustus Robinson, followed him into the civil service and spent most of his working life at the Local Government Board. He was appointed a temporary local government inspector in 1879, and joined the permanent staff of the Board as an inspector in 1882. In 1891 he was promoted to the position of junior commissioner and was appointed vice-president in 1898, a position he held until 1922 when the Board ceased to exist.

When making appointments, ministers generally sought to maintain a balance in the political and religious composition of the Local Government Board, and to match promotions from within the Board with appointments from outside. The Liberals had appointed George Morris, who held the vice-presidency from 1891 until 1898, a commissioner of the Board in 1880. A Catholic landowner and land agent, Morris had served as an ex-officio member and vice-chair of the Galway Board of Guardians for many years and had twice represented Galway Borough in parliament; firstly in 1867–68 and then again from 1874 to 1880. During the latter period he had aligned himself with Butt's Home Rule party, although he was never a member of it.[43] As the senior commissioner, Morris was the natural choice to succeed Henry Robinson as vice-president in 1891. Recommending Morris, the under-secretary, Sir West Ridgeway, advised that whoever was appointed commissioner in place of Morris 'must be a Protestant'.[44] H.A. Robinson was duly appointed from the senior inspectors. A few years later, the lord lieutenant, Lord Londonderry, insisted that Richard

Bagwell, the founder of the Irish Loyal and Patriotic Union, be appointed as an additional temporary commissioner, in order to provide 'an antidote' to William Micks.[45] Though a Protestant, Micks was known to be a supporter of home rule. As a local government inspector he had been censured for attempting to settle a dispute on the Vandeleur estate in County Clare, and had been transferred to the north-west.[46] Interestingly, when Micks was being considered for the post of Secretary of the Congested Districts Board in 1890, the fact of his being 'something of a Nationalist' was to work in his favour. This was regarded by Balfour as 'rather an advantage than not', presumably because it would enhance the credibility of the Board amongst the populace of the congested districts. Micks was appointed to the position the following year.[47]

For almost the entire period of its existence, the Local Government Board was led by men who by experience or training were both familiar with and attached to the principles and practice of the English poor law system. Throughout his career, Henry Robinson expressed firm adherence to the principles laid down by George Nicholls in the 1830s. In 1861, for example, Robinson declared himself opposed to the granting of any outdoor relief, except in cases of sickness, and in 1885 he resisted the abolition of proxy votes in poor law elections, arguing that Nicholls had judged proxy votes to be necessary to allow owners to protect their property.[48] H.A. Robinson shared his father's perceptions and prejudices. As inspector, commissioner and vice-president he strove to preserve the distinction between poverty and destitution and to restrict all relief, including emergency relief, to the destitute. During the 1880s and 1890s – the period on which this study concentrates – the Robinsons dominated the Local Government Board to such an extent that it has been difficult to prevent them dominating this book. Between them, they steered the Board through some very choppy political waters. And despite facing some formidable obstacles in the shape of guardians chaffing at central interference on the one hand, and ministers seeking more effective means of control over local boards on the other, they succeeded in maintaining a relatively steady course.

Given its bureaucratic roots, it is hardly surprising that the ethos of the Irish Local Government Board was very similar to that of the English Board. English poor law reformers regarded central supervision as essential if local authorities were to renounce the corrupt and improvident practices that had characterised their administration in their past. Lacking effective sanctions against recalcitrant local boards, the English Poor Law Commissioners, and subsequently the Local Government Board, were obliged to proceed by compromise and conciliation. In the words of its historian, the Board adopted a strategy aimed at 'building a hearts and minds consensus around the principles of sound administration'. To this end it was 'flexible and pragmatic, knowingly tolerating a great deal of variation in local practice, even against clear statutory prescription'.[49] The Irish Local Government Board possessed significantly greater sanctions, but it too pursued a cautious strategy aimed at educating local administrators in the art of government, and relying more on persuasion than coercion. The task of implementing this strategy in the localities fell to the field officers of the Board, local government inspectors and auditors, and it is to these officers that we will now turn our attention.

Local government inspectors

Local government inspectors were expected to perform a role that was both supervisory and advisory, and their recruitment reflected this dual function. Appointed by the president of the Board, inspectors, unlike other civil servants, were exempt from open competition and were not required to take a written examination. Individuals were chosen not for their formal qualifications, but for their ability to command respect. As the President of the English Board, James Stansfield, explained in 1872, he 'wanted men of experience and tact, accustomed to deal with men, knowing the boards of guardians and having their confidence'.[50] The civil service enquiry commission put forward a similar view with regard to the Irish inspectorate in 1873, observing that the qualifications required to make good inspectors were 'peculiar and not ascertainable by competitive examination'. They required 'not only good intellect and education, but also firmness of character, combined with mature age and experience'.[51] To this end inspectors tended to be drawn from the junior ranks of the landed gentry and from the higher professions. Typical recruits were the retired militia officer Major Richard Ruttledge-Fair who was appointed in 1886, and the barrister R. Kelly, appointed in 1892. Other inspectors had backgrounds in local administration. R.C. Lynch, for example, who was appointed in 1888, was described in an official return as 'Grand Juror, Poor Law Guardian, Magistrate, Vice-Guardian'.[52] Having a father within local government service was a definite advantage to an aspiring inspector. H.A. Robinson followed his father into the inspectorate, as did Edmund Bourke who was appointed in place of his father, Richard, when the latter retired in 1886 after forty years' service. The *Mayo Examiner* reported that there were 120 candidates for this and another vacant inspectorship.[53] Both Edmund, who was 29 on his appointment, and H.A., who was 32, were comparatively young for inspectors, the average age on appointment being around 40.

By the end of the century, the normal practice in both England and Ireland was to make appointments from among the ranks of temporary inspectors employed by the Boards, thus ensuring that those appointed had some familiarity with the work. H.A. Robinson outlined the advantages of this system to a committee of inquiry in 1913, explaining that if a temporary appointee proved unsuitable, 'he goes when his time expires. If he has the makings of a valuable official he is nearly always kept on, and if not too old he generally gets on to the permanent staff. We thus avoid the risk of getting a man on to our permanent staff of inspectors until we know he is thoroughly trained and has been tried'.[54]

One effect of the Board's recruitment policy was that Protestants always outnumbered Catholics among its senior staff. Even in the early twentieth century there were twice as many Protestants among the general inspectors as Catholics, while out of 17 auditors, only 5 were Catholic.[55] Noting the imbalance, an article in the *Leader* in 1907 called for competitive examinations for these posts. It was, the author suggested unkindly, 'quite possible to imagine that some of these gentlemen might do rather poorly under almost any kind of examination'.[56] But this was to miss the point. The real issue was not that those appointed were incompetent or unsuitable, but that they were of a particular type, conservative, unimaginative men who would follow instructions and uphold the authority of the Local Government Board.

Independence of thought was not a recommendation for employment. H.A. Robinson opposed the appointment of Dr Joseph Smyth as medical inspector for Dublin in 1898, arguing that while Smyth had 'some ability of a certain kind', he was 'full of incoherent ideas and fads about the functions of Government in relation to the control of local authorities', and was 'not the sort of gentleman that would get on well with Boards of Guardians'. Smyth had been recommended by the nationalist leader, John Redmond, as someone who would command confidence amongst all sections of the population. 'The Local Government Board and their officials', Redmond warned the Chief Secretary, Gerald Balfour, 'have not the influence or respect they ought to have in the country because they have been so exclusively recruited from the class of officialism and an opportunity now offers to remedy this state of things'.[57] Having been passed over in 1898 in favour of another Catholic, Dr Edgar Flinn, Smyth was eventually appointed to a medical inspectorship in 1902. Whether this did much to change perceptions of the Board and its officials is open to doubt. As Robinson characteristically remarked, Smyth's name, 'as spelt, had a Protestant flavour about it, and it was not generally known in areas remote from his home, that he was an inside pillar of the Catholic Church'.[58]

The proportional number of inspectors was considerably higher in Ireland than in England. The English inspectorate in the later nineteenth century consisted of between 13 and 17 general inspectors supported by a small number of assistant inspectors. The Irish establishment of between 8 and 10 general inspectors plus a number of temporary inspectors was only slightly smaller. This meant that whereas each English inspector was responsible for around 50 unions, their Irish colleagues inspected an average of just 15 unions in the 1870s. The workload of the Irish inspectors was revised in the mid-1880s when it was decided to separate the medical and general work with responsibility for the former assigned to dedicated medical inspectors drawn from the ranks of experienced surgeons and physicians. Ireland was divided into eight districts for general purposes and four districts (roughly corresponding to the four provinces) for medical purposes, giving each of the eight general inspectors a district of around 20 unions.[59] The Local Government Board insisted that the discrepancy between the relative size of the Irish and English establishments was justified by the greater level of responsibility carried by Irish inspectors. The latter were said to have more numerous and more demanding duties to perform than their English colleagues. For while they were in charge of fewer unions, they had longer distances to travel, greater numbers of indoor poor to monitor, and more buildings to inspect. According to a statement prepared in the late 1860s, over a period of three years an English inspector travelled 19,561 miles compared to the 22,613 miles travelled by an Irish inspector, and made 234 inspectional visits compared to 498. It was further argued that Irish inspectors were required to maintain a closer watch on the local authorities within their districts than was thought necessary in England.[60] As the Irish Poor Law Commissioners explained in a submission to the Treasury in 1869, they had felt it necessary to protect themselves from the responsibility which the power to dissolve defaulting boards of guardians had created, 'by maintaining a constant and uniform supervision of all the proceedings of every Board of Guardians in Ireland, and it is in this department of its business that it derives far greater value from the services of its Inspectors than can by possibility be the case in England'.[61]

The contrast between the Irish and English inspectorates was often exaggerated. All inspectors were required to make twice-yearly reports on every poor law institution in their district and most visited the major institutions, such as workhouses, more frequently. The regularity with which individual inspectors visited particular unions depended on local conditions and their own assiduity. Urban unions with large workhouses required closer supervision than rural unions in both England and Ireland. Topography also influenced patterns of inspection. The far west of the country remained relatively inaccessible even in the second half of the nineteenth century, and inspection rates reflected this. Whereas unions in remote coastal districts rarely saw an inspector more than two or three times a year, those in the major cities received regular visits at least once a month.[62]

Except in periods of exceptional distress, pressure of work

was undoubtedly greater in England than in Ireland and it is difficult not to agree with Treasury officials who concluded that the pay differential between English and Irish inspectors was 'just and reasonable', given 'the relative number of paupers, and the amount of money spent in poor relief in England and Ireland, and the comparative number of unions, and the acreage of the two countries'.[63] The real significance of the comparisons made by Irish officials, lies less in the insight provided into the actual work of inspectors than in the level of complacency they reveal within the Local Government Board. Members of the Irish Local Government Board believed themselves to possess a more complete knowledge of and thus to exert a stricter control over local administration than was possible in England. Appearing before the civil service enquiry commission in 1872, Alfred Power asserted that cases of workhouse mismanagement that had occurred in England could not have occurred in Ireland, 'without being detected or exposed at once'.[64] Power's certitude was, however, soon to be called into question. A general circular issued by the Local Government Board to its inspectors in 1879 noted that while the reports of some inspectors were fully comprehensive, those of others were 'not so full and satisfactory'. Serious defects in the management of a number of workhouses had been brought to light at special inquiries, yet the periodical reports received had made no mention of these, 'although the defects existed at the time of the inspections'. In order to try to remedy this, the Board produced a form which inspectors were required to complete following each inspection. Attention was particularly directed to the treatment of the aged and the sick and infirm, since these classes now accounted for a significant proportion of workhouse inmates.[65]

An inspector's duties were to attend meetings of boards of guardians, to inspect and report upon workhouses and other poor law institutions, to hold inquiries and to give advice on all matters relating to poor law administration and local government.[66] He acted as adviser and friend to local guardians, but also as censor and judge. The attitudes and prejudices of most inspectors reflected their class and background, and as such aligned them more closely with ex-officio than elected guardians. While this was also the case in England, the implications were more serious in Ireland where, as Mary E. Daly notes, 'such attitudes were more politically contentious'.[67] By the end of the century inspectors had little in common, either in terms of class background or politics, with the majority of poor law guardians with whom they came into contact. What were seen as declining standards of administration in unions under nationalist control, were attributed as much to personal as to political failings. As Richard Bourke explained to a select committee in 1885, ex-officio guardians were better qualified 'from their habits of thought and education ... to deal with large public subjects'. Elected guardians were well intentioned but lacked experience: 'They save money upon some things where they should spend it, and spend it lavishly very often where they should save it; it is their ignorance chiefly, I think, of public affairs which leads to that.'[68]

The majority of boards maintained good relationships with their inspectors, and it is clear from newspaper reports of board meetings that both guardians and inspectors were careful to treat each other with courtesy and respect, even when they were in conflict. A telling example of this is provided by a report of a meeting of the Westport guardians in November 1888. The board was close to bankruptcy and had been threatened with dissolution unless it struck a viable rate. H.A. Robinson was sent to attend the meeting at which the rate would be reconsidered. He suggested reducing the clerk's estimate by half the amount the guardians had originally proposed, commenting diplomatically that the Local Government Board was anxious to avoid sending paid guardians, 'seeing that the guardians acted so well, and did their work so creditably'. The guardians accepted his recommendation. It was 'characteristic of Mr Robinson', one observed, 'always to be friendly towards them and willing to serve them'. Guardians were pragmatists by necessity. The chair of the Westport Board reflected the view of many when he reminded his colleagues that the Local Government Board 'are stronger than we. We cannot be fighting with them; they have the law on their side.'[69]

Some inspectors appear to have been held in particular regard. When William Micks was transferred from the mid-west to the north-west all the boards of guardians in his district passed resolutions regretting his departure. One guardian from Killadysert Union declared that he 'had never observed any

Inspector to take such an interest in the welfare of the poor and the ratepayers', while the clerk of the Kilrush Board recalled that Micks had regularly given money to be divided amongst applicants for outdoor relief, believing the amounts granted by the guardians to be inadequate.[70] The death of Captain F.S. Sampson from typhoid fever later that year prompted tributes in all the local newspapers. The strongly nationalist, *Connaught Telegraph* reported the death with the comment that 'no more courteous, honourable, or high-minded gentleman ever did duty in a public capacity'.[71]

The local government inspectorate in England, Bellamy concludes, remained a 'cadre of field agents' whose approach was reactive rather than strategic. Lack of resources and pressure of work confined their supervisory role to the inspection of the indoor poor, and their role as mediators between centre and locality to the exertion of 'personal pressure on Guardians and the personal assessment of local opinion on the shifting issues of the day'. This, she argues, reflected the priorities of a central authority without the resources to 'dominate either the process of policy formulation or its implementation'.[72] In Ireland, the inspectorate was better resourced but Board officials lacked the will and, with the Chief Secretary only intermittently involved in their affairs, the political resources to shape government policy. Here too, departmental priorities focused on ensuring efficient administration and guaranteeing individual rights, not on developing public services.

Local government auditors

Local government inspectors had great authority but little power. If guardians refused to listen to their advice or to follow their recommendations, their only recourse was to report the matter to the Local Government Board. Auditors, by contrast, were in a position to impose an effective check on extravagant or illegal activities on the part of the boards through the disallowance of illegal payments and the surcharging of individual guardians. (Where an illegal payment had been made, the guardians who had signed the cheque were surcharged individually, even if the board as a whole had approved the payment.)

The centralised nature of the audit system in Ireland reflected early doubts about the competency and impartiality of Irish guardians. Under the English poor law act of 1834, boards of guardians appointed their own auditors. Not until 1868 did the appointment of auditors become the responsibility of the Poor Law Board, and it was 1879 before the district auditor became a full-time salaried position under the Local Government Board. In Ireland, the Poor Law Commissioners were empowered to appoint full-time, salaried officials to audit union accounts from 1838.[73] According to Nicholls, these appointments were intended 'to secure regularity and efficiency in the collections, and the proper keeping of union accounts', and thus to be 'the means of establishing a greater degree of uniformity as well as accuracy throughout all the unions in Ireland'.[74]

In the 1850s there were five auditors, each auditing a district of about 32 or 33 unions.[75] By the early 1880s this number had increased to nine, with districts of 18 or 19 unions. Auditors were directly appointed by the Poor Law Commissioners and later the Local Government Board. Many came from the legal profession; a number were retired army officers; others had been union or township clerks.[76] No formal qualifications were required but candidates were expected to have relevant experience. The post of auditor was less prestigious than that of inspector, but it was relatively well paid and there appears to have been no shortage of candidates. By the end of the century a senior auditor received a higher salary than an inspector – £800 p.a. compared to £700 p.a. – but could claim less in expenses. As with the appointment of inspectors, technical ability was judged less important in a candidate that personal character. Auditors, like inspectors, needed to be able to command respect and impose their authority.

Senior members of the Local Government Board regarded the audit as crucial to the success of the poor law system, and to the administration of local government generally. Discussing a number of new appointments shortly before the passage of the Local Government Act in 1898, H.A. Robinson reminded the Chief Secretary, Gerald Balfour, that the local government audit was 'the sheet anchor ... on which you rely to prevent abuse'. It might, therefore, be better, he suggested, to select 'a trained official or sound lawyer or competent accountant', rather than a militia officer. Robinson acknowledged that military men had proved satisfactory in the past, but 'none of them exercised the same influence over Local Authorities as the shrewd, lynx-eyed, trained business men'. Auditors such as J.W. Drury and W.E. Ellis had 'taught their local authorities to look at every penny they spend from the auditor's point of view, and to have a wholesome dread of the auditor'. Recommending one candidate, he summed up his qualifications as 'good social position (which is very important), a trained official, the right age (about 40), special knowledge of grand jury procedure and popular with the people'. Another candidate was described as 'just the sort of pertinacious self-opinionated sort of man who would keep the local bodies in splendid order'.[77]

Local guardians also took a close interest in the selection of auditors, believing the most important qualification to be a knowledge and understanding of union business. When Cornelius Pelly was moved from the southern to the northern district in 1888, a number of unions protested against the appointment being given to J.W. Drury who had been secretary to Rathmines Township, and thus had no direct experience of poor law administration. The Youghal Board of Guardians, for example, passed a resolution calling on both the Local Government Board and local MPs, 'to see that the post of Local Government Auditor, when vacant, shall be offered to a clerk of a union or his assistant, as they alone possess a practical knowledge of union accounts'.[78]

Surcharges imposed on guardians were often controversial, prompting angry resolutions by boards and critical comment in the popular press. If there were fewer complaints about trivial surcharges than in England, this is probably because Irish guardians were less likely to spend ratepayers' money on items such as toys or Christmas treats for workhouse children. Where such things were provided, they were paid for by individual guardians or by donations from local people, rather than charged to the rates. Some surcharges, such as those imposed for expenses incurred by deputations, caused annoyance in both England and Ireland.[79] By far the most controversial surcharges were those relating to outdoor relief for evicted tenants, a subject dealt with in some detail in Chapter 3. Reporting the surcharges imposed on members of the Athy Board in 1888, *The Nation* condemned them as 'Castle-instigated' attempts, 'on the part of the so-called Local Government Board, to abet the enemies of the people'.[80] To the Local Government Board, however, the auditor's power of surcharge was an essential means of safeguarding ratepayers. Noting that in a period of less than three years auditors had made disallowances in 21 cases involving the administration of excessive or illegal outdoor relief to evicted tenants, Henry Robinson remarked to Balfour in 1888 that it was 'fortunate that the ratepayers can be protected by the Auditors from such extravagant expenditure'.[81]

Widely assumed to be hostile to nationalist guardians, auditors did sometimes confound expectations. Elected members of the Limerick Board were delighted when Drury rejected objections raised by two ex-officio guardians to the payment of legal costs incurred by the Board in bringing a prosecution for trespass against a local Royal Irish Constabulary sergeant. The sergeant had brought a party of armed police into the workhouse and had refused to leave when asked to do so by the chair of the board. Drury ruled that since the guardians had obtained a favourable decision in court (the sergeant had been fined a farthing) their action could not be judged either unwarranted or illegal. Welcoming the auditor's report, the chair of the board, Dr William O'Shaughnessy, praised the 'manliness' with which he had delivered it. That Drury would need to be prepared to defend his decision was taken for granted.[82]

The exercise of audit powers in Ireland, as in England, was 'essentially negative and reactive, not positive and strategic'.[83] But in a far more politicised system, the negative and reactive could appear strategic. To nationalist critics of the Castle system of government, the district audit represented another shackle on local democracy. Local government auditors, the Home Rule MP, J.J. Clancy, observed in 1886, possessed powers that were 'extensive and far-reaching; and they, too, of course are practically irresponsible to Irish public opinion'. Clancy's criticisms formed part of a wider attack on the powers of the Local Government Board. Almost everything boards of guardians did, he complained, was 'interfered with and controlled' by the Board. Its officials could 'refuse to approve the "minutes" of their meeting, they may set aside their resolutions, they may dismiss their officers by "sealed orders", they may even dismiss and dissolve the local boards themselves – every one of them – and appoint paid guardians of their own nomination to their posts; and, moreover, all those powers are actually exercised from time to time'.[84]

Local guardians resented interference from the centre. As they became more anxious to assert their independence from central government their resentment became stronger and more politically charged. The following chapters examine a number of cases in which the Local Government Board resorted to the ultimate sanction of dissolution, much to the fury of the boards of guardians involved and their supporters. At such times the underlying tensions that were an integral part of the relationship between central and local government were starkly exposed. These cases were, however, exceptional. The primary objective of the Local Government Board was to maintain the operation of the relief system in accordance with statutory regulations. Members of the Irish Board, like their English colleagues, believed that this could best be achieved through a policy of compromise and conciliation. Only if this policy failed was coercion resorted to. As this chapter has shown, there was a fundamental similarity between the administrative and supervisory context in which the Irish and English poor law systems operated. If open conflict between central and local authorities was more common in Ireland than England, this should be seen as a consequence of deeper political divisions in Ireland and of the greater powers possessed by the Irish Board, not of a more combative attitude amongst its officials.

Notes

1 Sir George Nicholls, *A History of the Irish Poor Law* (London, John Murray, 1856), p. v.
2 Joanna Innes, 'The Distinctiveness of the English Poor Laws, 1750–1850', in Donald Winch and Patrick K. O'Brien (eds) *The Political Economy of British Historical Experience, 1688–1914* (Oxford, British Academy/Oxford University Press, 2002), p. 405–6. See also Rosalind Mitchison, 'Permissive Poor Laws: The Irish and Scottish Systems Considered Together', in S.J. Connolly, R.A. Houston and R.J. Morris (eds), *Conflict, Identity and Economic Development: Ireland*

and Scotland, 1600–1939 (Preston, Carnegie Publishing, 1995), pp. 161–71.

3 *Third Report of the Commissioners for Inquiring into the Condition of the Poorer Classes in Ireland*, Parliamentary Paper (hereafter PP), 1836 (43), xxx, 4.

4 Cited in Christine Kinealy, *This Great Calamity: The Irish Famine 1845–52* (Dublin, Gill and Macmillan, 1994), p. 20.

5 Cited in Nicholls, *History of the Irish Poor Law*, p. 152.

6 Ibid., p. 168.

7 Ibid., p. 165.

8 *Hansard 3*, xxxvi, 455 (13 Feb. 1837); ibid., xxxix, 492 (1 Dec. 1837).

9 Nicholls, *History of the Irish Poor Law*, p. 176.

10 1 & 2 Vict., c. 56.

11 Nicholls, *History of the Irish Poor Law*, pp. 187–8.

12 Mulgrave to Russell, 4 Dec. 1836, cited in Angus Macintyre, *The Liberator: Daniel O'Connell and the Irish Party 1830–1847* (New York, Macmillan, 1965), p. 216.

13 *Hansard 3*, xl, 1021 (12 Feb. 1838).

14 Cited in Macintyre, *The Liberator*, p. 222.

15 Nicholls, *History of the Irish Poor Law*, p. 271. The number of unions was increased to 163 in 1850. By the end of the nineteenth century, following the amalgamation of a number of unions, the number stood at 159. Nicholls was appointed permanent secretary of the English Poor Law Board in 1847. He retired in 1851.

16 Kidd, *State, Society and the Poor*, p. 30.

17 For resistance to poor rates see, Gerard O'Brien, 'The establishment of poor-law unions in Ireland, 1838–43', *Irish Historical Studies*, 23 (November 1982), p. 97–120, and 'A Question of Attitude: Responses to the new Poor Law in Ireland and Scotland', in Rosalind Mitchison, Rosalind and Peter Roebuck (eds), *Economy and Society in Scotland and Ireland 1500–1939* (Edinburgh, John Donald, 1988), p. 160–70.

18 Kidd, *State, Society and the Poor*, p. 34. See also Lees, *The Solidarities of Strangers*, p. 185.

19 10 Vict., c. 31; 10 & 11 Vict., c. 90.

20 Kinealy, *This Great Calamity*, p. 181.

21 25 & 26 Vict., c. 83. The age limit for boarding-out was gradually increased over subsequent decades to 15.

22 *Return showing the Area, Population, Pauperism and Expenditure for the Relief of the Poor in Ireland*, PP, 1874 (409), lvi, 933–1043; Kidd, *State, Society and the Poor*, p. 48.

23 *Annual Report of the Commissioners for Administering the Laws for the Relief of the Poor in Ireland*, PP, 1870 [C.156], xxxvi, 87.

24 *Annual Report of the Commissioners for Administering the Laws for the Relief of the Poor in Ireland*, PP, 1866 [3668], xxxvi, 10, 17; *Annual Report of the Local Government Board for Ireland*, PP, 1896 [C.8153], xxxviii, 228–9.

25 *Return of the Numbers in Receipt of Relief on the First Saturday in January, the First Saturday in March, and the First Saturday in June in each of the Years 1878, 1879, and 1880*, PP, 1880 (420), lxii, 289; *Annual Report of the Local Government Board for Ireland*, PP, 1896 [C.8153], xxxviii, 228–9.

26 Feingold, *Revolt of the Tenantry*, pp. 178–80. See also Mary E. Daly, *The Buffer State: The Historical Roots of the Department of the Environment* (Dublin, Institute of Public Administration, 1997), p. 21.

27 *United Ireland*, 13 Aug. 1887.

28 Isabella Tod, 'The Place of Women in the Administration of the Irish Poor Law', *The Englishwoman's Review*, ciii, 15 Nov. 1881, 484–5.

29 *Poor Law Union and Lunacy Inquiry Commission (Ireland)*, PP, 1879–80 [C.2239], xxxi, 123, 133.

30 Youghal Board of Guardians Minutes, 25 Jan. 1896: Cork Archives Institute, BG163/A91, 313.

31 *Annual Report of the Local Government Board for Ireland*, PP, 1888 [C.5455], l, 74–6.

32 *Tyrone Constitution*, 27 Jan. 1899.

33 *Report of the Vice-Regal Commission on Poor Law Reform in Ireland*, PP, 1906 [Cd.3202], li, 424.

34 John Muldoon and George M'Sweeny, *A Guide to Irish Local Government* (Dublin, Eason and Son, 1899), p. 3.

35 Virginia Crossman, *Local Government in Nineteenth-Century Ireland* (Belfast, Institute of Irish Studies, 1994), p. 52.

36 35 & 36 Vict., c. 69.

37 *Hansard 3*, ccxii, 1587 (23 July 1872).

38 Noting the striking similarity between the English Local Government Board of the 1870s and the Irish Poor Law Commission of the 1860s, Ronald D. Cassell has detected the influence of Sir John Lambert, the first Secretary of the English Board, who was familiar with the Irish system of local administration following a number of visits to the country in the 1860s. However, it is clear that the similarity owed more to accident than design. Irish models were rarely seen as suitable for translation to England since levels of economic development and social progress in the two countries were assumed to be quite different. Ronald D. Cassell, *Medical Charities, Medical Politics: The Irish Dispensary*

System and the Poor Law 1836–1872 (Woodbridge, Boydell Press, 1997), pp. 149–50.

39 These included the power to alter local government boundaries, and to approve applications from town councils to levy additional rates and to amend or repeal local acts.

40 R.B. McDowell, *The Irish Administration 1801–1914* (London, Routledge and Keegan Paul, 1964), p. 188, cited in Cassell, *Medical Charities*, p. 149; *Freeman's Journal*, 26 Sept. 1872.

41 Balfour to Robinson, 25 May 1889: Balfour Papers, British Library (hereafter BL), Add. MS 49828, f. 27.

42 For other comments on relations between Ridgeway and the Local Government Board, see Sir Henry Robinson, *Memories: Wise and Otherwise* (London, Cassell, 1923), p. 97; Daly, *The Buffer State*, p. 18.

43 David Thornley, *Isaac Butt and Home Rule* (London, MacGibbon and Kee, 1964), pp. 46–50, 212. A conscientious and unassuming man, Morris appears to have been content to adopt the policies and administrative style of his predecessors.

44 Ridgeway to Balfour, 12 Feb 1891: BL, Balfour Papers, Add MS 49811, f. 297.

45 Robinson to Gerald Balfour, 16 Aug. 1898: National Archives, London (hereafter NA), Balfour Papers, PRO 30/60/15; Lawrence McBride, *The Greening of Dublin Castle: The Transformation of Bureaucratic and Judicial Personnel in Ireland 1892–1922* (Washington, Catholic University of America Press, 1991), p. 80.

46 See below, pp. 71–105.

47 Balfour to Ridgeway, 18 Apr. 1890: BL, Balfour Papers, Add MS 49828, f. 812.

48 *Report from the Select Committee Appointed to Inquire into the Administration of the Relief of the Poor in Ireland...*, PP, 1861 (408), x, 335; *Report from the Select Committee of the House of Lords on the Poor Law Guardians (Ireland) Bill ...*, PP, 1884–85 (297), x, 298.

49 Christine Bellamy, *Administering Central–Local Relations 1871–1919: The Local Government Board in its Fiscal and Cultural Context* (Manchester, Manchester University Press, 1988), p. 139.

50 Cited in Bellamy, *Administering Central–Local Relations*, p. 144.

51 *Civil Service (in Ireland) Enquiry Commission, 1872*, PP, 1873 [C.788], xxii, 9.

52 *Return of all the Inspectors Now in the Services of the Local Government Board ...*, PP, 1906 (297), civ, 670–1.

53 *Mayo Examiner*, 22 May 1886.

54 *Royal Commission on the Civil Service*, PP, 1914 [C.7340], xvi, 565. See also John S. Harris, *British Government Inspection: The Local Services and the Central Departments* (London, Stevens and Sons, 1955), p. 26.

55 *Light on the Local Government Board* (National Library of Ireland (hereafter NLI), undated pamphlet), pp. 3–4.

56 Ibid., p. 4.

57 Redmond to Balfour, 26 Apr. 1898: Robinson to Balfour, 29 Apr. 1898, NA, Balfour Papers, PRO 30/60/15.

58 Sir Henry Robinson, *Further Memories of Irish Life* (London, Herbert Jenkins, 1924), p. 234. For Flinn see, Robinson to Balfour, 3 May 1898: Scottish Record Office (hereafter SRO), Balfour Papers, GD 433/2/114/2.

59 *Annual Report of the Local Government Board for Ireland*, PP, 1885 [C.4400], xxxiv, 43. This was to revert to an earlier arrangement that had been abandoned in the 1860s in order to give the Poor Law Commission more flexibility in its deployment of inspectors during a period of retrenchment. See, Cassell, *Medical Charities*, pp. 85–7.

60 *Civil Service (in Ireland) Enquiry Commission*, 34.

61 *Annual Report of the Commissioners for Administering the Laws for the Relief of the Poor in Ireland*, PP, 1870 [C.156], xxxvi, 85.

62 *Return of the Number of Visits made by each Inspector to the Workhouses of each Union in each of the Years 1857, 1858 and 1859*, PP, 1860 (294), lviii, 876–87.

63 Treasury minute, 19 Sept. 1868, cited in *Annual Report of the Commissioners for Administering the Laws for the Relief of the Poor in Ireland*, PP, 1870 [C.156], xxxvi, 86. Inspectors in England could earn up to £900 per annum. A senior inspector in Ireland received £650 plus an annual expenses allowance of £150. By the end of the century Irish salaries had increased to £700 with no fixed allowance for expenses. Individual amounts claimed in expenses in 1905/06 ranged from around £150 to around £400. *Return of All the Inspectors Now in the Services of the Local Government Board ...*, 670–1.

64 *Civil Service (in Ireland) Enquiry Commission*, 30.

65 *Annual Report of the Local Government Board for Ireland*, PP, 1880 [C.2603], xxviii, 57–9.

66 See Harris, *British Government Inspection*, p. 26; Robinson, *Further Memories*, p. 565.

67 Daly, *Buffer State*, p. 33.

68 *Report from the Select Committee of the House of Lords on the Poor Law Guardians (Ireland) Bill...*, 326.

69 *Connaught Telegraph*, 24 Nov. 1888.

70 *Munster News*, 10, 14 Nov. 1888. See also 17, 21 Nov. 1888.

71 *Connaught Telegraph*, 8 Dec. 1888.

72 Bellamy, *Administering Centra–Local Relations*, p. 153, 155.

73 Ibid., pp. 167–9.
74 Nicholls, *History of the Irish Poor Law*, pp. 298–9.
75 *Name and Residence of each Poor Law Auditor in the Years 1857, 1858 and 1859, and the Number of Poor Law Unions in the District of Each*, PP, 1860 (294), lviii, 888.
76 *Return giving the Names of Auditors and Assistant Auditors of the Local Government Board in Ireland, with the Dates of their Appointments, the Amounts of their Salaries, and their Occupations previous to Appointment, respectively*, PP, 1902 (146), lxxxviii, 357–9.
77 Robinson to Balfour, 6 Aug. 1898: SRO, Balfour Papers, GD 433/2/114/5. See also Robinson to Balfour, n.d. (Aug. 1898): ibid., GD 433/2/114/7.
78 Youghal Board of Guardians Minutes, 17 Mar. 1888: Cork Archives Institute, BG163/A75, 409. See also *Munster News*, 4 Apr. 1888, for a similar resolution by the Glin Board of Guardians.
79 See, *Mayo Examiner*, 5 Mar. 1887, for a report of the censure of Colonel James O'Hara for surcharging three members of the Westport Board of Guardians, including the chair, J.J. Louden, for expenses incurred in travelling to Dublin to lobby the Chief Secretary.
80 *The Nation*, 11 Feb. 1888.
81 Henry Robinson to Balfour, 10 Feb. 1888: National Archives of Ireland (Hereafter NAI), Chief Secretary's Office Registered Papers (hereafter CSORP), 1888/20832. The annual reports of the Local Government Board include statements of the sums disallowed by auditors and whether these were recovered.
82 *Limerick Reporter*, 10 Aug. 1888.
83 Bellamy, *Administering Central–Local Relations*, p. 155.
84 J.J. Clancy, *The 'Castle' System* (Dublin, Irish Press Agency, 1886), pp. 7–9.

2

Poor law boards and the advance of Irish nationalism

From the late 1870s the character of poor law administration across much of Ireland underwent a transformation. Poor law boards ceased to operate as a branch of landlord-dominated local government and became tenant-controlled assemblies committed to the achievement of Irish self-rule. Established as a means of promoting economic development and political stability, thereby facilitating the assimilation of Ireland into the United Kingdom, the boards came to provide a forum from which Irish nationalists could advance the cause of Irish independence. In a memorandum on local administration compiled in 1892, the Local Government Board recounted how

> guardians who had hitherto been elected on account of experience or interest in Union affairs had to give place to persons whose claim to be elected was that they had figured prominently in the land league agitation. The new class of elected guardians, naturally intelligent and fertile in resource, perceived at once that the poor laws might possibly furnish a powerful weapon of aggression against the landlords, and every effort was made to distort the law with that object and politics became the ruling factor in the acts and decisions of the poor law boards.[1]

How did the rise of elected guardians and the growing politicisation of the system affect the conduct of union affairs, and how did ministers and officials react to the injection of politics into poor law administration?

Poor law boards and politics

The poor laws were intended to have political as well as social consequences, promoting economic and social progress and helping to cement the union. Under their influence, it was hoped, Ireland would become more like Britain: more industrious, more ordered, more responsible, more prosperous. The particular character of the system, with its combination of local initiative and central control, was seen as conferring positive benefits that would encourage development within a regulated environment. In their annual report for 1841, the Poor Law Commissioners revealed that they had always considered the creation of a 'local machinery' for the administration of the poor law 'would afford important facilities for the introduction of other local improvements in Ireland'.[2] It was the existence of that machinery that was to encourage government ministers to augment the powers of poor law boards in the post-Famine period so that by the 1880s, poor law boards had become the most important branch of local government in rural areas.

Convinced that the poor law had been 'framed by the legislature to promote the interests of all classes, and was intended to become a bond of union not a ground of party contention', the Poor Law Commissioners deprecated the intrusion of 'party feeling' into poor law affairs commenting that there should be 'no contrariety of interest, the interest of each individual ratepayer being the interest of all'.[3] The belief that party politics had no place in local administration remained a guiding principle within central government. Reminding the Ennistymon Board of Guardians in December 1880 that they were 'constituted and hold their meetings for the purpose of administering the Poor Law, Medical Charities and Public Health Acts', the secretary of the Local Government Board observed that it was a cause of 'great regret that the Guardians should occupy their time in discussing political questions which are entirely outside and unconnected with their legitimate duties'.[4] Some years later the guardians of Kenmare Union were advised that since the board-room of a workhouse 'must necessarily accommodate gentlemen who may differ widely in political opinions ... the introduction into the board-room of anything calculated to offend the susceptibilities of Guardians ought carefully to be avoided'.[5]

However much the poor law authorities would have liked to isolate poor law administration from politics, it was clear from the early years of the system that contested elections were likely to be fought on party lines. Gerard O'Brien has outlined the 'vicious power-and-influence struggle between local priests and landlords' that marked poor law elections in County Wexford in 1839. Having studied the poor law elections of 1839–42 throughout the country he concluded that, 'politics generally eclipsed the pure selection of men who sympathised with the plight of the poor'.[6] Politics impacted on the functioning of poor law boards as well as on the progress of poor law elections. In 1848, Lord Carew advised the viceroy, Lord Clarendon, that 'repeal agitators' had taken control of poor law boards in County Wexford, prompting local proprietors to seek, unsuccessfully, to have 'paid, impartial, responsible guardians' sent down, 'at least for the present'.[7] With the emergence of home rule as a political issue, poor law elections became an even stronger focus of political activity. In 1874, *The Nation* published an editorial urging that 'every position which is open to popular election must be captured and held for Ireland – all poor law boards, town councils, parliamentary representation'.[8] This call had little immediate impact on the composition of the majority of poor law boards, but it is an indication of the growing importance attached to challenging the landed elite for positions of local and national influence.

The erosion of landlord domination

Until the 1870s landowners dominated local administration. As justices of the peace they formed the grand jury and petty sessions, and as ex-officio guardians they dominated poor law boards. Their influence largely determined the outcome of local elections, whether these were for town commissioners or poor law guardians. Vaughan has described landed estates as 'great centres of social, economic and political power, providing employment, capital for improvements and political patronage'.[9] Their owners expected to be able to direct local affairs either in person or through their agents and loyal tenants. In the early part of the century, the dominant position of the landed elite seemed impregnable. Tenants vastly outnumbered land-lords, however, and once they began to operate collectively, the illusory nature of landlord pre-eminence was exposed. The economic power of landlords was gradually eroded by the land acts while their political power faded with the advance of democracy at both local and national level. The speed and entirety of this process should not be exaggerated; landlords continued to exercise considerable influence even at the end of the nineteenth century, but this derived more from tradition and status than from actual political or economic power.

The fragile foundations of landlord domination were clearly revealed in the struggle for control of poor law boards. Landlords who engaged in this struggle enjoyed a number of advantages over tenants. Up to half the places on any poor law board were occupied by local magistrates sitting as ex-officio guardians. Since magistrates were largely drawn from the ranks of the landed classes, ex-officio guardians were generally landowners or their agents. Sharing the same powers and responsibilities, ex-officio and elected guardians were thus drawn for the most part from different social groups. As the chair of the Newport Board of Guardians explained to a parlia-mentary committee in 1861, ex-officio guardians attended the boards 'as gentlemen'; the elected guardians were 'the frieze-coated men'.[10] This divide was quite intentional and was designed to ensure that local property-owners had a role in the administration of the poor law. Changes to the composition of the Irish magistracy with the recruitment of a growing number of Catholics appear to have had little impact on the general body of ex-officio guardians who remained more likely to be land-lords than tenants.

In addition to being guaranteed a voice on the boards as ex-officio guardians, landlords could also influence the outcome of poor law elections through the exercise of multiple votes. In order to prevent the beneficiaries of poor relief from controlling its distribution, property owners had multiple votes under the poor law franchise. Ratepayers were entitled to between one and six votes according to the value of any property either owned or occupied in a union, up to a maximum of eighteen. While the majority of tenants possessed only one vote in poor law elections, landowners could generally claim the maximum entitlement of eighteen votes. And since property-owners were entitled to vote by proxy their votes could be concentrated in particular electoral divisions. These advantages were, however, rarely sufficient to overcome the sheer weight of tenant votes in populous areas. Where an organised effort was made to mobilise tenant votes in opposition to the landed interest, tenants were generally able to select the candidate of their choice.[11]

Elected guardians and nationalist MPs maintained that proxy votes could decide an election.[12] Local Government Board officials denied this. Asked in 1885 whether he had ever known a case in which the proxy votes swamped the occupational votes, local government inspector Richard Bourke, replied, 'No, never; it is impossible'.[13] In the absence of poll books, it is difficult to test the validity of such assertions. In private, however, officials acknowledged that landlords could 'work' the proxy votes to their own advantage. In response to complaints in 1889 that local landowners could no longer send an elected member to the Athy Board of Guardians in County Kildare, H.A. Robinson, observed tartly that he could not 'but think that if they took any trouble to work the proxy votes properly they could secure the seats for certain divisions, and if they would do this and attended occasionally at the Board I am convinced that they would be able to lessen or prevent much of the abuse which they now from a distance protest against'.[14] The main reason the Local Government Board and its inspectors consistently opposed the abolition of proxy votes was precisely because this would have lessened the influence of the landed class.[15]

Despite the potential strength of popular representation, landlords succeeded in dominating the vast majority of poor law boards until the period of the Land War. William L. Feingold estimated that 99 per cent of board chairmanships and 88 per cent of all board offices – chair, vice-chair and deputy vice-chair – were held either by landowners or justices of the peace in 1877. This, as Feingold observed, could only have been the case if local people were willing to accept this situation.[16] Moreover, electoral success did not automatically translate into control of the boards since the elected guardians still had to contend with the presence of ex-officio guardians. The latter retained control of board offices in many unions until 1898, when ex-officio guardians were abolished. Ex-officio dominance was in part a reflection of their willingness to exercise leadership and take responsibility. Many elected guardians were content to be led by their ex-officio colleagues, much to the annoyance of nationalist activists. In September 1882, for example, two letters appeared in *United Ireland* criticising guardians who refused to oppose the ex-officios, but rather voted with them. Such guardians, one correspondent complained bitterly, 'can be led to any dirty length by the smile of an aristocrat'.[17]

Ex-officio reactions

Having lost their hold on board offices, ex-officio guardians often responded by absenting themselves from meetings. There had always been a problem with non-attendance among ex-officios, many of whom were either non-resident or too busy to attend the weekly meetings.[18] The increasingly combative character of board meetings acted as a further disincentive. Appearing before a select committee in 1885, Colonel H.D. Carden, an ex-officio guardian from Mountmellick Union, attributed the non-attendance of his colleagues to the great disrespect that was shown to ex-officio members of the board, and the 'very offensive language used'.[19] Ex-officio members of the Athy Board were said to have been 'systematically insulted', until they were 'eventually driven from the boardroom, and the fact publicly exulted in'.[20] The sensitivity of ex-officio guardians to their treatment by their fellow guardians derived from their assumption that they had a natural right to influence the proceedings. Once that right was challenged, the boards became a hostile environment acting as a constant reminder of their declining influence.

Complaints about disrespectful treatment carried little weight with Local Government Board officials who argued that ex-officio guardians could hardly object to the activities of elected members if they themselves failed to attend board meetings. Many ex-officios, Richard Bourke maintained 'had absented themselves rather more readily than they might have done'.[21] Commenting on the disappearance of ex-officios from the Athy Board, H.A. Robinson expressed surprise that they had allowed themselves 'to be deterred by nationalist insults from attending the Board and making an effort to protect their interests'.[22] A return compiled in 1888 revealed the extent of the ex-officio exodus with board meetings across the country being attended on average by just three ex-officios. In Castletown Union in County Cork not a single ex-officio attended the board.[23] This return caused concern and frustration within the Irish government. The Chief Secretary, Arthur Balfour, was driven to the conclusion that 'the condition of many of the unions is undoubtedly to be attributed to the neglect of the ex officio guardians'. Ridgeway went so far as to consult the Local Government Board on the advisability of removing the most negligent of the ex-officios in order to replace them with 'more active representatives of the property interest'. Explaining that this was not possible under existing legislation, Henry Robinson promised to direct the inspectors to monitor the situation and report the name of any magistrate who was willing to act but was not currently an ex-officio, a course of action that appears to have had little practical effect. [24]

The 'nationalisation' of Irish poor law boards

As their social and political power grew in the aftermath of the Famine, tenant farmers came to demand a greater role in the administration of local affairs. Feingold's study of the 'nationalisation' of Irish poor law boards, convincingly demonstrates that these demands were given added impetus by the campaign for self-government. Poor law elections were being contested as part of national political campaigns from the early nineteenth century. But it was not until the 1880s that a sustained assault was made on the boards by tenant activists under the auspices of the Land League, and its successor, the National League. Key figures within the Land League, including Charles Stewart Parnell, were fierce critics of the system of local government in Ireland arguing that local affairs should be in the hands of people who commanded the confidence of the governed.[25] Founded in 1879, the Land League brought together campaigners for tenant rights, land reform and self-government. Its leaders were anxious to maximise political organisation and activity throughout the country and quickly realised the potential of poor law elections for mobilising support and demonstrating the strength of the popular movement. In 1881 Parnell called on tenant candidates to contest the poor law elections in order 'to wrest the local government of the country from the landlord classes'.[26] The following year, *United Ireland*, repeated the call, explaining that the poor law was 'the first rung of the ladder of national self-government. Win at the Poor Law Boards and we will presently win at the Castle'.[27]

The number of contested elections increased significantly in the early 1880s. As more tenant guardians were elected so the number of board offices held by tenants increased. According to Feingold's calculations, tenant guardians made up 50 per cent of office holders on poor law boards in 1886, compared to 12 per cent in 1877, and held 35 per cent of chairmanships compared to just 1 per cent in 1877.[28] Furthermore, as Feingold noted, the unions in which tenants were dominant were clustered in the south and west of the country, while those in which landlords were dominant were in the north and east. After 1886, therefore, Ireland was roughly divided between those areas in which the landed elite remained ascendant, and those 'comprising about half of territorial Ireland [in which] this ascendancy was broken and local self-government by the tenantry was a reality'.[29]

National–local relations

In addition to charting the transfer of power on poor law boards across the country, Feingold attempted an analysis of national-local relations in respect of board nationalisation. He argued that the original motivation was predominantly local, gaining 'direction and impetus' from national events, and that this remained the pattern under the National League. Focused on achieving their primary objective of home rule, the National League's leaders concentrated their efforts on Westminster and paid little attention to developments within local government. It was left to local activists to continue and maintain the progress made at local level, supported by sympathetic figures within the leadership such as William O'Brien, who continued to give extensive coverage to poor law elections and board activities in the pages of *United Ireland*. Feingold maintained that 'the party did not attempt to use its formal authority or its machinery to promote the [board nationalisation] movement', and that the actions of tenant-controlled boards were not directed by the national leadership. Local branches, he observed, often held conventions to pick slates of candidates but 'the branches carried out these functions without any supervision from the central branch'. The local movement, he concluded 'was a separate movement, locally motivated though influenced indirectly by events on the national scene'.[30]

Whilst agreeing with Feingold's overall conclusion, my own research suggests that he underestimated the complexity of the national–local relationship. Local branches of the National League did not select candidates entirely free from central supervision. As secretary of the National League, Timothy Harrington was in regular contact with local branches concerning issues such as candidate selection, and while he did not get involved in individual cases, he was forthright about the approach to be adopted. In 1886, for example, he instructed branch officers that, where more than one nationalist candidate came forward, branches should not indicate a preference between them. It was, he explained, 'no part of the National League to interfere where Nationalists are opposing one another, as this opposition only shows the strength of the National movement in the locality'. Harrington was anxious to prevent the League being presented as intolerant and oppressive. He warned the Roscrea Branch against expelling members over incidents that had taken place during poor law elections, observing that such expulsions, 'if used by our opponents against us, would do a great deal to throw back the progress of the National Cause'.[31]

Harrington's strictures displayed little understanding of local politics or local feeling. Allowing electors a choice between competing candidates threatened to split the popular vote. In March 1887 the *Leinster Leader* instructed its readers that 'it was the bounden duty of Nationalists to vote for the person selected by the National League because there are unfortunately too many who will record their votes against the Nationalist'.[32] Local activists could not afford to allow ratepayers the luxury of a free vote. Chairing a meeting of the Ballincollig National League prior to the 1888 poor law elections, W. Higgins noted that while the sitting candidate advocated leaving the selection of a candidate to the ratepayers, he believed that in the present state of the 'National crisis the representative of the people should come from the National League'. This remark was greeted with applause.[33]

National politicians did concern themselves with developments in local government, although they were wary of becoming too closely involved. Irish MPs of all political parties were expected to represent the interests of unions within their constituencies, and they were assiduous in questioning ministers regarding union affairs. Poor law boards lobbied their local MPs on a regular basis. It was common practice to send copies of political resolutions to local MPs as well as to the Chief Secretary. MPs were also expected to help to arrange meetings with government ministers and, on occasion, to accompany deputations of guardians.[34] Many Nationalist MPs were, however, wary of allowing local issues to impinge on national campaigns, fearing that the pursuit of local interests would undermine the unity and strength of the wider movement. T.M. Healy declared in 1885 that the electoral aim of nationalists must be 'to efface and blot out every local distinction and recognise only the interests of the country at large'.[35] Thus while nationalist victories in poor law elections were welcomed as indications of popular support for the movement, their significance for the conduct of local administration was seen as being of secondary importance.

Poor law elections offered an opportunity for people to demonstrate their commitment to the nationalist movement and to reject both landlordism and unpopular government policies. Nationalist victories in 1881, and particularly the election of a number of those detained as 'suspects' under the Protection of Person and Property Act, enabled the movement to reject claims that its support was only maintained through fear and intimidation. As William O'Brien later recalled, the elections had torn away 'the last rag of verisimilitude from the plea that the people were only pining to be delivered from the Parnell despotism'.[36] Similarly, *The* success of nationalist candidates in 1888 provided, according to *The Nation*, 'the best possible answer to the vain boast' of the Chief Secretary, Arthur Balfour, that the coercion act had freed people from the tyranny of the National League.[37] At times when political meetings were liable to be banned and activists detained, the activities of poor law boards took on an added significance. According to Higgins, people looked upon the boards of guardians as 'the second line of defence when the front position, viz, the House of Commons, had been rendered untenable through their members being caught and thrown into prison'.[38] In Limerick, nationalist guardians preparing to attend the first meeting of the new board in April 1888, were reminded that since

> the rights of public meeting and freedom of speech are suppressed in Ireland, the people will be compelled to have recourse to the public Boards to make known their wants and aspirations ... If all our men attend we can return the Nationalists by an overwhelming majority; and thus supply to Mr Gladstone and the people of England the answer of the elected representatives of 150,000 Irishmen, demanding Home Rule for Ireland.[39]

Politics and prestige

As the only administrative body in rural areas with a popularly elected element, poor law boards provided tenant farmers and rural businessmen with a rare opportunity to participate in local government. Many had been seeking to play an active role in local affairs well before the land campaign boosted the number of popularly elected guardians. Frustrated by the severely restricted range of positions open to them in local government, they were quick to take advantage of the opportunities provided by the formation of the Land League to establish themselves as figures of influence within their localities, and thus to mount an effective challenge to landlord power. The career of John T. Heffernan exemplifies this process. Heffernan, whose father held 56 acres from the Duke of Leinster, had considered emigrating in the 1870s because of the poor prospects in Ireland. In March 1880 he helped to form the Kildare town branch of the Land League. Having worked as a League organiser in County Kildare, he was elected to the Naas Board of Guardians in the spring of 1882. He went on to make a successful career in local politics serving as chair of the Naas No. 1 District Council, and subsequently as secretary of the Kildare County Council.[40] Patrick Fulham followed a similar path in County Meath. Having been an active member and paid organiser of the Land League in Counties Louth and Meath, he was elected to the Drogheda Board of Guardians, becoming vice-chair in 1886. In 1892, he was elected MP for Meath South but was unseated on petition. Fulham was described in a special branch report in 1892 as holding around 100 acres, being 'of good appearance and address' and having 'considerable influence among the people in his neighbourhood'.[41] For men such as Heffernan and Fulham, becoming a poor law guardian was a means to both personal and political advancement.

Membership of a poor law board brought access to power and influence. Guardians had considerable patronage at their disposal in terms of jobs and contracts as well as control over local expenditure on matters that directly affected people's lives such as water and sewerage services. Poor law guardians were thus significant figures in the local community. As W.E. Vaughan notes, 'if the use of the abbreviation 'PLG' in petitions and newspaper reports is an indication of social prestige', then guardians 'had considerable prestige'.[42] Indeed, Samuel Clark has suggested that tenant victories on poor law boards in the 1880s were 'largely prestigious', arguing that the assault on the boards was undertaken less for pragmatic reasons than 'because it accorded unprecedented status in the local community to the shopkeepers and large farmers who came to manage these government bodies so recently under the patronising rule of the landed elite'.[43] However, this is to underestimate the extent to which local activists sought control of the poor law boards in order to utilise the power of the boards for their own ends.

Representing the nation

As elected guardians began to flex their political muscles so the likelihood of their coming into conflict with the Local Government Board increased. By insisting on strict adherence to poor law regulations, the Local Government Board was seen as attempting to hinder nationalist campaigns and frustrate the popular will. Local activists, as Feingold noted, identified two

main enemies: the Local Government Board as the representative of government, and the ex-officio guardians as the
representatives of landlordism. But while political rhetoric
presented the relationship between the Local Government
Board and nationalist-controlled boards as one-dimensional, the
reality was far more complex. As we shall see, Feingold's assertion that 'as the representative of British rule, the board's
authority was to be opposed and obstructed whenever possible',
is not borne out by the evidence. Primarily concerned with
tracing the process of board nationalisation, Feingold did not
attempt to assess the consequences of that process, beyond
commenting on the increase in outdoor relief.[44] The remainder
of this chapter seeks to explore the impact of board nationalisation both on poor law administration and on the relationship
between central and local administrators, and to assess the
extent to which elected guardians attempted to use their powers
to advance nationalist campaigns. In order to do this, it is necessary first to examine the way in which nationalist guardians
perceived their role within the movement, and to appraise the
powers that they possessed.

Nationalist elected guardians acted as representatives of the
nation, of their locality and of the ratepayers to whom they were
accountable. The nature of this accountability was made quite
explicit in some cases. Thus the Kilcoleman branch of the
National League in County Limerick, bound the guardian of the
Dunmoylan division of Glin Union to give an annual report of
his 'stewardship' to his constituents. A large number of ratepayers and labourers were reported to have attended the first such
meeting held in February 1888. Taking the chair, the Revd S.
Frost declared that the branch 'took a pardonable pride in being
the first to introduce so healthy a practice, which he hoped
would be followed by each of the electoral divisions, not only in
this but in other unions'.[45] In some unions, nationalist guardians
met outside board meetings to agree a strategy. National League
members elected to the Limerick Board in 1888, for example,
resolved to constitute themselves the 'National League Party of
the Limerick Board of Guardians', and bound themselves 'to act,
sit and vote together as a party on all questions on which the
party should decide to take action'.[46] As with the selection of
candidates, local practices were often disowned by the national

leadership. Writing to Revd P. Keran of Ennis in County Clare, Harrington condemned the conduct of local National League branches in attempting to interfere in the affairs of the Ennis Board. He totally rejected the idea that 'a Nationalist guardian, returned to discharge the duty of the ratepayers, is, out of pure gratitude to you for his return, bound to sink his own opinions, and do whatever you bid him to do. If that rule held good, the position of representative men on public boards would be a mere sham'.[47] Here again, Harrington was out of touch with local sentiment. What was the point of ratepayers electing someone like them to represent their interests, unless he was going to act as their surrogate?

Anxious to retain the support of the ratepayers, elected guardians often attempted to reduce the burden of rates by cutting the salaries and pensions paid to local officials, such as medical officers and union clerks. They were also suspicious of proposals that involved increased expenditure, such as the boarding-out of pauper children, and the creation of new offices.[48] Poor law officials often attributed this to inexperience. Elected guardians had a great desire to be economical, one local government inspector observed in 1885, but they did not always know the most effective means of achieving this.[49] While there may have been some truth in this analysis, the actions of elected guardians in such cases undoubtedly reflected popular feeling. In 1886, *United Ireland* castigated ex-officio members of Ballycastle Union who were trying 'to create a new office ... that of midwife – to be paid by the Union'. The medical officer received £120 a year and the ratepayers believed that if he needed any assistance he should pay for it.[50] Reporting on the decision of the Ballyshannon Board not to grant a pension to their retiring medical officer, the local inspector observed that he did not believe the pension was refused on political or religious grounds. 'The people', he explained, 'are much opposed to granting any pensions, and the guardians knowing this, dare not risk their popularity with their constituents ... Even the ex-officio guardians were very callous about it.'[51] In such cases poor law guardians were clearly placing their responsibility to protect the interests of ratepayers above their responsibility either to the poor, or to their own officers.

The increasing influence of elected guardians from the late

1870s led to a more open and accessible style of poor law administration. Instead of being held in private, as had generally been
the case earlier in the century, most board meetings were
opened to members of the press and the public. This practice
provided further cause for complaint amongst ex-officio
guardians. In May 1881, Richard Notter, an ex-officio on the
Schull Board of Guardians in County Cork, wrote to the Chief
Secretary complaining about the behaviour of Land Leaguers on
the Board. Their intention, he claimed, was 'merely to convert
the Board-room into a Land League meeting. A resolution was
lately passed to have strangers admitted, we have also labourers
nearly every Board-day in attendance, and I feel certain they
come for a purpose from Ballydehob perhaps to intimidate Mr
George Swanton and myself'.[52] The allegation that elected
guardians were attempting to use their position to carry on the
work of the League was to become increasingly common as the
number of nationalist-controlled boards rose. In September
1889, Balfour noted that the difficulties in poor law administration in County Clare were 'largely due to the fact that Boards of
Guardians have shown a desire to use the machinery of the Poor
Law to fill the gap caused by the suppression of the National
League. Nothing could be more pernicious in itself or more
inconsistent with the due administration of the Unions'.[53] What
substance was there to this charge?

Advancing the cause: political resolutions

In seeking to support and advance nationalist campaigns,
elected guardians had a range of options. Perhaps the most
common action, and also the easiest to take, was to pass a resolution supportive of the Land or National League, commending
national figures such as Parnell, or condemning government
policies. Such resolutions attracted media attention in both
Ireland and Britain, and had the satisfying result of annoying ex-
officio guardians and, in some cases, ministers. The practice was
increasingly evident from the early 1880s when boards began to
pass motions supportive of the Land League, and condemning
the arrest of activists under the Protection of Person and
Property Act of 1881. Prior to 1883, boards were free to discuss

political topics and pass political resolutions at any stage of their proceedings. This was found to be problematic since so much time could be taken up in political discussions that the ordinary business was left unattended, or postponed until a later date. In his book of satirical sketches published in 1880, the stipendiary magistrate, Henry Blake, portrayed a weak ex-officio chair bowing to the determination of a nationalist guardian, 'that his resolution, on fixity of tenure and free right of sale, of which he had given no notice of motion, must be discussed before the less important business on the books as to the expediency of grant-ing out-door relief'.[54] Following discussions within the Irish government, the Local Government Board issued new regula-tions governing the proceedings of boards of guardians in December 1882. These included the stipulation that 'No matter or question shall be brought forward at the Meeting until all the business of the Meeting ... shall first have been disposed of'.[55] From then on the Local Government Board adopted a policy of ignoring political resolutions, whilst recommending that if any attempt was made to raise matters outside the scope of the guardians' powers, the proper course for the chairman to take was to leave the chair.[56] Nationalist chairmen, needless to say, declined to follow this advice and continued to allow such reso-lutions to be introduced.

The Board adhered to its policy throughout the 1880s and 1890s despite furious protests from ex-officios and constabulary officers. In October 1887, the District Inspector of the Royal Irish Constabulary in Kilrush reported that the Kilrush Board of Guardians had passed resolutions declaring that the agent of a local estate 'should be boycotted and holding him to public censure for acting as bailiff'. The case, he believed, was serious enough to warrant prosecution. On examination of the minutes, it emerged that the guardians had merely condemned the action of the bailiff, who was described as 'acting as an emergency man to suit the services of the Balfour's coercion act'. But having ruled that there was insufficient evidence to bring a prosecution, the Attorney General recommended that the Local Government Board should consider taking action 'in cases of resolutions of this class'. The Board insisted that there was nothing it could do since the offending resolution 'appears by the minutes not to have been brought forward till all the regular business had been

disposed of'.[57] The best response to such resolutions, Board officials maintained, was to disregard them. When the Lismore
Board passed a resolution condemning the prison treatment of
William O'Brien and declaring that should he die, 'his name
shall live to fire with freedom every Irish heart and light the
funeral pyre of his Tory Executioners', Henry Robinson, advised
Ridgeway that no good 'would be effected by taking notice of
the resolution of the Lismore Guardians. It would give them an
excuse for passing some other violent resolution, and would
have no effect in checking such ebullitions.'[58]

What constituted a political or inflammatory resolution was a
matter of debate. As *The Nation* pointed out in November 1886,
those who attempted to ridicule nationalist guardians for
passing patriotic resolutions were content to listen 'with bated
breath to ungrammatical elogiums [*sic*] on the virtues of the
"Royal family", or the latest landlord come of age from the local
captain of militia – in the chair of course'.[59] When Lord
Inchiquin was re-elected to the chair of the Ennis Board in 1885,
he had promptly moved an address welcoming the Prince of
Wales to Ireland.[60] Most landlord-dominated boards, however,
operated self-denying ordnances with regard to political resolutions, in part to emphasise the contrast between well-run
unionist boards and unruly nationalist ones. In 1887 the Bandon
Board proposed to pass a resolution that 'no motion of a political character be received in future by the presiding chairman',
only to be informed by the Local Government Board that they
had no power to control 'the action of a future board in regard
to any matter which might legally be brought before them'.[61]
The Cookstown Board got around this difficulty by adopting a
standing order each year not to consider matters outside the
business of the board.[62]

Rather than use the poor law boards as a forum for expressing loyalty to government and the union, guardians
representing the landed interest consciously presented themselves as 'non-political', and their activities as limited to union
business. Landlord-dominated boards attracted far less media
attention than nationalist boards, partly because they deliber-
ately avoided such attention and partly because their meetings
were less interesting to the public. There were fewer rows
during board meetings, and fewer contentious items under

discussion. A typical report of an Ulster board was that of a meeting of the Antrim board that appeared in the *Belfast Newsletter* in April 1886. This consisted of the brief statement that 'the numerous items noted on the programme were disposed of with accustomed despatch, much unanimity characterising the entire proceedings'.[63] Such reports contrasted with those of the proceedings of southern, tenant-dominated boards that regularly included accounts of violent arguments between guardians and colourful exchanges of insults. Landlord-dominated boards rarely came into conflict with the Local Government Board, and prided themselves on acting in an efficient and businesslike manner. When the Clogher Board of Guardians found itself in dispute with the Local Government Board in 1898, the guardians made frequent reference to their previous unblemished record of orderly administration, thus seeking to differentiate their dispute from those of disorderly nationalist boards.[64]

Patronage

Passing political resolutions was a convenient way for nationalist guardians to express their support for the movement, and was useful for propaganda purposes, but as the Local Government Board privately acknowledged, this was 'probably the most harmless of their aggressive proceedings'. A more potent means of advancing the cause was through the distribution of patronage. There was a propaganda aspect to this, as the decision of a number of boards in 1881 to exclude from competition all but Irish manufacturers indicates.[65] But guardians were also demonstrating the power of the nationalist movement to benefit its supporters, and to effect change in the localities. The awarding of contracts was frequently cited as evidence of corruption on the part of nationalist boards. As the Royal Irish Constabulary inspector for County Kerry reported in 1888, 'the dealings of the Guardians are not as they ought to be and their contracts are always looked on as jobs and nothing seems to be done from an honest motive'.[66] But nationalist guardians were not doing anything that ex-officio guardians had not done in the past. Patrick Malone, parish priest of Belmullet had complained to the Poor Law Commissioners on a number of occasions between 1869 and 1871 regarding maladministration by Belmullet guardians, claiming that offices and contracts were given to friends of the guardians. These complaints were dismissed after the union auditor, James Martin, declared that board had acted with full legal authority in all they had done.[67]

However much the Local Government Board might disapprove of the way in which contracts were awarded, they had limited powers to intervene. In 1890 the proprietor of the *Leinster Express*, Michael Carey, complained to the Chief Secretary that the Athy Board of Guardians had awarded the union printing contract to the *Carlow Nationalist* even though the *Nationalist* had submitted a higher tender than the *Express* and was not local to Athy. Informing Ridgeway that there were no grounds for intervention, the secretary to Local Government Board explained that the guardians were not bound to accept the lowest tender, 'and the selection rests entirely with them, for, although we might interfere with the view of dissolving the Board of Guardians if a systematic practice of jobbery prevailed ... we cannot set aside a particular contract if it is entered into the Guardians in a legal manner'.[68]

Appointments within the patronage of poor law boards included workhouse officials, relieving officers, rate collectors, and medical officers, together with the union clerk and solicitor. As in the awarding of contracts, nationalist guardians took pains to appoint candidates who were active in or supporters of the movement, and to exclude their opponents. In July 1890, *United Ireland* welcomed the appointment of an evicted tenant, Patrick Hickey, as a rate collector in Kilrush Union, and commended the action of the other eleven candidates in withdrawing when they learned about the latter's application, thus exemplifying the 'spirit of patriotism and unselfishness which animates the people of Ireland'.[69] When this appointment was queried by the Chief Secretary's Office, Robinson replied that they were inquiring into Hickey's qualifications. But if he satisfied the Board that he was competent to perform the duties of a rate collector, there was no reason to object. 'I do not think we can refuse to confirm his appointment', Robinson explained,

> merely because he is an evicted tenant, and a newspaper report attributes his election to the bias on the part of the guardians in

favour of a nationalist. The vacancy was duly advertised – the election formally conducted – he had no legal disqualification – we have nothing official before us showing the reasons which influenced the guardians in giving their votes ... I do not think we have sufficient grounds to set aside their decision if it is found that the man is competent to keep the books and accounts of a relieving officer.

Hickey's appointment was subsequently confirmed.[70]

The following year, the Board confirmed the appointment of John Leyden as a rate collector in Killadysert Union, despite the objections of the local constabulary. The District Inspector at Ennis described Leyden as 'a thoroughly bad character' who, as 'an organiser of outrages', was 'quite unworthy of such an appointment'. This assessment failed to impress the Local Government Board. Their own inspector, William Micks, had concluded that Leyden would make 'a fairly good officer', and as Robinson explained to Ridgeway, if the Board was to cancel Leyden's appointment it would have to have good grounds, 'and it would be impossible, or at all events not right, to do so merely because more than two years ago Leyden was fined for assault, or on account of the suspicions or opinion of the District Inspector, unless he can state fully to the Guardians the facts on which he bases his assertion that the man is unfit for the post of Collector'.

Whilst admitting that he was unable 'to give evidence of the facts', the District Magistrate, Colonel Turner, strongly endorsed the District Inspector's judgement. Whatever Micks might believe, the police were 'much better able to judge' and they strongly opposed 'such a man being appointed'. Anticipating a bruising conflict with the board of guardians, Robinson warned Ridgeway that the government would have to be prepared to dismiss Leyden if the guardians insisted on retaining him, and that 'neither the circumstances mentioned by Colonel Turner ... or any other facts disclosed in this file would, in our opinion, afford grounds for adopting that course'. Under the circumstances, the Chief Secretary reluctantly agreed to accede to the appointment.[71]

One reason for the Local Government Board's caution can be found in their previous unhappy experience in the case of Dr Magner. Magner was dismissed as medical officer of the

Courseys dispensary district of Kinsale Union in January 1888, having been convicted of criminal conspiracy under the Crimes Act for proposing a series of resolutions at a National League meeting. He also served as medical officer of Timoleague in Clonakilty Union and in March 1888 he was unanimously re-elected to this position by the dispensary committee. At the behest of the Chief Secretary's Office, the Local Government Board refused to approve his re-appointment unless he under-took not to connect himself with any illegal associations.[72] This he refused to do pointing out that the National League was not an illegal association in the Timoleague district. The Local Government Board was eventually forced to sanction his appointment when no other candidate for the post could be found. Magner's victory had caused much rejoicing in the nationalist press. *The Nation* had congratulated the doctor on his 'splendid triumph over the red-tape administrators of the Local Government Board', noting that it was 'in matters like this that the spirit of Irish nationality may well be said to be indomitable'. Condemning the action of the Local Government Board in trying to block the appointment, *United Ireland* declared that 'never, we are glad to say, has arbitrariness of meanness got a severer check'.[73] It was hardly surprising that the Board was anxious to prevent a similar outcome in Leyden's case.

Reactions within government

The official position of the Local Government Board was strongly to deprecate the introduction of politics into board proceedings, but since there was no enactment or regulation on the point much had to be left to the discretion of the guardians. In 1884, the Board had quietly retreated from a dispute with the Enniskillen Board of Guardians over the use of a dispensary building for storing the instruments of an Orange lodge band. The issue had been taken up by the local paper, the *Impartial Reporter*, and by nationalist MPs, such as T.M. Healy, who relished an opportunity to embarrass both the Local Government Board and the government. Would the Local Government Board, Healy enquired of the Chief Secretary, 'sanction the employment of the dispensaries throughout the three southern provinces as store-rooms and meeting places for the national party?'[74] Conscious that the Local Government Board had no legal control over dispensary buildings, Henry Robinson was reluctant to interfere. The guardians stalled for time, hoping to delay any investigation until after the commons had risen for the summer. It was not until late August that Robinson was able to inform the under secretary, Sir Robert Hamilton, that in letting the building to the guardians the owner had reserved two upstairs rooms for the use of the Orangemen and that this arrangement had been in force for more than thirty years. The guardians, he noted, 'therefore, seem to have no control over the two rooms used by the Orangemen'. The matter was then allowed to drop, much to the relief of both the board of guardians and the Local Government Board.[75] When bringing the matter before the Commons, Healy had questioned whether nationalist boards would be allowed the same latitude as the Enniskillen guardians. The evidence suggests that, in many cases, they were.

Taking their cue from senior officials, local government inspectors were careful not to over-react to what could be interpreted as the political posturings of boards of guardians. In contrast to the exaggerated and alarmist accounts of board activities that appeared in some sections of the press, and in some constabulary reports, local government inspectors adopted a tone that was studiously measured and laconic, generally playing down any political element in incidents under investigation. Since many of the allegations that inspectors were required to investigate concerned the language used by elected guardians, their conclusions were often largely a matter of interpretation. And whenever they were required to infer intentions or motivation, inspectors generally opted for the most innocuous explanation.

In 1880 an incident at a meeting of the Killadysert Board of Guardians in County Clare was referred to Richard Bourke for investigation. According to a report that had appeared in the *Dublin Evening Standard*, one of the guardians had 'refused to sign a cheque for an officer of the Board recently boycotted, unless he promised to join the [Land] League at once'. Bourke made enquiries of the clerk of the union who assured him that 'the entire matter from beginning to end was a joke on both sides'. The clerk explained that a guardian named Kennedy, who was a prominent member of the Land League, had been the last of three guardians to sign a cheque made out to the medical officer for duties performed under the public health act. In doing so Kennedy had 'jocularly remarked that he would not sign a cheque for anyone who was not a Land Leaguer, [saying], "What would the poor doctor who was boycotted do if he did not get his cheque". The doctor joined in the joke which was carried on good humouredly to the end by all who were present and was concluded by the signing of the cheque.' According to the clerk, this was not the first time that 'undue importance' had been 'given to trivial circumstances at the Board and elsewhere in this locality by having them transmitted to the central news and then communicated to the newspaper press of the country'. None of the local newspapers had thought the incident worth reporting. Bourke concluded that the clerk's explanation might be relied on as correct, and no further action was taken.[76] Having established that the most serious allegation in the *Standard's* report – that Kennedy had refused to sign the cheque – was without substance, Bourke decided not to inquire further. Yet it seems unlikely that the exchange was really as light-hearted as the clerk maintained. Kennedy was effectively reminding the doctor that by setting himself against the Land League he was setting himself against the community and its representatives, and thus putting his own interests at risk. The use of humour softened but did not remove the underlying threat in Kennedy's remarks.

By sticking resolutely to the facts, and avoiding interpretation, inspectors sought to prevent the operation of the poor law system from being unnecessarily disrupted. In 1887, local government inspector George Spaight was directed to report on a story that had appeared in *The Times* alleging that the Kanturk Board of Guardians had instituted sanitary works in order to provide employment for labourers who had given up their jobs on the boycotted Curass estate. Having inquired into the matter, Spaight reported that 'the statements made are not correct ... The only sanitary work contemplated was the enlargement of Kilbrin grave yard (very much required) and recommended by the medical officer and Father O'Keefe; it was not contemplated for any other purpose'.[77] This explanation ignored the fact, reported in the *Cork Examiner*, that John Dillon had urged that the Curass labourers be employed on the Kilbrin sanitary works, as this 'would be a great saving of those much needed [National League] funds'. A number of the Kanturk guardians had also strongly advocated this course arguing that 'we would be no men if we did not give the work to the Curass labourers who so well deserve it'. The matter was not, however, put to vote and the work was executed by contract.[78] That Spaight, who on other occasions was fiercely critical of the malign effect of National League influence upon poor law boards, decided not to mention any of this in his report suggests a conscious decision to avoid reference to politics.

The reluctance of Local Government Board officials to look beyond the facts and to consider what was implicit as well as explicit in matters that came before them was rooted in the desire to prevent unseemly and unproductive disputes with boards of guardians. To enter into arguments that the Board could not be sure of winning would be to risk undermining the authority of the Board. Direct intervention was, therefore, reserved for cases in which poor law regulations were being contravened or the welfare of the poor endangered. During the early 1880s, this approach created no obvious disquiet within the Irish government. Liberal ministers were equally anxious to avoid unnecessary confrontations with popular representatives, and had little sympathy with the grievances of ex-officio guardians. When Richard Notter complained to the Chief Secretary, W.E. Forster, about attempts made to intimidate ex-officio members of the Schull Board of Guardians, the under-secretary, T.H. Burke, dismissed the affair as a 'tempest in a teapot and quite unworthy [of] the attention of Government or of the House'.[79]

Balfour and the boards

Such matters were perceived in a very different light during the period of Arthur Balfour's chief secretaryship. At a time when other sections of government were busy trying to portray the National League and its supporters as a threat to law and government, the cautious, non-interventionist approach of the

Local Government Board appeared not only inappropriate but damaging, and provoked considerable frustration within the Chief Secretary's Office and the constabulary. Indeed, the failure of the Local Government Board to prevent boards of guardians in County Clare from promoting National League campaigns, and the apparent refusal of their inspector, William Micks, even to acknowledge the political nature of the board's activities, nearly drove the District Magistrate, Colonel Turner, to distraction.

At the end of January 1888, the Royal Irish Constabulary inspector at Kilrush, J.N. Brown, reported that he had good reason to believe that 'the Kilrush Board of Guardians has now adopted the principles and practice of the suppressed Branch of the National League in Kilrush by calling before them on Board days persons who offend against National League Law'. Brown cited a recent incident in which the dispensary doctor, Dr Connihan, had been called before the Board 'to account for his conduct in dealing with a number of his tenants ... against whom he had to take out ejectment decrees for non-payment of rent'. He would not be surprised, Brown added, 'if the Doctor will be reported for some alleged offence to the Local Government Board because he refuses to be dictated to by the Board of Guardians'. Micks undertook to investigate the report, assuring the Local Government Board that it was a matter 'about which I can easily learn the true facts'. Having interviewed the doctor and the clerk of the union, Micks confirmed that Connihan had been asked to appear before the guardians. This request had only been made, however, after the board had received a memorial from three or four of Connihan's tenants requesting the guardians' interference. The doctor had provided a satisfactory explanation and the guardians had taken no further action in the matter. Micks acknowledged that the guardians had acted 'most improperly' in summoning Connihan, but concluded that, with the exception of this incident, he been 'unable to ascertain that anything occurred in the proceedings of the Kilrush Guardians' to justify Brown's statement that the board had constituted itself a branch of the National League.[80]

This was not the first time that the activities of the Kilrush Board of Guardians had attracted attention. The board had appointed the evicted tenant, Hickey, as a rate collector, they had passed a number of 'improper' resolutions, described by Turner as 'exactly similar to those which are characteristic of the League', and, earlier in January they had ejected a boycotted farmer, George Pilkington, from a board meeting as an 'obnoxious' individual. This last incident, which had prompted Turner to seek unsuccessfully to have the board dissolved, was discounted by Micks on the grounds that the 'resolution about Pilkington was brought forward and passed upon the spur of the moment without any previous discussion or arrangement by the guardians'.[81] Turner was astounded by the local government inspector's report. Brown had been 'perfectly justified' in his description of the board, Turner insisted, and he 'thoroughly concur[red] with him'. Ridgeway was equally mystified, commenting that he 'quite agree[d] with Col. Turner', and could not 'understand how Mr Micks had any doubts'. Micks's assessment was, however, accepted by the Local Government Board without question. Henry Robinson had rejected Turner's earlier recommendation that the Kilrush Board be dissolved, stating that the ejection of Mr Pilkington did not provide sufficient grounds. He was also to resist Balfour's proposal that 'an inspector ad hoc ... should henceforth attend all meetings of [Kilrush] Board'.[82]

The idea of appointing a special inspector to attend the meetings of any board of guardians suspected of acting as a branch of the National League had first surfaced at a meeting of the Local Government Board in November 1887. Described by Balfour as involving 'semi-police duties', the post was an extension of the government's campaign to criminalise the National League. Special, or ad hoc, inspectors would provide information on resolutions or actions by boards of guardians that contravened the Crimes Act and assist in initiating prosecutions against individual guardians, duties that the ordinary inspectors had been unable to perform. Robinson had agreed to the plan in principle but as soon as Balfour proposed that it be put into operation, he raised practical objections. No agreement had been reached on the exact nature of the post, whether it was to be paid, or for how long any appointment was to last. This lack of clarity allowed Robinson to block the entire plan. Since the services of an ordinary inspector could not be utilised 'as it would materially interfere with his usefulness in discharging his poor law work', an additional inspector would have to be appointed, but this, as he helpfully reminded Ridgeway, would require Treasury sanction. Undeterred, Balfour directed that sanction for an appointment should be obtained and a suitable person selected.[83]

By this time, however, it was mid-March and the poor law elections were approaching. Robinson now advised deferring the appointment until after the elections in the hope that the composition of the Kilrush Board might change. The elections saw no change in the political complexion of the Board, but the defeat of the 'advanced nationalist', M.G. Gibson, by the more moderate John Mahoney was seen as a positive sign, as was the election of Michael Behan as chair in Gibson's place. District Inspector Brown described Behan as 'a steadier and more reliable man than Gibson', even if 'his principles and ideas of the N. League' were no different. Ignoring Turner's observation that Behan appeared to be 'little improvement upon his predecessor', Ridgeway took the opportunity to suggest to Balfour that since the Local Government Board seemed 'so averse to the proposal that an inspector should be sent to attend the meetings of this Board, perhaps you will agree to wait and see how the new Board works'.[84] No more was heard of ad hoc inspectors. Robinson had succeeded in preventing the creation of a local government official whose first loyalty would be to the Chief Secretary's Office rather than the Local Government Board, and whose reports could not be relied upon to filter out all but the worst instances of political strife.

It would appear from local press reports that Micks was correct in concluding that the political commitment of the Kilrush guardians was manifest more in their words than their deeds. There is no doubt that the guardians took every opportunity to assert their identification with, and support for, the nationalist movement. At a meeting in late September 1887, Gibson had described himself and his colleagues as 'the elected representatives of West Clare', and had proposed that they should make the boardroom available for 'any meetings for the welfare of the county, whenever our much revered and respected parish priest, Dr Dynan, sanctions it'. However, no resolution to this effect was passed, and no action appears to have been taken. The following month the suggestion that 'no poor law guardian ought to drink and converse with an enemy of our cause' met with general agreement, but again did not lead to a formal resolution.[85] The change of chairman appears to have made little difference to the character of board proceedings. In April 1888, the *Clare Journal* reported a board meeting at which it was argued that 'no man should get any position except members of the [National] League'. A man named Bourke was then voted off the dispensary committee. He was said not to attend National League meetings, but more importantly perhaps he was also revealed to have attended only one meeting of the dispensary committee over the whole of the previous year.[86]

In the 1890s the National League succeeded in imposing its own laws on large areas of the country. Indeed, Donald Jordan has suggested that during this period the League was the only popularly recognised authority in Ireland.[87] If this is the case, then nationalist controlled poor law boards played a significant role in maintaining the authority of the League, particularly in districts where its branches had been suppressed. Reports of board meetings in local newspapers served the same purpose as reports of branch meetings in publicising and reinforcing League edicts and boycotts. Constabulary officers thus had good reason to regard the proceedings of boards such as Kilrush as constituting a manifest threat to law and order. However, their belief that poor law boards were fulfilling the same functions as League branches was unwarranted. People could be held answerable to their local branch of the League, but not to their local poor law board. League branches could act as 'courts'; poor law boards could not. Far from having any direct power over local ratepayers, poor law guardians were answerable to them. And local opinion was intolerant of guardians who neglected their administrative duties, however sound their politics. In November 1888, an editorial in the *Munster News* regretted the poor financial state of the Kilrush Union, commenting that a board 'comprising so much intelligence and so many most capable businessmen' ought to be able 'to place the Kilrush Union in a better financial position'.[88] As elected representatives nationalist guardians were in a position of authority, but they were also dependent on popular support.

The Local Government Board had been content to support Micks in his exoneration of the Kilrush guardians, but even the Board objected when he became involved in attempts to bring about a settlement on the Vandeleur estate, where tenants had adopted the Plan of Campaign. Turner had remained deeply suspicious and resentful of Micks, complaining to Ridgeway in August 1888 that he had 'constantly' reported the 'seditious and improper resolutions' that had been passed by boards of guardians in County Clare to government, but had 'never heard of any check being put on them by Mr Micks'.[89] Turner seized upon Micks's attempt at mediation as further evidence of the inspector's maverick and unreliable character. His intentions might have been good, but this did not alter the fact that 'the public co-operation of a government official in Mr Micks' position with the confessed promoters of the Plan of Campaign ... is mischievous and misleading in the extreme'.[90] Ridgeway and Balfour concurred. The Chief Secretary asserted that it was clearly the duty of the local government inspector 'to use every method open to him' to prevent boards of guardians from abusing their position. He could only do this effectively, 'if he rigidly abstains from everything which can give the slightest handle to the imputation that he takes a part in local controversies, political or social or that he views with anything like indifference the operations of an association which is illegal and dangerous'.[91]

The Local Government Board acknowledged that Micks had demonstrated 'want of judgement' and revealed that it had already been decided to transfer him to another district. On learning of this decision, the Bishop of Limerick wrote to Balfour asking him to reconsider. Micks's removal, the Bishop warned, would be seen as 'a punishment for an attempt on his part to settle ... the unfortunate dispute on the Vandeleur estate', and thus 'as the very extreme of hostility to the people in this agrarian movement'. Balfour declined to intervene, explaining that Micks had 'impaired his usefulness by the manner in which he has traversed the limits of his official duties'. It was imperative, the Chief Secretary reminded the bishop, that inspectors should 'rigidly abstain from even the appearance of being mixed up with any of the controversies which unhappily divide society in Clare and elsewhere, and which the Boards of Guardians them-

selves, whose duties should be strictly confined to the economical and humane administration of the Poor Law, are too apt to
take a part'.[92]

Local Government Board officials generally sought to operate
outside politics. By allowing himself to be drawn into a political
controversy, Micks became vulnerable to the accusation that he
was siding with the National League. In the struggle between
the government and the League, officials were not at liberty to
chose which side they were on. They could only affect not to
notice that there were sides.

During the closing decades of the nineteenth century, poor
law administration became an important sphere of nationalist
activity in Ireland providing a platform from which nationalists
could advertise and advance their aims. Through the awarding
of contracts and the appointment of officials, nationalist
guardians were demonstrating their power to assist their
supporters, whilst also reinforcing the authority of the movement within local communities. Beyond the immediate
beneficiaries, the impact of such activities was largely symbolic.
The Local Government Board could ignore the adoption of political resolutions precisely because this represented no direct threat
to the operation or integrity of the poor law system. But as the
Board noted in the memorandum cited at the beginning of this
chapter, nationalist guardians sought to control the poor law
boards primarily as a means of prosecuting the fight against
landlordism. And their powers in this respect were of much
greater potential significance. Through the distribution of relief,
nationalist guardians could reward activists and punish opponents, and by granting relief to evicted tenants they could
intervene directly in rent disputes. The consequences and implications of such interventions form the subject of the next chapter.

Notes

1 [Local Government Board] Memorandum as to administration by
 Local Governing bodies in Ireland, 2 Apr. 1892: NAI, CSORP,
 1892/4813.
2 *Seventh Annual Report of the Poor Law Commissioners*, PP, 1841 (327),
 xi, 360.

3 *Sixth Annual Report of the Poor Law Commissioners*, PP, 1840 (245), xvii, 397.

4 Banks to Clerk of Ennistymon Union, 29 December 1880: NAI, CSORP, 1880/34318.

5 Workhouse – Display of Party Ensigns in Board-Room, Local Government Board Precedent Book: Public Record Office of Northern Ireland (hereafter PRONI), LGB/D2/1, 36450–89/ Kenmare.

6 Gerard O'Brien, 'The Establishment of Poor-law Unions', 110, 115.

7 Cited in Crossman, *Local Government*, p. 53.

8 *The Nation*, 15 Aug. 1874, cited in Feingold, *Revolt of the Tenantry*, p. 87.

9 W.E. Vaughan, *Landlords and Tenants in Mid-Victorian Ireland* (Oxford, Clarendon Press, 1994), p. 104.

10 *Report from the Select Committee Appointed to Inquire into the Administration of the Relief of the Poor in Ireland ...*, PP, 1861 (408), x, 301, 306.

11 Feingold, *Revolt of the Tenantry*, pp. 123–58.

12 See, for example, the evidence of James Daly, *Report from the Select Committee on Poor Law Guardians*, PP, 1878 (297), xvii, 559.

13 *Report from the Select Committee of the House of Lords on the Poor Law Guardians (Ireland) Bill ...*, 322. Henry Robinson cited the example of Rathdown Union where there were 5,130 occupier votes and 248 proxies. Ibid., 301.

14 Observations by H.A. Robinson on Mr Carey's letter, 26 Apr. 1889: NAI, CSORP, 1890/7728.

15 See evidence of Henry Robinson and G.C. Spaight, *Report from the Select Committee of the House of Lords on the Poor Law Guardians (Ireland) Bill ...*, 298, 353.

16 Feingold, *Revolt of the Tenantry*, p. 49.

17 *United Ireland*, 16 Sept. 1882. See also 23 Sept. 1882.

18 In the early 1860s, elected guardians were found to have attended an average of thirteen meetings a year, while ex-officio guardians attended only four. *Return for each Union in Ireland of the Attendance of Ex-officio and Elected Guardians respectively at the Board during the Two years ended 31st December 1860*, PP, 1861 (408), x, 502–4.

19 *Report from the Select Committee of the House of Lords on the Poor Law Guardians (Ireland) Bill ...*, 520. See also evidence of G.C. Spaight, ibid., 360.

20 Michael Carey to A.J. Balfour, 14 Jan. 1889: NAI, CSORP, 1890/7728.

21 *Report from the Select Committee of the House of Lords on the Poor Law Guardians (Ireland) Bill ...*, 325.

22 Observations by H.A. Robinson on Mr Carey's letter, 26 Apr. 1889: NAI, CSORP, 1890/7728.

23 Return showing the number of meetings held by the boards of guardians of each union and the average attendance of ex officio guardians during the year ended 30th September 1887: NAI, CSORP, 1889/ 3812.

24 Note by A.J. Balfour, 22 Oct. 1888; Ridgeway to Robinson, 13 Aug. 1888; Robinson to Ridgeway, 16, 25 Aug. 1888; Robinson to Balfour, 1 Nov. 1888: ibid.

25 Alan O'Day, *Charles Stewart Parnell* (Dundalk, Historical Association of Ireland, 1998), p. 31.

26 Cited in Feingold, *Revolt of the Tenantry*, p. 114.

27 *United Ireland*, 4 Feb. 1882.

28 Feingold, *Revolt of the Tenantry*, p. 174. Feingold's conclusions were derived from an analysis of board office-holders. Individuals were categorised either as a landowner or a tenant, and their political affiliation determined on this basis. While this methodology is somewhat crude, since it fails to take account of radical landowners and conservative tenants, it can be justified by reference to the increasingly polarised nature of Irish politics in these years. My own research has largely confirmed Feingold's categorisations and his results have therefore been assumed to provide a reasonably accurate picture of the rate and scale of board 'nationalisation'. The object of this study is not to replicate Feingold's work but to build on it.

29 William Feingold, 'The Tenants' Movement to Capture the Irish Poor Law Boards, 1877–1886', *Albion*, 7, 3 (1975), 230.

30 Feingold, *Revolt of the Tenantry*, pp. 164, 169, 173.

31 Harrington to J. Lyons, 25 Mar. 1886: NLI, 'Proofs of Letters from Timothy Harrington as Secretary of the Irish National League, 1883–1888', 55; Harrington to Rev. P. Kennedy, 3 Apr. 1886: ibid., 58.

32 *Leinster Leader*, 12 Mar. 1887.

33 *Cork Examiner*, 27 Feb. 1888.

34 See, for example, the request from the Swinford Board of Guardians to John Dillon in 1893, and from the Clogher Board of Guardians to T.W. Russell (and others) in 1898: Clerk of Swinford Union to Dillon, 10 Oct. 1893: Trinity College Dublin (hereafter TCD), Dillon Papers, MS 6803, f. 12; Resolution of Clogher Board of Guardians, 10 Sept. 1898: PRONI, BG9/A/41, 299–300.

35 Cited in Frank Callanan, *T.M. Healy* (Cork, Cork University Press, 1996), p. 96.

36 Cited in Feingold, *Revolt of the Tenantry*, p. 157.

68 *Politics, pauperism and power*

37 *The Nation*, 14 Apr. 1888.
38 *Cork Examiner*, 27 Feb. 1888.
39 Letter addressed to Members of the National League Party of the Limerick Board of Guardians, 30 Mar. 1888: NAI, CSORP, 1892/4813.
40 Thomas Nelson, *The Land War in County Kildare* (Maynooth, Dept. of History, St Patrick's College, 1985), pp. 18–26.
41 Report on Patrick Fulham PLG, 4 July 1892: NAI, Crime Branch Special, 1892/5403/S.
42 Vaughan, *Landlords and Tenants in Mid-Victorian Ireland*, p. 203.
43 Samuel Clark, *Social Origins of the Irish Land War* (Princeton, Princeton University Press, 1979), p. 329.
44 Feingold, *The Revolt of the Tenantry*, pp. 178–81.
45 *Munster News*, 15 Feb. 1888.
46 Resolutions adopted at a meeting of the National Party of the Corporation and Limerick Board of Guardians, 25 Feb. 1888: NAI, CSORP, 1892/4813.
47 Harrington to Revd P. Keran, 9 Feb. 1887: 'Proofs of Letters from Timothy Harrington as Secretary of the Irish National League', 121.
48 See, for example, evidence of Patrick Meehan, Mountmellick, and Edward Fenelon, Naas, *Report from the Select Committee of the House of Lords on the Poor Law Guardians (Ireland) Bill...*, 490–1, 511.
49 Evidence of Richard Bourke, ibid., 326.
50 *United Ireland*, 2 Jan. 1886.
51 Report of R. Kelly, 30 June 1892: NAI, CSORP, 1892/10204.
52 Richard Notter JP to Forster, 4 May 1881: NAI, CSORP, 1881/16442. Swanton and Notter were the only two ex-officio guardians who still attended the board.
53 Note by A.J. Balfour, 13 Sept. 1888: NAI, CSORP, 1888/21874.
54 Terence McGrath, *Pictures from Ireland* (London, C. Keegan Paul and Co., 1880), p. 83.
55 *General Order of the Local Government Board for Ireland for Regulating the Meetings and Proceedings of Boards of Guardians in Ireland and the Appointment and Duties of Union Officers, 18 December 1882* (Dublin, Alex Thom & Co., 1883), p. 13.
56 Guardians' Proceedings, Local Government Board Precedent Book, PRONI, LGB/D2/1, LO/181/M/83 Misc.
57 Report of DI Irwin, 31 Oct. 1887; Note by JEG, 11 Nov. 1887; Robinson to Ridgeway, 15 Nov 1887: NAI, CSORP, 1887/20962.
58 Robinson to Ridgeway, 14 Nov. 1887: ibid. See also Robinson to Balfour, 19 Feb. 1889: NAI, CSORP, 1889/4026.
59 *The Nation*, 27 Nov. 1886.
60 *The Times*, 2 Apr. 1885.

61 Guardians' Proceedings, Local Government Board Precedent Book, PRONI, LGB/D2/1, 44042–87/Bandon.

62 *Belfast Newsletter*, 13 Feb. 1893.

63 Ibid., 3 Apr. 1886.

64 See below, pp. 199–211.

65 See, for example, *United Ireland*, 20 Aug. 1881, 27 Aug. 1881, 10 Sept. 1881, 17 Sept. 1881.

66 Monthly Confidential Report of CI T. Singleton, 2 June 1888: NAI, Crime Branch Special, CBS/DCCI, Carton 4. See also *Notes from Ireland*, 23 Feb. 1889, 27 July. 1889.

67 James Martin to Poor Law Commissioners, 13 Feb 1870; Banks to Malone, 17 Feb. 1870: NAI, CSORP, 1871/10622.

68 Carey to Balfour, 21 Mar. 1890; Wodsworth to Ridgeway, 17 Apr. 1890: NAI, CSORP, 1890/7728.

69 *United Ireland*, 12 July 1890.

70 Robinson to Balfour, 4 Nov. 1887, 12 Dec. 1887: NAI, CSORP 1887/20962.

71 Robinson to Ridgeway, 7 July 1888; Note by Colonel Turner, 10 July 1888; Turner to Inspector General, 25 July 1888; Robinson to Ridgeway, 25 July 1888: NAI, CSORP, 1888/15530.

72 Note by Ridgeway, 22 May 1888: NAI, CSORP, 1888/10982.

73 *The Nation*, 18 Aug. 1888; *United Ireland*, 18 Aug. 1888. See also *United Ireland*, 4 Feb 1888.

74 *Hansard 3*, cclxxxix, 1864 (3 July 1884).

75 Robinson to Hamilton, 21 June 1884; Robinson to Hamilton, 30 Aug. 1884: NAI, CSORP, 1884/20092. At least two of the Enniskillen guardians were anxious to take the matter further, arguing at a meeting in late July that the Board should vacate the building in question and rent or build new premises. But they were clearly in the minority. See *Impartial Reporter*, 31 July 1884.

76 *Dublin Evening Standard*, 25 Dec. 1880; MacMahon to Bourke, 30 Dec. 1880; Banks to Burke, 3 Jan. 1881: NAI, CSORP, 1884/401.

77 *The Times*, 29 Nov. 1887; Note by Spaight, 14 Dec. 1887: NAI, CSORP, 1887/20682.

78 *Cork Examiner*, 26 Nov. 1887.

79 Notter to Forster, 4 May 1881; Note by Burke, 16 May 1881: NAI, CSORP, 1881/16442. Exchanges between Notter and his fellow guardians appeared in the local press, prompting T.M. Healy to raise the matter in the Commons. *Eagle and Cork Advertiser*, 14 May 1881; *Hansard 3*, cclxi, 792–3 (19 May 1881).

80 Report of DI Brown, 28 Jan. 1888; Report of William Micks, 21 Feb. 1888: NAI, CSORP, 1888/17324.

81 Turner to Inspector General, 25 Feb. 1888; Report of William Micks,

21 Feb. 1888: ibid. The guardian who had proposed the resolution had been charged with intimidation, and bound over for 12 months. See, report of J. Brown, 5 Jan. 1888: ibid.

82 Turner to Inspector General, 25 Feb. 1888, with note by Ridgeway, 27 Feb. 1888 and Balfour, 1 Mar. 1888; Robinson to Ridgeway, 20 Jan. 1888: ibid.

83 Balfour to Ridgeway, 9 Mar. 1888; Robinson to Ridgeway, 14 Mar. 1888, with note by Balfour, 16 Mar. 1888: ibid.

84 DI Brown to County Inspector, 14 Apr. 1888; Minute by Turner, 16 Apr. 1888, with note by Ridgeway, 18 Apr. 1888: ibid.

85 *Munster News*, 1 Oct. 1887, 19 Oct. 1887.

86 *Clare Journal*, 12 Apr. 1888. See also Memorandum on Mr Micks, n.d. (Nov. 1888): NAI, CSORP, 1888/21874.

87 Donald E. Jordan, 'The Irish National League and the "Unwritten Law": Rural Protest and Nation-Building in Ireland 1882–1890', *Past and Present*, 158 (Feb. 1998), 146–71.

88 *Munster News*, 28 Nov. 1888. See also *Clare Journal*, 15 Nov. 1888.

89 Turner to Ridgeway, 16 Aug. 1888: NAI, CSORP, 1888/17324. See also Memorandum on Mr Micks, n.d. (Nov. 1888): ibid., 1888/21874.

90 Turner to Inspector General, 4 Sept. 1888: ibid. See also Turner to Inspector General, 1 Sept. 1888; Turner to Ridgeway, 9 Aug. 1888: ibid.

91 Minute by Ridgeway, 11 Sept. 1888, with a note by Balfour, 13 Sept. 1888: ibid.

92 Robinson to Ridgeway, 1 Nov. 1888: NAI, CSORP, 1888/21874; Edward Thomas O'Dwyer, Bishop of Limerick, to Balfour, 7 Nov. 1888: ibid., 1888/22789; Balfour to O'Dwyer, 22 Nov. 1888: BL, Balfour Papers, Add. MS 49827, f. 386. Micks was sent to Londonderry, a district in which there were few nationalist boards. His transfer did nothing to harm his subsequent career. He served on the Donegal Light Railway Commission in 1890, and in 1891 was appointed by Balfour as secretary to the newly created Congested Districts Board. He became a commissioner of the Local Government Board in 1898 and a permanent member of the Congested Districts Board in 1910. He retired in 1924.

3

Poor relief and the prosecution of the land campaign

Shortly before the 1882 poor law elections, *United Ireland* announced that, 'if it were only in the matter of outdoor relief for evicted families, the Poor-law Guardians about to be elected may be made to play a great and influential part in the death-grip with landlordism'. A few years later, *The Nation* observed with satisfaction that whereas when landlords had held the union purse strings, they had ensured that

> those whom they had doomed to destruction should not be succoured ... Now the national guardians being in power, and having some humanity in their composition, take equally good care that the victims of a murderous system and a heartless class shall not die of want, no matter to what amount the outdoor relief bill may tot up ... Surely it is only strict justice that is done when landlords who have enjoyed a demonic dance of death above the homes of their ruined serfs are eventually made to 'pay the piper'.[1]

It was widely believed by those on both sides of the land war that nationalist guardians had played an important role in the tenants' campaign. But what could nationalist guardians do to support tenant activists and to what extent did their actions influence the outcome of the campaign at either local or national level? Two case studies are used here to explore these questions. The first examines an attempt by the New Ross Board of Guardians to relax workhouse rules in order to accommodate evicted tenants. The second focuses on the decision of the Athy

Board of Guardians to expend large sums on outdoor relief to
evicted tenants, and then to reimburse surcharged guardians
from union funds. Both cases were seen as trials of strength
between the Local Government Board, as the representative of
British governance, and the boards of guardians, as representatives of the Irish nation. The outcome in each case had relevance
for the prosecution of the land campaign and for the wider
nationalist movement. But the interest of these cases is not
confined to issues of land and politics. They are also important
in understanding how nationalist guardians thought about
welfare issues, and, in particular, how they interpreted and
applied concepts such as entitlement, able-bodiedness and
respectability.

Relieving evicted tenants

Why the relief of evicted tenants was so controversial needs
some explanation. Passed in 1848 with the aim of assisting the
victims of Famine clearances, the Evicted Poor Protection Act
enabled guardians to grant outdoor relief for one calendar
month to people made destitute by eviction, 'to the same extent
as destitute poor persons permanently disabled from labour'.[2]
Nationalist guardians were quick to realise that their powers
under this act could be used to support participants in the land
campaign. Such support was potentially of critical importance.
For tenants to risk eviction by withholding rent, they needed to
be confident that they would be assisted in the event of eviction
taking place. If poor law boards could be relied on to provide
assistance, tenants would feel more confident and would not
have to make demands on the limited financial resources of the
nationalist movement. Moreover, since landlords paid half the
poor rate on land occupied by tenants, and the whole amount on
land in their own hands or occupied by tenants rated at or below
£4, any increase in poor rates fell most heavily on landlords.

Granting generous relief to evicted tenants thus became a
means of sustaining tenant campaigners whilst at the same time
penalising evicting landlords. As a Kerry grazier explained to a
journalist from the *Birmingham Daily Gazette* in 1893, nationalist
guardians had been 'fighting the landlords with money raised

from the landlords by means of the poor rates. Evicted tenants generally receive a pound or twenty-five shillings a week out-door relief. This punishes the landlords, and saves the funds of the Land League, now called the National League.'[3] A good example of this practice is provided by the case of Major Mills Molony. In March 1882, the guardians of the Tulla Union in County Clare had granted outdoor relief to a number of families evicted by Molony. Since 'all the land in the division is his property, and principally comprises his demesne', the *Daily Express* had reported, 'he will find the impost a heavy one'. Having been directed to investigate the story, the local Royal Irish Constabulary inspector, Hubert Crane, confirmed that Molony was likely to end up meeting over half the cost of the relief granted, even though he was receiving no rents. Crane added that he believed the Local Government Board had 'the power to check these grants'. This was not in fact the case. Only the union auditor had the authority to disallow or reduce illegal or exorbitant payments. Informed of this fact, the resident magistrate of the district, Clifford Lloyd, was unimpressed. The guardians who had signed the cheques were, he observed, 'men from whom nothing could be recovered in many cases [and] in the meantime the expenditure goes [on] and is a premium on crime'.[4]

Landlords and officials believed that such payments sent out an inappropriate message to tenants, and to the ordinary poor. Appearing before a select committee in 1885, local government inspector George Spaight observed that evicted tenants were often granted sums larger than were necessary, and more than they would receive as ordinary recipients of relief. This 'had a most demoralising effect'.[5] Evicted tenants who were receiving 30 shillings a week outdoor relief, a Royal Irish Constabulary inspector in County Kerry remarked wryly in 1889, 'will be slow to settle with landlords'.[6] The apparent unwillingness of the Local Government Board to curb the generosity of nationalist guardians was the cause of much frustration amongst those attempting to combat the land campaign. The land agent, Samuel Hussey, complained to the Cowper Commission in 1886 that the Local Government Board had sanctioned payments of one pound a week to evicted tenants even though they had the power to stop them.[7] Many assumed the Board's attitude to reflect current political priorities. Reporting on the activities of western poor law boards in October 1886, a special correspondent of *The Times* speculated that the Local Government Board had 'probably felt that the principle of allowing people to manage their own affairs was being recognised in higher quarters, and that their interference had better be exercised only in extreme cases'.[8] Liberal ministers did have more sympathy for evicted tenants than evicting landlords. And while they did not condone illegal or excessive relief, they had sufficient confidence in boards of guardians to furnish them with additional powers. The Protection of Person and Property Act of 1881, for example, had empowered boards of guardians to give outdoor relief to the families of those detained for Land League activities.[9] Local Government Board officials were to find themselves under much greater pressure to curb the generosity of poor law boards following the return of the Conservatives to office in 1886, and the opening of a new phase of the land campaign.

Like the Land League agitation, the Plan of Campaign was intended to provide a structure and focus for the agrarian discontent, whilst at the same time advancing a broader nationalist agenda.[10] Under the Plan, tenants in dispute with their landlords over rent levels were to offer what they believed to be a fair rent. If this was refused, the money was to be paid into a fund that could then be used to support tenants evicted in the course of the dispute. The role of poor law guardians was potentially more significant during the Plan of Campaign than it had been during the Land League agitation. The strategy adopted in 1881–82 was to avoid actual eviction. Tenants would withhold rent as long as possible, and then pay up on the point of eviction. The Plan of Campaign, on the other hand, required tenants to refuse to pay 'unreasonable' rents, thereby courting eviction. Providing financial support for evicted tenants was thus a more pressing issue during the Plan of Campaign than it had been previously, and, as a number of boards of guardians were to discover, carried correspondingly greater risks.

The New Ross Board of Guardians and the Ely tenants

Evicted tenants who applied to boards of guardians for aid generally sought outdoor relief. Few were so lacking in resources that they needed to consider entering the workhouse, and most were anxious to stay close to their holdings in order to prevent their occupation by new tenants. Nationalist guardians looked favourably on such applications believing that evicted tenants were legally and morally entitled to support outside the workhouse. They were not paupers and should not, it was felt, be treated as such. As one Mallow guardian declared in 1889, 'we don't want the evicted tenantry to come into this house, to be the companions of a degraded class'.[11] When the New Ross Board of Guardians agreed to provide a special ward in the workhouse for the accommodation of a number of families evicted from Lord Ely's property at Fethard-on-Sea, they were, therefore, pioneering a novel method of assisting evicted tenants.

This policy appears to have been devised by Canon Thomas Doyle, parish priest of Ramsgrange and president of the Ramsgrange branch of the National League. In March 1886, Doyle persuaded tenants in dispute with Lord Templemore to threaten 'to throw their farms upon the landlord's hands, and let him do the best he can with them, whilst they will take up their quarters in the New Ross Union workhouse, and allow Lord Templemore the gratification of paying the cost for their maintenance'. Entering the workhouse 'for the advancement of this great cause', Doyle assured the tenants would be considered not a disgrace but an honour.[12] Within a few days, Templemore had offered his tenants a rent reduction of 25 per cent. Encouraged by this success, Doyle recommended the same course of action to tenants of the Marquess of Ely. Having resolved to hold out for an equivalent reduction, the Ely tenants were evicted from their holdings in mid-August.

Local branches of the National League condemned the evictions and called on their colleagues on the New Ross Board of Guardians to prepare a ward for the reception of the tenants, 'to be called in future "The Ward of Honour"'. Local people offered enthusiastic support and the eleven evicted families made their way to the workhouse accompanied by 'large contingents who

had travelled upwards of twenty miles to express their sympathy'.[13] Cheering crowds greeted the procession when it arrived
at New Ross. Special arrangements were made to accommodate
the tenants in the workhouse. They were allowed to stay
together as families and to remain apart from other inmates, to
wear their own clothes, to cook food brought in for them, and to
receive frequent visitors. According to the master, William
Harrington, some relaxation of workhouse rules had initially
been necessary to cope with the sudden influx of people. Further
measures had then been introduced, 'by special directions of the
Guardians who visited the house and made arrangements for
admission and treatment'.[14]

The case of the Ely tenants attracted much comment in the
press. Anxious to maximise support for the tenants, the
[*Wexford*] *People* presented the extremity of their action as
evidence of their desperation, commenting that when 'a whole
estate elect, not alone to be evicted, but to enter the Union
Workhouse … the evidence is clear that the tyranny under
which they have groaned must have been of the most grinding
character, and of their utter inability to suffer its continuance'.[15]
Entering the workhouse under these conditions was an action
deserving of sympathy and support, not, as would normally be
the case, approbation. National newspapers took a broader
focus and considered the wider implications of the case.
Welcoming an addition to the national movement's 'stock of
strategic information', *The Nation* commended this method of
proceeding 'to the consideration of all the National League officials'. *United Ireland* could see 'no reason why the New Ross idea
should not be extensively imitated', and hailed the Ely tenants
as having done as much to popularise the workhouse ward as
nationalist prisoners had done 'to rob the prison cell of its
lugubrious associations. It is disgraceful to enter the workhouse
as a loafer; it is in the highest degree honourable to occupy it as
an encampment against landlordism'.[16]

Conservative publications were alarmed by the way in which
the keystones of the poor law were being eroded. Deploring the
'decadence of that spirit which made the entrance to the poorhouse to the more decent of the farmers and labourers a
humiliation bitter as death', the *St James Gazette* looked back to
the time when the Irish pauper 'crept to the poorhouse down-

cast and shunning observation'. For the unionist weekly, *Notes From Ireland*, the case demonstrated 'that the administration of poor relief in Ireland is of a most peculiar character, and open to the most serious impeachment; and that no effort is spared to popularise lawlessness, and to foster discontent between classes by those whose position and responsibilities should make them thoroughly impartial'.[17] Local landowners regarded the treatment of the Ely tenants as an abuse of the poor laws, and could not understand why the Local Government Board took no action. As one Wexford landowner protested in a letter to the Board, none of the tenants were destitute,

> very far from it, and I am informed that they have not to conform to the rules of the Workhouse; they wear their own clothes, get special food, can go in and out as they like … According to my idea the whole matter is a gross abuse of the Poor Relief Acts … and I protest against paying rates perfectly unnecessary and expenses incurred simply for political purposes.[18]

When finally challenged by the Local Government Board in late October, the guardians defended their conduct on the grounds that the tenants were entitled to 'special treatment on account of [their] being so suddenly cast out of comfortable homes'. They did, however, assure the Board that the tenants were now conforming to workhouse rules, 'except in the matter of some trifling privileges known to and approved by the Guardians'. These privileges included the supply of 'comforts' from supporters outside the workhouse. The guardians maintained that this practice was 'no expense to the ratepayers and does not interfere with the discipline of the establishment and we also understand this is customary in all the Unions we know of'.[19] The Local Government Board took a different view, observing that 'distinguishing certain paupers by granting them privileges which are not enjoyed by others of the same class is entirely at variance with the proper administration of the Poor Laws and cannot be permitted to continue'. The Board ordered the guardians to instruct the Master 'to enforce the rules strictly', and threatened to remove him if he failed to do so.[20]

Poor law regulations were framed so as to render life inside the workhouse less commodious than that outside, the intention being to ensure that people would only enter the workhouse if they had no alternative and would leave again as soon as possible. The New Ross guardians were subverting the poor law by providing a certain level of comfort for the Ely tenants, thus enabling them to remain as long as they needed. They were not, however, seeking to improve conditions in the workhouse generally. Following a tour of the workhouse on 4 December, the board's visiting committee reported that they had found all the wards to be 'clean and in excellent order' with the exception of those occupied by the evicted families, 'which we consider quite inadequate for their health and comfort'. The committee recommended that two wards, one male and one female, be 'exclusively set apart' for evicted families who should be allowed 'to keep their clothes in the wards and if necessary to wear them if their health require it'. It was further recommended that the master be directed 'to allow any comforts sent in by the friends of the evicted families to be given to them'.[21] It was not suggested that such privileges should be extended to the ordinary inmates. Unlike paupers, the evicted tenants had not forfeited their membership of respectable society. As the *People* commented, the tenants had been 'allowed privileges their respectability entitled them to'.[22]

When the board of guardians unanimously adopted the visiting committee's report, it became clear that they had abandoned any attempt to appease the Local Government Board. In a resolution adopted at the same time as the report, the guardians announced their determination,

> as the elected representatives of the ratepayers [to] defy the threats of a non-representative body, which in the present instance as on all other occasions has taken the side of the landlord faction. The Board of Guardians refuse to treat persons who have been rendered homeless and destitute by the tyranny of a brainless agent as ordinary paupers and if they require any justification for ordering those people to be treated in an exceptional manner they have only to point to the exceptional circumstances of the times. The Guardians believe that many of the regulations framed by the Poor Law Commissioners were intended to degrade the victims of landlordism, and they refuse to be parties to such a vile attempt.

This resolution presented a direct challenge to the power of the Local Government Board. The Board's authority to regulate the poor law was rejected, and that of the guardians asserted. The guardians rested their claim to authority on popular legitimacy and support. Daring the Local Government Board to send down vice-guardians, the guardians declared confidently that 'relying on the soundness of public opinion they have no doubt as to the issue of the contest forced upon them'. [23] This confidence was ultimately to prove misplaced.

The dissolution of the board of guardians

As the guardians must have expected, the Local Government Board's response to their defiant resolution was to dissolve the board of guardians and appoint vice-guardians to manage the union.[24] The guardians had already discussed tactics in the event of dissolution, and, with the support of local branches of the National League, they immediately embarked on a campaign of resistance and defiance. Ratepayers were urged not to pay 'a single penny [in] rates so long as the Union is managed by the representatives of Dublin Castle', and a boycott was established. 'Let the Plan of Campaign be applied to the New Ross Workhouse by the New Ross traders', the *People* proclaimed, and the vice-guardians 'will be starved into surrender'.[25] Resistance to the new regime was also promoted within the workhouse. All the officers of the workhouse, with the exception of priests and schoolteachers, were called on to resign. Seven of the officers answered this call: the matron, three of the four rate collectors, the boot-maker, the carpenter and the tailor. The master had already resigned. Accompanying him on a farewell tour of the workhouse, the deputy vice-chair of the deposed board, Michael M'Grath, reminded the female inmates of the disturbances that had erupted the last time vice-guardians had been in charge of the union during the Famine. If they were harshly treated, he advised the women, they should 'do the same thing'.[26]

The boycott was successful in disrupting the administration of the union. The vice-guardians were obliged to move the union account from the National Bank to the Bank of Ireland, and union officials were forced to travel out of the county to obtain supplies, 'local dealers having refused to deal directly

with the Vice Guardians'.[27] The poor were also affected. In mid-
February a reporter for the *People* described meeting a number
of distressed people at the gate of the workhouse who had not
received relief for some weeks because the relieving officers had
been unable either to obtain food or to cash cheques. Supplies
for the workhouse were similarly affected causing, according to
the *Irish Times*, 'a feeling of something like rebellion among the
inmates'.[28] The failure of the vice-guardians to provide
adequately for the poor became another grievance against them.
The Nation reported that the poor of the district were 'suffering
severely by the state of things brought about by the Dublin allies
of evicting landlords', while the *People* claimed that the vice-
guardians' boasted reduction in expenditure had been achieved
by 'the shameless sacrifice of the poor'.[29]

The deposed guardians continued to meet as a body on a
regular basis both to direct the campaign of resistance, and to
demonstrate their disregard for the Local Government Board's
edict. Their meetings were mostly taken up with the rates strike
but they also discussed ways of helping those removed from the
relief lists by the vice-guardians. At a meeting held on 8 January,
one of the elected guardians, James Dooley, recommended that
the money withheld in rates should be paid into a charitable
fund for people whose relief had been stopped. A few weeks
later the guardians passed a resolution calling on National
League branches to form divisional committees to collect funds
to relieve the poor wherever there was a need. Local leaders of
the National League such as Canon Doyle supported this
suggestion. Here again, the guardians were asserting their right
to distribute relief and the legitimacy of their interpretation of
the poor laws. It would appear, however, that local people were
reluctant to provide more than moral support. The call for a
relief fund was repeated in January, in February and again in
June.[30]

The vice-guardians' administration

Under the vice-guardians' administration, expenditure, particularly on outdoor relief, was reduced, and workhouse rules were
strictly enforced. The movement of people in and out of the

workhouse, for example, was curtailed and steps were taken to introduce a stricter classification of workhouse inmates. Mothers of two or more illegitimate children were to be placed by themselves and married women and children provided with their own quarters.[31] Classification within workhouses was a contentious issue throughout the post-Famine period with critics of the workhouse system insisting that only a strict system of moral classification could save the respectable poor, and particularly women, from corruption by the non-respectable. Official policy was to encourage the provision of separate accommodation for prostitutes but to leave the internal layout of workhouses to boards of guardians and workhouse masters. By separating single mothers from married women, the vice-guardians were addressing one of the main complaints made on behalf of the evicted tenants, that the women of the party were being forced to mix with 'the very dregs of society – mothers of illegitimate children and prostitutes'. Compelling the wives and sisters of 'sturdy farmers ... to sleep in dormitories set apart for the most disreputable female characters in the house', was, *The Nation* had proclaimed, 'a scandal that must not be tolerated'.[32] The moral indignation expressed on the tenants' behalf depended for much of its force on the depiction of their social status. They were portrayed as respectable farmers, people for whom the workhouse was a totally alien environment, while the workhouse inmates with whom they were forced to associate were presented as social outcasts. In reality, however, the tenants were not 'sturdy farmers'. They were not farmers at all, but household tenants who worked as tradesmen and labourers. As such they occupied the very social groups that featured most frequently on relief lists. The social gulf between the tenants and the inmates was in fact much narrower than their supporters implied.

The campaign by the deposed guardians proved very effective in stirring up anger and resentment against the vice-guardians, both within and outside the workhouse. That anger erupted on 17 February when the vice-guardians and the new master, Timothy McAuliffe, were attacked 'by upwards of 100 women, beaten with sticks, pelted with stones and mud, and forced to retreat'. According to the *People*, 'the subsequent skedaddling of the vice-guardians with all the female paupers in full hue-and-cry after them through the streets of New Ross' was 'a picture for another Cruikshank'. Order was restored to the workhouse by the police, but serious disturbances broke out in the town the following week when eight of the principal rioters appeared before the local magistrates.[33] The riot and its aftermath highlighted the deficiencies of the vice-guardians' administration, and thus provided a further opportunity for the deposed guardians to present themselves as the only people with the authority to administer the poor laws effectively. At a meeting on 19 February the guardians unanimously resolved to request the Local Government Board to recall the vice-guardians, 'and hand over the affairs of the union to the ratepayers by ordering a new election of guardians and we will guarantee for the safety of the house and not have law and order outraged as it is'. The Local Government Board declined this offer. Observing that the riot was 'unquestionably attributable to the obstruction given by the late guardians and their supporters to the administration of the poor law in the New Ross Union, and the encouragement thus afforded to insubordinate inmates of the workhouse and other ill-disposed persons outside', the Board warned that the guardians would not be restored 'while the illegal and disorderly conduct alluded to above is promoted and encouraged, and until the authority of the law is fully established'.[34]

The main concern of the Local Government Board following the riot was to reassert the authority of the vice-guardians and to ensure that rates were paid. The Assistant Secretary of the Board, Thomas Mooney, noted on 3 March that the 'point of greatest importance now is … to pay particular attention to the actions of the collectors and to keep them up to the mark and to enforce the payment of rates'. The Board was much relieved when concerted action by rate collectors and bailiffs in mid-March secured payments totalling £80. Reporting on the operation, the Royal Irish Constabulary inspector for County Wexford expressed the hope 'that the success of the two days collection and the paying of those who said they would not, may cause others to do likewise'. But he warned that should the remainder of the defaulters hold out, 'the collection will be attended with enormous difficulty'.[35] Maintaining the strike became more difficult following the departure of all the Ely tenants from the workhouse in early June.

The tenants return home

The evicted tenants had been kept under strict supervision in the months following the riot and were required to adhere to workhouse rules. On 1 June a number of the tenants were discharged on the grounds that they were 'able-bodied men who should have no difficulty in obtaining employment'. The following week the master reported that this 'course appears to have had the effect of nearly the whole party quitting the House'.[36] In contrast to their entry to the workhouse, the tenants departed quietly and unaccompanied. They were, a police report noted, 'obliged to employ cars at their own expense to convey them back to Fethard'. Having left the workhouse 'in opposition to the wishes of the Ramsgrange National League', the tenants were said to have been publicly denounced by Canon Doyle who maintained that they had acted against advice and called on people not to associate with them. The tenants' decision was regarded with much satisfaction by the authorities. Noting that they had gained nothing by going into the work-house and remaining there so long, District Magistrate Owen Slacke predicted that their return, against Doyle's wishes, 'will do good'.[37]

At the beginning of August, Doyle judged that the tenants had been 'punished sufficiently for all practical purposes' and recommended that they should be allowed 'to live as they can'. Any further resistance to rates might also be abandoned, 'since the cause of the resistance – the oppression of the unfortunates of Fethard' had been removed. The tenants, he noted bitterly, had 'proved themselves utterly unworthy of an honour that O'Connell or Charles Stewart Parnell might be proud to receive – to be surrounded, cheered, and applauded by 70,000 Wexford, Carlow and Kilkenny men. Such a compliment should have made cowards brave.' Everything possible had been done to alleviate 'the little inconvenience they had to endure', and victory had been within their grasp. Yet 'they preferred to skulk home, a sham and a disgrace to their native village'. Far from stressing the respectability of the tenants, Doyle now drew attention to their relatively low social status, asserting that most of them 'had better food and clothes in the workhouse than they had a home'. Doyle's recommendations were endorsed by a

meeting of local representatives on 10 August. Public appetite
for the fight was acknowledged to be waning. As one delegate
commented, 'when the Fethard tenants, for whom they were
fighting, were after turning tail, it was but right that they should
give up'. After some discussion it was agreed

> that as the original cause of the resistance to the payment of the
> poor-rates has ceased, and as the people have made a sufficiently
> emphatic protest, and shown the power they possess to prosecute
> evil doers, they may now pay the outstanding rates, if they wish,
> when called upon, and avoid troubling themselves further about
> the matter in the hurry of the harvest.[38]

Attitudes to the tenants underwent a striking reversal in the
months after their return home. Condemned as cowards by
nationalists, they were acclaimed by unionists as victims of
National League bribery and intimidation. The *Daily Express*
had alleged on 30 June that 'a prominent member of the Land
League [*sic*] offered £5 a-piece if they held out for another fort-
night. They held out for a month but not one of them saw a
penny, much less £5.' When they finally left the workhouse,
'after their ten or eleven months martyrdom', they were
boycotted by the League.[39] Balfour cited the case in a Commons
debate in late August as demonstrating 'how the National
League interferes in matters altogether outside the sphere of
land and landlordism'. He was, he declared melodramatically,
unable to conceive 'any form of tyranny more gross and scan-
dalous and unwarrantable than this case discloses'. Balfour's
account was challenged by the Ramsgrange National League.
There had, they insisted, been no compulsion. The tenants had
required an abatement of their rent 'just as much as landholders,
as they being labourers, petty shopkeepers, and poor fishermen,
depended entirely upon the surrounding landholders for their
sustenance'. They were boycotted not because they had left the
workhouse, but for 'having boastingly and defiantly entered
into a contest in which they behaved cowards and runaways'.[40]

Within a few months, the Ely tenants had been restored to the
nationalist pantheon. In December they accepted a 50 per cent
reduction on all rents due. This was considerably more than the
25 per cent reduction originally requested but as the tenants
were no longer part of the Plan of Campaign, Ely's agent could

settle with them without appearing to be giving in to the Plan. Wexford nationalists rejoiced. 'The victory has been won', the *People* trumpeted, 'bad landlordism defeated and the banner of the Plan of Campaign floats triumphantly'. At a meeting held on 1 January 1888, speakers congratulated the tenants on their 'splendid victory ... over landlordism' and lauded the sacrifices made by them, 'for the sake of principle and the cause of their fellow tenants'.[41] The change in language could hardly be more striking. Cowards had become heroes, and labourers had become the fellows of tenant farmers.

The restoration of the board of guardians

With the authority of the vice-guardians and the law firmly restored, the Local Government Board felt able to return the administration of the union to the board of guardians in the spring of 1888 following the poor law elections. The elections saw all twenty elected members of the deposed board (with two exceptions) returned unopposed.[42] The example of the New Ross guardians was not widely imitated. Boards of guardians in at least four other unions made plans to set aside a special ward to accommodate evicted tenants and to provide a special diet, but none implemented them. The Local Government Board attributed this to warnings that it had issued to the boards that workhouse rules could not be varied for political reasons.[43] More to the point perhaps, tenants had shown no sign of wishing to take advantage of the arrangements. Even *United Ireland*, one of the strongest advocates of what it termed 'the New Ross experiment', acknowledged that outdoor relief provided a better method of supporting evicted tenants, and placed a greater financial burden on the evicting landlord. Only in exceptional circumstances, arising from 'special local pressure', would it be 'advisable to utilise the Wards of Honour'.[44] Turning the workhouse into a sanctuary for evicted tenants proved ineffective as a policy for a number of reasons. The necessary infringement of workhouse regulations rendered boards of guardians vulnerable to dissolution. Popular attitudes were hostile both to the workhouse and to those who took refuge in it, thus undermining support for a campaign focused on workhouse inmates. Evicted tenants were reluctant to enter the workhouse and risk being stigmatised as paupers. Few were persuaded by the analogy drawn between prison and the workhouse. Political prisoners were a traditional and respected element of Irish campaigns. Political paupers were not.

The New Ross guardians maintained that their treatment of the Ely tenants had been justified 'by the dictates of decency and humanity'. Their duty to protect the respectable from the stigma of pauperism had thus outweighed their duty to adhere to poor law regulations. The Local Government Board, they believed, had no real objection to this principle, only to its application. Had the Ely tenants been 'Orange emergencymen', one elected guardian asserted, the Local Government Board would have overlooked the infringement of the regulations. According to this interpretation, it was the officials of the Local Government Board, seeking 'to prop up a landlord system that pauperises the people', not the guardians, who were bringing politics into the boardroom.[45] Throughout their conflict with the Local Government Board over the Ely tenants, the New Ross guardians sought to present themselves as the only legitimate arbiters of relief policy. By so doing they were challenging the authority of the Local Government Board and of the poor law system. If the poor law could not be used for the benefit of the people, the *People* proclaimed in December 1886, 'it must go'.[46] But as the Ely tenants were to discover, while the New Ross guardians might have adopted their own definition of eligibility, they would continue to differentiate between applicants and to privilege 'respectability'. The respectable were entitled to be treated in a humane manner that preserved their dignity. The non-respectable had no such entitlement. The Ely tenants were deserving of special treatment so long as they remained loyal to the nationalist cause and did what they were told. Public perception of their social status also fluctuated according to their political activism. Having been elevated to the status of respectable tenant farmers whilst following the Plan of Campaign, they reverted to labourers as soon as they abandoned the Plan. The message for those on the margins of society was clear. Just as respectability had to be earned, behaviour rather than need was to be a central factor in determining eligibility to relief.

The Athy guardians and the Luggacurran evictions

In June 1888, the Local Government Board dissolved the Athy Guardians on account of their wilfully misapplying the union funds for the pecuniary advantage of a member of their own body who had been surcharged by the Local Government Auditor on account of relief granted to evicted tenants.[47]

In the wake of the New Ross experiment, most boards of guardians followed *United Ireland's* advice, and their own inclinations, and granted evicted tenants outdoor relief. While the sums granted were often generous in comparison with those given to ordinary applicants, relief was generally discontinued after one month unless the applicant qualified on other grounds such as sickness. The Athy guardians contravened poor law regulations and established practice by granting sums well in excess of £1 a week and continuing the relief beyond the one-month time limit. Their aim was to administer relief in a way that was responsive to political exigencies and popular sentiment. Their response to dissolution was to attempt to mobilise the local community in defiance of central government. Once again, nationalist guardians were asserting the right as elected representatives to shape the relief system to meet local needs and to manage their union as they saw fit.

The Luggacurran evictions

On 17 November 1886, tenants on Lord Lansdowne's estate at Luggacurran in the Queen's County had adopted the Plan of Campaign after being refused the same rent reductions as tenants on Lansdowne's property in County Kerry.[48] Leading the campaign were two of Lansdowne's largest tenants, described in the local press as 'gentlemen of extensive means', John W. Dunne of Raheenahone who rented more than 1,300 acres, and Denis Kilbride of Luggacurran who held 700 acres. Dunne and Kilbride could afford to pay their rent but had declared their refusal to do so as long as poorer tenants were refused just concessions.[49] Both Dunne and Kilbride were evicted in March 1887, followed by a number of their sub-tenants and other tenants. In all 31 tenants and 18 sub-tenants were evicted, a total, including their families, of 239 people.[50] It was widely believed that Dunne and Kilbride had been singled out in order to set an example. Addressing a large meeting in Athy at the end of March, the sub-editor of *United Ireland*, James O'Connor, declared that by allowing themselves to be evicted the two had 'acted like men – they were noble standard bearers ... for all Ireland'.[51]

Shortly after the evictions, the Athy Board of Guardians held their annual election of officers. Dunne was elected chair, Kilbride vice-chair and Daniel Whelan deputy vice-chair. Whelan was also a tenant of Lansdowne, though not on the Luggacurran estate, and had been evicted from his farm near Athy after joining the Plan of Campaign in support of the Luggacurran tenants. In electing three 'Campaigners of the Queen's County', the guardians were said to be consulting not only their own wishes, 'but the feeling of every Nationalist in Ireland'. Thanking the guardians for the honour conferred on him, Dunne welcomed the fact that the union now had an elected guardian in the chair. The people, he declared, had 'taken that office in their hands and he hoped they would keep it'.[52] Dunne had in fact been chair of the board since 1883, but he had held the post as an ex-officio rather than an elected guardian. Having been removed from the commission of the peace for his promotion of the Plan of Campaign, he was invited to stand as an elected guardian by the Athy National League and had been returned for the Luggacurran division in March 1887. For tenants such as Dunne, Kilbride and Whelan, the Plan of Campaign offered both a political and an economic opportunity. Unlike tenants in the south-west who embraced the Plan as a means of economic survival, many of the Luggacurran tenants did so in the hope of forcing Lansdowne to sell off land at a favourable price. Participation in the Plan allowed them to engage in a public struggle with landlordism whilst also potentially improving their economic and social status.[53]

The officers of the Athy Board and their supporters were determined to use their powers as guardians to support the Luggacurran tenants and to advance the Plan of Campaign. Providing support for poorer tenants was essential if the campaign was to be successful. While large tenants such as

Dunne and Kilbride were in good circumstances, many of the sub-tenants were not. Moreover, since many of them worked for their immediate landlord as labourers, eviction meant the loss of their jobs as well as their homes. Addressing a meeting held in the locality in late April, the Kildare MP, James Leahy, assured the evicted tenants on behalf of the Irish Parliamentary Party, the Irish National League, and the Irish people, that 'they would never want or suffer in the least'.[54] Funds were collected by public subscription and the National League erected 20 wooden huts for the accommodation of some of the evicted tenants.

The Athy guardians had already taken steps to ensure that Leahy's pledge was honoured. Following a discussion of the tenants' situation on 29 March, the guardians had unanimously agreed a motion

> that all the families evicted on the Lansdowne estates in the Queen's County within the Union be granted a sum of £1 per week for each family of eight and under that, but that families of over eight in number be granted 2s 6d per head per week. In no case is any family to receive a lesser sum than £1.

As a result of this decision, 42 applicants had been granted £1 a week for a month. Three others had been granted 22s 6d, 25s and 35s respectively. (Of the 45 applicants, 41 were from the Luggacurran electoral division, three from Timoleague and one from Moone.) All but one of the applicants continued to receive relief after the first month but generally at the lower rate of 10s. For example, Michael Cranny, who had a wife and 14 children ranging in age from 14 years to 6 months, had initially received 35s a week. This was later reduced to 15s and then to 10s.[55] Cranny had previously worked for Kilbride earning 12s a week, and had grass for a cow said to be worth a further 2s 6d. In November, Cranny came before the Board asking either for an increase in the amount of outdoor relief he was receiving, or to be admitted to the workhouse. The guardians decided to maintain the grant of outdoor relief at 10s a week. This, together with what Cranny was receiving from the National League 'War Chest', should, Whelan argued, be enough to support him.[56] Given the size of his family, and his inability to find employment, Cranny undoubtedly qualified for relief, but, as an able-bodied man, he was ineligible for outdoor relief after the

first month. The guardians were clearly anxious to prevent sub-
tenants such as Cranny, who were dependent on either Dunne
or Kilbride for their livelihoods, ending up in the workhouse.

Criteria for support

Ordinary recipients of outdoor relief were treated far less gener-
ously. In late May, James McLoughlin, a guardian from
Stradbally in Queen's County, and president of the Stradbally
branch of the Irish National League, sought to reduce the
amount of relief being given to a man from his district who, he
claimed, could get employment 'if he liked'. Such considerations
did not apply to the Luggacurran tenants. They, McLoughlin
declared, were 'worthy of anything they get'. Another guardian
pronounced the tenants to be 'objects of compassion a great deal
more than the ordinary recipients of relief'.[57] Lynn Hollen Lees
has noted the growing use of moral criteria to assess eligibility
to relief in England in the later part of the nineteenth century. In
many unions guardians denied outdoor relief to applicants
judged to be immoral, indolent or improvident. Criteria for
support became more rigorous, 'as guardians articulated a
model of morality to which paupers were expected to
conform'.[58] A similar development is evident in Ireland but here
attention was focused more on those who offended against
political, rather than moral, codes of behaviour. In May 1887, for
example, Thomas Orford, a member of the Athy Board of
Guardians and president of the Moone branch of the National
League, recommended that Mary Nolan be struck off the
outdoor relief list until she explained her conduct in providing
an evicting party with 'a comfortable dinner'. The Board
agreed.[59]

A more extreme example of this policy is evident in the case
of the Dandys that came before the Athy Board in October 1887.
Patrick Dandy, together with his wife, his eldest son, William,
aged 21, and four younger children, applied for admission to the
workhouse on 13 October and were provisionally admitted.
When the case came before the guardians on 18 October, they
ordered the family's discharge on the grounds that both Patrick
and William were able-bodied. It was also alleged that since

William Dandy had been working as an emergencyman on Lansdowne's estate over the summer, he could not be 'destitute or badly off'. The *Leinster Leader* had no sympathy for the family, expressing the wish that the same fate might 'overtake all the enemies of our country'. Patrick was discharged with his son, but his wife, who was sick, and the younger children were allowed to remain. Within a short time, however, the two men were readmitted to the workhouse as destitute. The guardians again ordered their discharge. They were able-bodied men, one guardian observed, 'and if they have squandered away their money must we admit them here?' What, he enquired of his colleagues, 'will you turn the workhouse into if you admit such people?' The pattern of discharge and re-admittance looked set to be repeated indefinitely until, on 8 November, the relieving officer managed to persuade the guardians to leave the matter in his hands.[60]

By this time the case had come to the attention of the both the Chief Secretary and the Local Government Board. Lansdowne's agent, Townshend Trench, had written to the Local Government Board complaining that the Dandys had been refused relief because William Dandy had been in Lansdowne's employment. Asked to report on the case, the local Royal Irish Constabulary inspector described it as one of 'persecution on the part of the members of local branches of the National League'. Ridgeway, shared this view, commenting that it was evident that the motive of the guardians in evicting the Dandys from the work-house was 'political and that they propose to employ the money of the ratepayers in order to attain their end'. The Local Government Board asked their inspector to inquire into the affair but, as Robinson warned Ridgeway, there was 'consider-able difficulty in dealing with such a case' as 'the Irish Poor Relief Act expressly prohibits interference by the Local Government Board in any individual case for the purpose of ordering relief'. The Board subsequently wrote to the guardians pointing out that since 'the only question they ought to consider in determining whether an applicant should be relieved is whether or not he is destitute', they would be acting 'in a very improper manner if they were to allow any consideration of a political nature to influence their decision in the matter', and reminding them that the relieving officer was duty bound to afford provisional relief in cases of urgent necessity.[61] The guardians justified their action by referring, once again, to the fact that the Dandys 'were able-bodied men, and, therefore, not eligible for relief'.[62] This response demonstrates the determination of nationalist guardians to apply poor law principles on their own terms.

The surcharges

The conduct of the Athy guardians came under further scrutiny in January 1888, when the union auditor, George Finlay, conducted his half-yearly audit of the Athy Union accounts. Finlay disallowed payments totalling £38 15s and surcharged the three guardians who had authorised them. Daniel Whelan was surcharged £136, James Byrne £2 and James McLoughlin 15s. The surcharges included illegal payments of relief made after the expiry of the one-month time limit, together with amounts disallowed as exorbitant. Finlay later explained that in calculating the amount of exorbitant relief granted in the first month, he had been 'very much influenced by the guardians' own measure of the wants of each family, as evidenced by their allowance at the end of the month; and I believe that in every case, with, I think, one exception, I allowed a sum considerably in excess in that measure'.[63] It was not uncommon for guardians to be surcharged, but the sums involved rarely exceeded £10. The level of surcharge in Whelan's case was exceptional. The Athy guardians protested vigorously against all the surcharges arguing that they had considered it much cheaper to relieve the tenants outside the workhouse, 'having no accommodation for so many', and protesting that the Local Government Board had failed to advise them that they were acting illegally.[64]

These arguments made no impression on the Local Government Board whose secretary pointed out that it was up the guardians to decide on the amount of relief in individual cases and then for the auditor to determine whether the amounts granted were warranted.[65] Byrne paid the surcharge. Whelan and McLoughlin did not. Warrants were obtained against the two men and on 21 May the police seized cattle and farm implements belonging to Whelan which were to be sold at auction two days later. Before the auction could take place, Whelan's friends settled the claim.[66] The Local Government Board regarded this as the end of the affair, observing that it had been brought 'to a very satisfactory conclusion'. This view was reinforced by a report from their inspector, H.A. Robinson. Noting that the large grants of outdoor relief made by the Athy guardians had 'attracted a considerable amount of attention' when they were given, and that 'the guardians and ratepayers of all the unions in these midland counties were much exercised as to what the result of such a proceeding would be', Robinson concluded that 'Mr Finlay's prompt and successful action has taught the guardians a lesson, the salutary effect of which it is impossible to exaggerate'.[67]

Nationalist newspapers condemned the interference of the Local Government Board as an attempt 'to abet the enemies of the people'. Insisting that it was the duty of poor law guardians 'to interpose the shield of charity between ravaging landlordism and its victims', *The Nation* urged the guardians to stand firm 'remembering that the pauper-ward and emigrant ship have ever been the favourite "remedies" of the enemy for the manu-factured misery of our people'. The *Leinster Leader* welcomed Whelan's refusal to pay the surcharge as a 'manly and effective protest ... against a system of government which is rotten to the core', commenting that the guardians' actions had been endorsed by the rate-payers of Luggacurran when they had once again returned Dunne as guardian for the division by a majority of almost 60 votes. The *Leader* urged the Board of Guardians to reimburse Whelan, declaring that the 'little shred of Local Government that Irishmen have left is of no value if its administration is to be hampered at every turn ... Better have Local Government swept away altogether than that it should exist only in name'.[68] The idea of reimbursal was strongly supported by *United Ireland* as well as by nationalist MPs such as John Dillon and J.E. Kenny.[69] The guardians were initially reluc-tant to take such a step. A motion proposing that Whelan be given a cheque to cover the amount of the surcharge failed to find a seconder on 22 May. On 12 June, however, a similar motion was passed unanimously despite a warning from the Local Government Board that if such a payment was made,

not only will the Guardians who sign the cheque be made personally liable for the amount but that the Board of Guardians who as
a body authorise the expenditure must be regarded as failing to
perform their duties in accordance with the intention of the Irish
Poor Relief Acts.

A cheque was duly made out to Whelan for £136 and signed by
Dunne, as chair of the board, and two other guardians.[70]

The appointment of vice-guardians

On learning of the guardians' action, Henry Robinson promptly
wrote to Balfour requesting his approval for superseding the
Athy Board of Guardians, and on 18 June the board was
dissolved. C.L. Fitzgerald and W.J. Burke were appointed vice-
guardians.[71] Burke was subsequently transferred to Dungarvan
Union in October, being replaced by C.R. Lynch-Staunton of
County Galway. As in New Ross, the vice-guardians immediately set about instituting a more economical administration.
The outdoor relief lists were reduced and able-bodied men
encouraged to leave the workhouse. On 29 August, for example,
seven able-bodied men were called before the vice-guardians to
show why they should not be discharged to work on the
harvest. James Doogue claimed to be suffering from pains in his
arms and shoulders but was discharged when the vice-
guardians were informed that he was known as 'the strong man
of the house'. Vice-guardian Burke urged the men to 'try and
earn a living outside the workhouse', telling them that it was for
their own good 'as well as that of the ratepayers' that they were
being discharged. Five of the men were discharged, the master
being directed to obtain the medical officer's opinion as to the
health of the other two.[72]

Encouraged by the vice-guardians' revision of the outdoor
relief lists, a deputation of ex-officio guardians was organised to
protest against individual relief cases in their own districts.
These objections were sustained in some cases; in others the
relieving officer was able to make a case for the continuance of
relief. Relief was allowed in the case of Mary Bowe, for example,
who was receiving 1s 6d a week despite living with her son-in-
law, after the relieving officer explained that the son-in-law had

two children, 'and had enough to do for himself'.[73] The readiness of Fitzgerald and Burke to accept the opinion of the relieving officers suggests that they were anxious not to remove relief from deserving cases. While this approach might conciliate some sections of local opinion, it was at variance with official policy. Earlier that month an enquiry by the vice-guardians concerning a woman with six children, who had been receiving provisional relief for seven months, her husband having been committed to a lunatic asylum, elicited a frosty response from the Local Government Board. Explaining that 'under the circumstances described the Vice Guardians cannot afford outdoor relief to this woman or to her children unless any of them should be suffering from infirmity or sickness', the secretary of the Board noted that the action of the relieving officer in the case 'was not in accordance with the spirit and intention of the Irish Poor Relief Extension Act' and that he should not in future use his powers 'to meet cases of sudden and urgent necessity with the object of retaining on the relief lists persons to whom outdoor relief cannot be legally afforded.'[74]

The Local Government Board regarded the appointment of vice-guardians as an opportunity to provide a practical demonstration of efficient and economical administration. It was, therefore, essential that they adopted only the narrowest interpretation of poor law regulations. H.A. Robinson exemplified this approach when he temporarily replaced Burke as vice-guardian in October, following the latter's transfer to Dungarvan. Outdoor relief, Robinson reminded the relieving officers, 'was only intended to meet cases of emergency or illness', and in cases of illness a medical certificate was required. The elderly were required to enter the workhouse. When Mary Kealy applied for a grant of 1s a week to be renewed claiming that she was starving, Robinson informed her that she would be much better off in the workhouse. Kealy disagreed, declaring, 'I don't want to come in; I wish to be buried with my children outside'. She was refused relief.[75]

Critics of the deposed guardians welcomed the new regime. The *Leinster Express* reported that 309 people had been struck off the outdoor relief lists effecting a saving of £750. Arguing that the vice-guardians had 'conducted the business of the union, and reduced the expenditure to such an alarming extent, that we do not see why they should not be continued in office', the *Express* noted that the 'majority of the largest ratepayers had not object to the present arrangement, because they have profited considerably by it'. Robinson endorsed this view, noting that many ratepayers would regret the return of the elected board having seen what substantial savings could be effected 'by careful and judicious management'. The substantial reduction in outdoor relief brought about by the vice-guardians afforded 'ample proof that there was very great laxity in this respect by the late Board'.[76] It is evident, however, that not all ratepayers supported the new policy on relief. On 7 November one of the elected guardians made representations to the vice-guardians on behalf of a number of people struck off the outdoor relief list in his own division of Castledermot. These were elderly people considered by the ratepayers to be entitled to relief. 'All the ratepayers', he claimed, 'are very willing to give these people outdoor relief. They have worked amongst them all their lives. They have never been a burden to anybody, and we think it is very hard now to make them come into this establishment, which we all know is not a good place for young or old to enter'.

Fitzgerald promised to review the cases but warned that relief could only be granted in certain circumstances. Having reviewed the cases of nine people, the vice-guardians granted outdoor relief to six and offered the other three the house.[77] Popular support for the elected guardians, and for their administration of relief, clearly existed within the union, but it proved difficult to convert this into positive action to secure their return.

The rates strike

Like their colleagues in New Ross, the deposed Athy guardians had attempted to resist the imposition of vice-guardians by means of a rates strike. The strike was supported by local representatives such as the Athy Town Commissioners, by local National League branches, and by the local nationalist press. An editorial in the *Leinster Leader* proclaimed it to be the proud privilege of the Athy Board of Guardians, 'to strike a blow for the freedom and independence of Irish representative bodies', predicting that when the Local Government Board found that the cost of collecting the rates was 'ten times the amount of the rate itself, they will begin to realise that they have entered into a foolish struggle against popular rights with a people organised to resist them'. But as the *Leinster Express* smugly observed, such threats 'need not give much concern'. Rates strikes had been 'tried, and failed, in other places where guardians have been superseded'.[78] As the *Express* suspected, a rates strike was easier to call than to enforce. Having expressed surprise at the end of July that the vice-guardians were being treated with respect in the town, the *Leader* was forced to admit on 18 August that the inhabitants of Athy had so far 'made no manful effort to clog the work of those who have grabbed an office peculiarly the people's'. This, the paper reminded its readers, was a question of principle. They could 'either be brave or craven'. On 21 October, a convention of all National League branches within the Athy Union passed a resolution calling on ratepayers 'to support the principle of "No taxation without representation" with reference to the rate struck by the Vice Guardians of Athy Union'. The *Kildare Observer* was in no doubt about the significance of the resolution. The meeting, it pronounced, had 'practically issued a No Rate manifesto and the result will be watched with eagerness'.[79]

The attempt to galvanise ratepayers into a concerted campaign of non-payment failed. Frustrated by the lack of activity, local newspapers turned to other topics. The board of guardians was restored in July 1889, a few months later than had originally been anticipated. Ridgeway had advised Balfour at the time of the dissolution that 'if things go on smoothly without opposition, [the Local Government Board] proposes to allow the guardians to be reinstated at the next election'.[80] In the event, the restoration was postponed from the spring until the summer. The delay would suggest that while the rates strike did cause the authorities some concern, it did not seriously disrupt the administration of the union. Most of the elected guardians were returned unopposed at the poor law elections. However, neither Whelan nor Dunne returned to boardroom. No nomination was received for Whelan's division of Barrowhouse, while Edmund Lynch replaced Dunne as the representative of the Luggacurran division. It would appear that, having been evicted from their farms, the two men were unable to fulfil the property qualification required of electoral candidates. At the first meeting of the restored board, Matthew Minch was elected to the chair with Thomas Orford and James McLoughlin taking the positions of vice-chair and deputy vice-chair.[81] All three were prominent within the local nationalist movement and had taken an active part supporting the Plan of Campaign on the Luggacurran estate.

With the restoration of the board of guardians, both sides claimed victory. *United Ireland* declared that the Local Government Board had once again come off second best in its attempt to support 'Balfourian tyranny'. Congratulating the people of Athy for getting rid of the vice-guardians, Denis Kilbride commended the way in which the town had 'come out in the most extraordinary manner in supporting the evicted tenants'. Balfour might have suppressed the Board of Guardians but 'he had not succeeded in suppressing or abating the Nationalist spirit of Athy or the Athy Union'. The poor people who had suffered from the withdrawal of outdoor relief would, he suggested, 'bless the day the elected guardians take their place', knowing that they 'will act in no niggardly spirit towards them'.[82] Relief policy was here being presented as a symbol and a product of nationalist administration, reinforcing the movement's claim to represent the popular will. The Local Government Board, on the other hand, continued to maintain that the surcharge of the guardians and the dissolution of the Athy Board had taught Irish guardians a salutary lesson and had thus prevented other boards from attempting to evade the auditor's power to surcharge illegal relief.[83] There does appear to be some truth to this claim. While guardians continued to grant illegal relief, particularly to evicted tenants, no further attempt was made to grant such large amounts, or to reimburse surcharges from union funds. Guardians were reimbursed, but from funds raised by voluntary subscription.[84]

During 1888–89 the Athy Union experienced the replacement of one kind of poor law administration by another. The guardians' administration was characterised by a loose definition of eligibility based on factors such as behaviour, character and connections. Evicted tenants were eligible for outdoor relief as active participants in the Plan of Campaign, as victims of landlordism and, in some cases, as dependents of members of the board. The elderly were eligible for outdoor relief as respectable and deserving members of the community. The vice-guardians' administration was characterised by its close adherence to poor law regulations and by a narrow definition of eligibility. Local people were divided in their response. Both regimes commended some support, but whereas the vice-guardians received their strongest backing from landowners and large ratepayers, the elected guardians' most enthusiastic supporters were, as Kilbride suggested, probably to be found amongst the poor. This may help to explain why the rates strike failed to attract sufficient support to be effective. Ratepayers had their own interests and their own pockets to protect.

Conclusion

Granting relief to evicted tenants enabled poor law guardians to make a substantive contribution to the land campaign by shifting the balance of power in land disputes away from landlords and towards tenants. This was one reason why Balfour was far more concerned about the activities of boards of guardians than Liberal ministers such as Forster. Having identified the government so closely with landlordism, any challenge to landlord power also represented a challenge to the authority of government. But if guardians were able to provide symbolic and material support for tenant activists, that support was subject to the limitations imposed by poor law regulations and by public attitudes to relief. Providing indoor relief proved unsatisfactory for the reasons outlined above. Outdoor relief provided a more flexible and more acceptable form of assistance. By granting outdoor relief to all evicted tenants regardless of circumstances, boards of guardians were able to categorise them as victims without stigmatising them as paupers. But to grant such relief for more than a month, or at levels considerably in excess of those given to ordinary recipients, was to run the risk of surcharge by the auditor. The standard rate for the relief of evicted tenants was one pound a week for one month. So widespread was this practice that the Local Government Board rarely intervened so long as relief remained within these limits. When the Athy guardians exceeded them, they found themselves subject to the full force of official sanctions.

With the force of law on its side, the Local Government Board was always likely to have the final word in any dispute. As the Board noted with typical, but not unjustified, complacency in 1892, the general effect of dissolutions over the previous twenty years had been

> in every instance satisfactory. The abuses were remedied, the financial embarrassments were removed, an example of proper and careful administration was set to the guardians on re-election, and the action of our Board had a most salutary effect in checking a tendency to similar irregularities on the part of Boards of Guardians elsewhere in Ireland.[85]

Whilst generally seeking to avoid public conflict with local guardians, Board officials appreciated the power of exemplary dissolutions. Where guardians were clearly acting in breech of poor law regulations, and where the Local Government Board was confident of victory, confrontation provided an opportunity to remind guardians where power ultimately lay. In defying the authority of the Local Government Board, the New Ross and the Athy guardians were asserting their right as popular representatives to rewrite or reinterpret the poor laws. In so doing they were publicly aligning themselves with the people against the government. They presented their administration as more caring, more generous and more in tune with local feeling. By categorising applicants for relief as deserving of sympathy or condemnation and treating them accordingly, nationalist guardians could claim to be reflecting popular sentiment. But the introduction of politics into the decision making process alienated many larger ratepayers.

Both sets of guardians found it more difficult to resist the imposition of vice-guardians than they had anticipated. Rates strikes proved difficult to organise and to maintain. Unlike a rent strike, where the target was a landlord and the strikers were tenants whose own livelihoods were at stake, a rates strike involved a less emotive target, and the strikers were a far more disparate group. Moreover, those adversely affected by the strike included the poor themselves. The immediate objective of the strikes was to remove the vice-guardians. In the event, they merely extended their terms of office. The longer-term objective of the action was far from clear. The guardians were variously claimed to be acting on behalf of the evicted tenants, the ratepayers, the poor and the nation. But the interests of these groups did not necessarily coincide. The failure of the rates strikes demonstrated the limits of the guardians' power and of community action. Working within the existing system of government, nationalist guardians could challenge but not evade the power of the Local Government Board to regulate that system. Poor law administration provided a weaker focus for communal consensus and cohesion than landlord–tenant relations and was, therefore, less effective as a springboard for nationalist campaigns. Conflict over the relief of evicted tenants exposed the growing divergence between local and central authorities regarding appropriate criteria for, and objects of, poor relief. The provision of emergency relief was to prove equally emotive and divisive.

Notes

1 *United Ireland*, 4 Feb. 1882; *The Nation*, 27 Nov. 1886.
2 11 & 12 Vict., c. 47, sect. 4. For details of famine evictions, see James S. Donnelly, jr, 'Landlords and Tenants', in W.E. Vaughan (ed.), *A New History of Ireland. V. Ireland Under the Union, 1801–70* (Oxford, Clarendon Press, 1989), pp. 333–42.
3 R.J.B., *Ireland As It Is and As It Would Be Under Home Rule: 62 Letters Written by the Special Correspondent of the Birmingham Daily Gazette between March and August, 1893* (Birmingham, Birmingham Daily Gazette, n.d.), p. 267.
4 *Daily Express*, 30 Mar. 1882; Crane to Lloyd, 7 Apr. 1882; Wodsworth to Burke, 17 Apr. 1882; Lloyd to Burke, 21 Apr. 1882: NAI, CSORP, 1882/19779. See also Robinson to Morley, 21 June 1886: ibid., 1886/11762.
5 *Report from the Select Committee of the House of Lords on the Poor Law Guardians (Ireland) Bill...*, P.P., 1884–85 (297), x, 364. See also evidence of George Morris, ibid., 340.
6 T. Singleton, County Kerry, Monthly Confidential Report for Oct. 1889, 1 Nov. 1889: NAI, Crime Branch Special, CBS/DCCI/Carton 4.
7 *Report of the Royal Commission on the Land Law (Ireland) Act, 1881, and the Puchase of Land (Ireland) Act, 1885*, P.P., 1887 [C.4969–1], xxvi, 583.

8 *Letters from Ireland, 1886, by a special correspondent of the The Times* (London, 1887), p. 169.

9 44 & 45 Vict., c. 4. Such relief was to be granted in food or fuel, rather than money, and required the approval of the Local Government Board. See, Circular to the Clerk of each Union, 14 Dec. 1881: NAI, CSORP, 1882/19779.

10 For the Plan of Campaign, see L.M. Geary, *The Plan of Campaign, 1886–91* (Cork, Cork University Press, 1986); Philip Bull, *Land, Politics and Nationalism: A Study of the Irish Land Question* (Dublin, Gill and Macmillan, 1996), pp. 101–6.

11 *Cork Examiner*, 5 Oct. 1889.

12 *People*, 10 Mar. 1886.

13 Ibid., 18 Aug. 1886; 25 Aug. 1886.

14 Ibid., 4 Sept. 1886; Harrington to Chairman of New Ross Board of Guardians, 13 Nov. 1886: Wexford County Library (hereafter WCL), New Ross Board of Guardians Minutes (hereafter NRBGM), July–Dec. 1886, 350.

15 *People*, 25 Aug. 1886. See also 21 Aug. 1886.

16 *The Nation*, 11 Sept. 1886; *United Ireland*, 18 Sept. 1886.

17 *St James Gazette*, quoted in *The Nation*, 11 Sept. 1886; *Notes from Ireland*, 9 Oct. 1886.

18 Hewitson to Secretary of Local Government Board, 6 Nov. 1886: WCL, NRUMB, July–December 1886, 308.

19 Resolution adopted 13 Nov. 1886: ibid., 351; Resolution adopted 27 Nov. 1886: ibid., 390–1.

20 Secretary of Local Government Board to Clerk of New Ross Union, 9 Dec. 1886: ibid., 429–30.

21 of the visiting committee, read 11 Dec. 1886, ibid., 426–7.

22 *People*, 15 Dec. 1886.

23 Resolution adopted 11 Dec. 1886: WCL, NRUM, July–Dec. 1886, 430.

24 Sealed Order of Local Government Board, 14 Dec. 1886: ibid., 448–9.

25 *People*, 26 Jan. 1887. See also 12 Feb. 1887.

26 *People*, 12 Feb. 1887; ibid., 15 Jan. 1887. In November 1847 a crowd of around 300 people had threatened to attack the workhouse unless they were provided with either food or employment. See Kinealy, *This Great Calamity*, p. 202.

27 Resolution adopted 2 Mar. 1887: WCL, NRUM, July–Dec. 1886, 167; Minutes for 11, 28 May 1887: ibid., 382, 442.

28 *People*, 19 Feb. 1887; *Irish Times*, 18 Feb. 1887.

29 *The Nation*, 26 Feb. 1887; *People*, 25 May 1887.

30 *People*, 15 Jan. 1887; 12 Feb. 1887; 15 June 1887.

31 Order of the vice-guardians, 24 Dec. 1886: WCL, NRUM, July–Dec. 1886, 489; Order of the vice-guardians, 13 Apr. 1887: ibid., Jan.–June 1887, 287. See also *People*, 12 Mar. 1887; Order of the vice-guardians, 9 Feb. 1887: WCL, NRUM, Jan.–June 1887, 109.

32 *People*, 8 Jan. 1887; *The Nation*, 15 Jan. 1887. See also *United Ireland*, 15 Jan. 1887.

33 *People*, 19 Feb. 1887; Report of DI Gamble, 27 February 1887: NAI, CSORP, 1887/11223.

34 William Tobyn to Secretary of Local Government Board, 21 Feb. 1887: WCL, NRUM, Jan.–June 1887, 168; Assistant Secretary of Local Government Board (Thomas Mooney) to Clerk of New Ross Union, 24 Feb. 1887: ibid., 169.

35 Mooney to Robinson, 3 Mar. 1887: NAI, CSORP, 1887/11223; Report by CI Jones, 20 Mar. 1887: ibid.

36 *People*, 12 Mar. 1887; Minutes, 1 June 1887: WCL, NRUM, Jan.–June 1887, 470; Minutes, 8 June 1887: ibid., 487.

37 Report by DI Gamble, 9 June 1887: NAI, CSORP, 1887/11223; Report by DI Gamble, 11 June 1887, with note by DM Owen Slacke, 16 June 1887: ibid.

38 *People*, 6 Aug. 1887; 13 Aug. 1887.

39 Reprinted in *Notes from Ireland*, 9 July 1887.

40 *Hansard 3*, cccxix, 1870 (25 Aug. 1887); *People*, 3 Sept. 1887.

41 *People*, 17 Dec. 1887; 18 Jan. 1888.

42 Ibid., 7 Mar. 1888.

43 *United Ireland*, 16 Oct. 1886, 6 Nov. 1886. See also Memo. as to the administration of Local Governing bodies in Ireland, 7 Apr. 1892, NAI, CSORP 1892/4813. The four unions were Fermoy, Kanturk, Millstreet and Mallow.

44 *United Ireland*, 27 Nov. 1886.

45 'Much Ado About Nothing by An Elected Guardian', *People*, 26 Feb. 1887.

46 Ibid., 15 Dec. 1886.

47 Statement as to the Dissolution of Boards of Guardians, n.d. (1892): NAI, CSORP, 1892/4813.

48 The Kerry tenants had been offered a 30 per cent reduction. The Queen's tenants were offered 20 per cent off non-judicial rents and 15 per cent off judicial rents. See, Report by DI Aldworth, 19 June 1888: NAI, CSORP, 1888/12739.

49 Ibid.; Geary, *The Plan of Campaign*, p. 49. Kilbride had been prominent in the National League since its inception and had previously acted as secretary of the Luggacurran branch of the Land League.

50 Report by DI Aldworth, 19 June 1888: NAI, CSORP, 1888/12739.

51 *Kildare Observer*, 2 Apr. 1887.

52 Ibid., 9 Apr. 1887; 7 May 1887.
53 Geary, *The Plan of Campaign*, p. 49.
54 *Kildare Observer*, 23 Apr. 1887.
55 Ibid., 2 Apr. 1887; *Leinster Leader*, 15 Oct. 1887. Relief was granted for a month at a time.
56 Copy of Mr Finlay's Observations, 10 Feb. 1888: NAI, CSORP, 1888/12739; *Leinster Leader*, 19 Nov. 1887.
57 *Kildare Observer*, 4 June 1887.
58 Lees, *The Solidarities of Strangers*, p. 267.
59 *Kildare Observer*, 14 May 1887.
60 *Leinster Leader*, 22 Oct. 1888; 5 Nov. 1887; 12 Nov. 1887.
61 Report of DI Chatterton, 5 Nov. 1887; Ridgeway to LGB, 9 Nov. 1887; Robinson to Ridgeway, 8 Nov. 1887; MacSheahan to Clerk of Athy Union, 14 Nov. 1887: NAI, CSORP, 1887/20962.
62 *Leinster Leader*, 19 Nov. 1887. See also *Kildare Observer*, 19 November 1887.
63 Observations by Mr Finlay, 10 Feb. 1888: NAI, CSORP, 1888/12739; G.W. Finlay, Relief in Cases of Eviction, Luggacurran Electoral Division, 28 Jan. 1888: ibid. In Cranny's case for example, Finlay took the 15s a week allowed to Cranny after the first month as adequate for the family's needs, added 10s to this sum and allowed 25s a week for four weeks making a total of £5. Since Cranny had received a total of £20 from the guardians during the half year to 29 September 1887, Finlay disallowed £15.
64 Athy Union, Extract from Guardians' minutes dated 31st January 1888: ibid.
65 Mooney to Clerk of Athy Union, Feb. 1888: ibid.
66 *Kildare Observer*, 26 May 1888.
67 Note by Sir Henry Robinson, 31 May 1888: NAI, CSORP, 1888/12739; Observations of H.A. Robinson, 29 May 1888: ibid.
68 *The Nation*, 11 Feb. 1888; *Leinster Leader*, 9 June 1888.
69 *United Ireland*, 9 June 1888. See also 2, 16 June 1888.
70 Minutes, 22 May 1888, 12 June 1888: St Vincent's Hospital, Athy, County Kildare (hereafter AHK), Athy Board of Guardians Minutes (hereafter ABGM), Apr. – Oct. 1888, 188–9. Dunne had been re-elected chair of the Board in April 1888. With Kilbride now in parliament representing South Kerry, Whelan had been elected vice-chair and Thomas Orford deputy vice-chair.
71 Robinson to Balfour, 14 June 1888: NAI, CSORP, 1888/12739. Fitzgerald and Burke were both were experienced ex-officio guardians. Fitzgerald had been vice-chair of Castlebar Board of Guardians in County Mayo for around 25 years, effectively acting as chair in the absence of Lord Lucan who was non-resident. Burke

had also been in effective charge of a union as vice-chair of the Tuam Board of Guardians during the illness of the chair, Mr Bodkin. Burke described himself as a 'Conservative Roman Catholic', who had 'suffered much at various times for my Conservative opinions'. Applications for employment from Mr C.L. Fitzgerald and Mr W.J. Burke, n.d. (June, 1888): ibid.

72 *Kildare Observer*, 1 Sept. 1888; Minutes, 29 Aug. 1888: AHK, ABGM, Apr. – Oct. 1888, 470.
73 Minutes, 25 July 1888: ibid, 350; *Kildare Observer*, 28 July 1888.
74 Minutes, 25 July 1888: AHK, ABGM, Apr.–Oct. 1888, 348–9.
75 *Kildare Observer*, 27 October 1888.
76 *Leinster Express*, 1 Sept. 1888, 15 Dec. 1888; Robinson's observations on Mr Carey's letter, 26 Apr. 1889: NAI, CSORP, 1890/7728.
77 *Kildare Observer*, 10 November 1888.
78 *Leinster Leader*, 30 June 1888, 22 Sept. 1888; ibid., 23 June 1888; *Leinster Express*, 23 June 1888.
79 *Leinster Leader*, 28 July, 18 Aug. 1888; *Kildare Observer*, 27 October 1888.
80 Ridgeway to Balfour, 14 June 1888: NAI, CSORP, 1888/12739.
81 *Leinster Express*, 22 June 1889, 27 July 1889.
82 *United Ireland*, 15 June 1889; *Leinster Leader*, 6 July 1889.
83 Memo. as to administration by Local Governing bodies in Ireland, 2 Apr. 1892: NAI, CSORP, 1892/4813.
84 See, for example, remarks of Sgt. James McGlinn regarding surcharges imposed on Tim Clarke and Edward Kane, guardians of Portumna Union, 28 Mar. 1890: NAI, Crime Branch Special, S26.
85 Statement as to the Dissolution of Boards of Guardians, n.d. (1892): NAI, CSORP, 1892/4813.

4

Famine echoes: the relief of distress

For the majority of Irish people, the experience of famine was a memory not a reality in the second half of the nineteenth century. For those in the west, however, where land holdings remained small and agriculture continued to be heavily dependent on the potato, periodic harvest failures and economic downturns meant that famine and disease remained constant spectres. The poor law could provide only limited protection against economic insecurity in these regions since rateable values were low and levels of poor relief minimal even in relatively prosperous periods.[1] Having refused to supplement poor law resources or relax poor law regulations to combat distress in 1861–63 and 1867,[2] ministers were forced to do both in 1879–81 in the face of a major subsistence crisis. Subsequent occurrences of distress in 1886, 1890–91, 1894–95 and 1897–98 were met by a combination of poor relief, state aid and private benevolence. By the end of the century emergency relief had become an integral element of the economy and culture of the west,[3] a fact that caused considerable concern within government and more widely. Ministers and officials lamented the reliance on aid and the demoralisation of the rural population, fearing that people had been taught to look to government rather than their own resources. Irish landlords and their supporters criticised government interference in economic relationships in Ireland, and condemned what they saw as attempts to stifle Irish discontent with government grants. Irish nationalists attacked the unreliable nature of emergency aid and argued for a state-funded programme of economic development as the only solution to the chronic poverty of the west.

The following provides a chronological analysis of the relief measures adopted during the period from 1879 to 1898. Debates over the necessity for and provision of emergency relief focused attention not only on the operation of the poor laws, but also on the way Ireland was governed. Central to these debates were questions of rights and responsibilities. What was the nature of government's responsibility, local and central, for the relief of poverty and distress? How far did an individual's responsibility for his or her own welfare extend, and under what circumstances could it be legitimately surrendered? As the rigid divisions between categories such as paupers and independent labourers broke down under the pressure of food shortages, so the relevance of such categories in an Irish context was called into question. If relief under the poor laws proved inadequate during times of economic crisis, how far did this discredit the poor law system as a whole? As in other areas of poor law administration, central and local government tended to adopt different positions. Most chief secretaries believed that they had a responsibility to prevent starvation, but also to avoid undermining the integrity of the relief system and the principles by which it operated. To this end, they sought to ensure that local government retained responsibility for the administration and funding of relief measures. Poor law guardians, on the other hand, looked to central government to provide the resources to relieve distress, arguing that Irish ratepayers could not be expected to bear the cost of emergency relief.

Policy decisions on emergency relief had significance far beyond the immediate crisis, having political as well as material implications. Food shortages in the second half of the nineteenth century inevitably brought back memories of the Great Famine, and invited comparison with it. Ministers were acutely aware that should deaths from starvation occur, they would ultimately be held responsible. Irish politicians, community leaders, and officials, were well aware of ministerial sensitivity on this topic and had no qualms about exploiting it. When the Local Government Board wanted to persuade John Morley to support a request from a rate collector in Belmullet Union for police

protection in 1894, H.A. Robinson cannily warned the under-
secretary that he was worried that 'the food contractors may
suddenly stop supplies if they can't get paid, and if that
happened, and some old woman died, the Guardians would put
it down to the fact that they could not get the government to
give protection to their collector and you can easily see what
political capital the Chief Secretary's opponents would make
out of an occurrence like that'. This warning had the desired
effect. Morley gave his support, noting, 'I wish I had seen the
matter earlier.'[4]

All governments of the post-Famine era accepted that poor
law regulations might need to be relaxed in the event of severe
distress to enable those affected to receive assistance outside the
workhouse. Discussion of emergency relief measures generally
focused on three key questions: under what circumstances
should relief measures be introduced, what form should they
take, and who should take responsibility for their implementation? Over the course of the 1880s and 1890s the answers
provided by different ministers to these questions varied
according to personal temperament, ideological outlook and the
political climate in which they were operating. Thus, whereas
John Morley was determined to channel aid through poor law
boards in 1886 in order to demonstrate the administration's
commitment to the principle of self-government, Arthur Balfour
bypassed the local authorities altogether in 1890–91, placing the
responsibility for relief operations in the hands of government
officials. In contrast to the variable nature of ministerial attitudes, the approach of the Local Government Board remained
consistent throughout this period. Board officials were always
wary of responding to demands for emergency relief. They were
also anxious to limit the nature of any such relief and to provide
means of safeguarding the primacy of the poor law. They did
not object to the bypassing of poor law mechanisms so long as
the established principles of relief distribution were maintained.
Relief should be confined to the destitute and some test of destitution should be applied. That ministers often disregarded the
advice proffered by Board indicates the limitations of its influence within the executive.

The crisis of 1879–81[5]

In 1879 a combination of poor weather, the third consecutive bad harvest and depressed livestock prices precipitated a major crisis. In Connaught and Donegal supplies of food and fuel were virtually exhausted by the end of 1879 and it was clear that the winter months were likely to see serious and widespread distress among the poorer classes. Since many tenant farmers were in arrears with their rent they faced the very real prospect of eviction, and it was against this background that the Land League was formed. But the very conjunction of economic and political grievances that was so crucial to the popular success of the Land League, encouraged government to dismiss warnings about food shortages as political propaganda. Reports of famine conditions, H.A. Robinson recalled, were regarded as 'a move in the political agitation rather than a well-founded cry of distress.'[6]

Doubtful of the veracity of newspaper reports and of the representations of nationalist MPs and community leaders, the government relied heavily on information supplied by local government inspectors to provide an objective account of the situation in distressed districts. The inspectors had their own bias, however, viewing Irish distress through the prism of the poor law. Even though the experience of the Great Famine had clearly demonstrated the deficiency of the workhouse test during a period of exceptional distress, officials sought to apply it as a test of destitution and thus eligibility in 1879–80. As a temporary inspector in County Mayo, the young H.A. Robinson was confronted with one of the chief problems facing government in responding to distress: how to identify the point at which intervention was necessary. Reporting on the state of Ballinrobe Union in January 1880, he observed that the

> question as to whether there really is distress depends entirely on the definition which is put on the word. If a worthless supply of seed, a low price for stock, a complete withdrawal of credit and heavy encumbrances are signs of distress, then I have to report that distress there is, throughout the entire Union. But here the terms distress and starvation are often used in precisely the same sense although they are by no means synonymous.[7]

Robinson believed that maintaining a distinction between starvation and distress was central to a responsible relief policy. If mere distress was relieved the labour market and the economy would be weakened, and the poor law undermined. It was only by limiting emergency relief to the prevention of starvation that the government could protect the wider interests of the country. Robinson's views were significant since he was to play a leading role first in administering and then in shaping relief policy in the 1880s and 1890s.

Government relief measures introduced during the winter of 1879–80 were intended to maintain a central role for poor relief whilst making extra funds available. The Local Government Board warned poor law guardians to prepare for an increased number of applicants, and a circular was issued reminding landlords that they could borrow money from the Board of Works in order to undertake improvement projects that would provide employment. The sum of £500,000 was set aside for this purpose. When it became clear that few landlords were prepared to take any action, the terms of the loans were made more favourable.[8] In February 1880, ministers introduced a bill to provide a further £250,000 for relief works, making loans available to local authorities as well as landlords. This measure also empowered the Local Government Board to authorise the relaxation of restrictions on the granting of outdoor relief so that the able-bodied and small landholders could be relieved outside the workhouse. In addition, poor law boards were empowered to borrow money at a low rate of interest to meet their expenses. And, on the suggestion of Irish MPs, the government agreed to allow poor law boards to borrow from the Board of Works in order to supply distressed districts with seed potatoes.[9] This meant that crops could be planted for the following year thus preventing a repetition of the situation that had occurred during the Great Famine, when people had eaten their seed potatoes or planted diseased seed.

During the debate on the relief bill Irish MPs raised an important issue regarding the perception and rights of the recipients of emergency relief when they objected to the removal of voting rights from those receiving outdoor relief on the grounds that the situation in the distressed districts 'was a purely exceptional case, arising from a visitation of Providence'.[10] Acknowledging that disenfranchisement was 'fair and reasonable in regard of professed and helpless mendicants', the *Freeman's Journal* insisted that with 'an independent and mostly rate-paying population plunged into the agony of a sudden death' a different approach was needed. Any benefactor should aim to help the people 'without degrading them, and to preserve them from perishing without withdrawing their rights or lowering their self-respect'.[11] The issue was made more sensitive by the approaching general election. Since disenfranchising large numbers of Irish small holders was likely to reduce support for Home Rule candidates, the government could be accused of using money voted for the relief of distress, 'for the purpose of obtaining an electoral advantage'.[12] Following further protests, ministers were forced to amend the bill so that no voter would incur electoral disability on account of assistance received under the act.[13] This was a significant concession and set an important precedent.

The government's approach to distress in 1879–80 was intended to avoid the mistakes made during the Great Famine. Landowners were seen as appropriate initiators of relief works in 1879–80 because 'the public funds would be lent on good security and would be disbursed among the most necessitous of the people'.[14] In the event, many landlords declined to initiate works either through apathy or insolvency, or because they saw no reason to help tenants who were not paying rent. The primary providers of emergency relief over the winter of 1879–80 were voluntary and charitable organisations, as they had been in 1846–47. Speaking in the Commons in June 1881, E.D. Gray, who, as Lord Mayor of Dublin had presided over the Mansion House Fund, declared that it was solely owing to charitable organisations, 'that the people had been preserved from starvation. It certainly was not owing to anything that had been done by the Government'.[15] Those involved in the voluntary relief effort were equally critical of boards of guardians, many of which had refused to grant any outdoor relief so long as people were receiving help from charitable funds. Reporting on a tour of the west coast, the philanthropist James Hack Tuke noted that the poor law was 'in fact inoperative as regards outdoor relief'. Attempts to persuade guardians to grant outdoor relief to labourers and cottiers, so that charitable funds could be concentrated on small farmers, had met with little success. The chair of the Westport Board of Guardians, Lord John Browne, was said to have greeted this suggestion with a 'strong denunciation' of the demoralising effect of all outdoor relief.[16]

Irish nationalists denounced the relief measures as inadequate and inappropriate. The *Freeman's Journal* pronounced the government to be 'plainly ... unequal or unwilling to deal with the present issue in Ireland, and to be utterly regardless of the future'.[17] Many Liberals shared this judgement, and following Gladstone's return to power at the general election of April 1880, a more active and generous approach to distress was adopted. The Relief of Distress (Ireland) Act 1880 provided a further £750,000 for relief works, and eased the repayment terms of loans taken out by boards of guardians for the provision of outdoor relief.[18] Throughout the crisis, the Local Government Board took an active role in supervising and advising poor law boards in the distressed districts. Three temporary inspectors were appointed in November 1879 and another three in February 1880 in order to monitor the situation in the worst-affected areas and maintain a close watch on the actions of the guardians.[19] H.A. Robinson was to claim that in the first eight months of his appointment, he never slept two nights in succession in the same place.[20] In the summer of 1880, the Local Government Board dissolved the boards of guardians of three unions – Belmullet, Swinford and Newport – on the grounds that they had failed to strike and collect sufficient rates to provide relief.[21] The guardians maintained that ratepayers, who were themselves victims of crisis, were incapable of paying the amount required. Government, not the people, they argued should fund the relief effort.

The Belmullet Guardians had drawn attention in October 1879, 'to the danger which threatens the poorer classes of this isolated part of the country', and had 'respectfully, yet earnestly, implore[d] the Government to take immediate steps to afford employment to the people, or such other relief as to them shall seem fit'. The following month the board had been obliged to take out an additional loan with the Hibernian Bank in Belmullet, despite being already overdrawn by over £500. Without the additional loan the guardians judged that it would 'be impossible to carry on the business of the Union, considering the distressed state of the Ratepayers, and the pressing demands of the Contractors'. At the same time they decided to reduce rates across the union. The rate collectors were already behind with their collections and, in January 1880, the Local Government Board warned the guardians that if they did not 'exert themselves to the utmost ... to realise the rates required for the relief of the destitute poor', they would 'feel reluctantly called upon to dissolve the Board of Guardians'.[22] By May 1880, the Belmullet guardians owed over £1,700 to the bank and around £1,300 to contractors. Rate arrears stood at £1,153, nearly half the total of outstanding rates. When the guardians applied to the Local Government Board to sanction yet another loan, the Board carried out its earlier threat and appointed vice-guardians. Dismissing the guardians' assertion that they could not have avoided getting into their 'embarrassed financial state, which has been owing to several consecutive bad seasons etc., etc., and not to any fault on their part', the Board insisted that their indebtedness was due not to the cost of administering exceptional relief, but to the guardians 'failing to make and collect sufficient rates when they might have been collected'.[23]

Just how difficult a task the Belmullet Guardians had faced can be inferred from the fact that the vice-guardians found it impossible to place the union on a sound financial footing. In July 1881, the auditor of the union, Colonel James O'Hara, noted that the vice-guardians had failed to pay off the loan contracted with the Hibernian Bank despite having borrowed money under the Relief of Distress Act in order to discharge this liability. The vice-guardians explained that the workhouse was in such 'a neglected and dilapidated condition that they found it necessary to expend much more than they had anticipated and they were unable to discharge more than £600 of the loan [to the bank]'.[24] Even H.A. Robinson acknowledged that Belmullet was a special case. In his memoirs he recalled mentioning to Forster that the seed supply acts 'had been a tremendous success everywhere except in one district on the west coast, the most poverty-stricken in Ireland, where they had totally failed'. The problem there, he had explained, was that the 'valuation per head of the people was only about 5s 6d and they had no money'. Yet parliament could not be expected 'to legislate for an exceptional case'.

Forster's response had been to give Robinson a cheque for £1,000. This account is corroborated by a note in the vice-guardians' minutes recording their gratitude to Forster for his 'generous gift of champion seed potatoes' and their indebtedness to the 'untiring exertions of Mr Robinson in bringing their distressed condition' under Forster's notice, and for exercising his 'tact and judgement' in distributing the seed.[25] Forster, Robinson and the vice-guardians, all recognised that the Belmullet ratepayers were too poor to fund adequate relief measures. To admit this publicly, however, would have undermined the government's efforts to place the primary responsibility for relieving distress on boards of guardians.

The official verdict on the relief measures adopted in 1879–81 was a positive one. In their annual report for 1880–81 the Local Government Board declared the measures to have been 'effectual ... in dealing with the destitution which has existed in the country, and in meeting the exceptional distress which has prevailed'.[26] In private, judgement was much less favourable. Reports arriving in the Chief Secretary's Office revealed that the system of relief works had been beset by problems from the start. Improvement works undertaken by local authorities were generally executed by contract under the supervision of the county surveyor whose primary concern was not to provide employment for the needy, but to get the job done efficiently at the lowest possible cost. Captain Dorwood of the Royal Engineers concluded in September 1880, that 'small contracts have, in the majority of cases, more or less failed in their object as relief works'.[27] A resolution of the Board of Guardians of Mohill Union, County Leitrim, had complained in June 1880 that 'the contractors do not employ the unemployed labourers in the neighbourhood of the works, but monopolise the whole for the benefit of themselves and their families'. The Local Government Board concluded that there would have been 'a very heavy charge on the poor rates had it not been for the different charitable organizations that poured vast sums of money into the distressed districts of the west'. As poor law guardians were usually members of the local relief committees, 'they were able to divert the pressure of relief from the rates to these relief funds'.[28]

Official returns indicate that over £2m was expended in

government grants and loans 1879–81, with a further £624,000 being provided in the period up to 1884.[29] The bulk of this money (around £1.5 million) was spent on relief works. In addition, over £1.2m of private money was distributed. The various charitable funds were understandably self-congratulatory about their contribution to the relief effort. The Mansion House Committee took credit for its role in ensuring that famine had been successfully 'grappled with . . . by the almost unaided arm of private benevolence'.[30] None of these accounts – governmental or non-governmental – were disinterested; all needed to demonstrate the effectiveness of the measures undertaken. And despite the massive scale of the relief effort, getting access to aid could be a frustrating and capricious process. Employment on improvement works was in many cases confined to those with the right connections, and despite the lifting of restrictions on outdoor relief, boards of guardians often proved reluctant to grant relief to the able-bodied, or to those owning livestock. Even charitable aid was subject to unpredictable fluctuations. The different funds did not always co-ordinate their efforts effectively so that the level of assistance available could bear little relation to the level of need in a particular district. In April 1880, for example, the Mansion House Committee severely reduced the amount of assistance being afforded to the Cong district of County Mayo having been erroneously informed that a local landlord, Sir Arthur Guinness, was providing sufficient relief.[31]

While the relief operation as a whole did achieve the organisers' primary aim – to prevent starvation – R.V. Comerford's assessment that 'the general picture is one of successful aversion of threatened calamity through practical and sensible effort on many fronts', is over-generous.[32] It is difficult not to agree with the Local Government Board's conclusion that the

> powers placed in the hands of landowners, boards of guardians, magistrates and cesspayers, etc., would undoubtedly have sufficed to meet the distress could these classes have been prevailed upon to co-operate harmoniously with the common object of tiding over the crisis. But the political differences between them were too strong to make combination for any purpose possible and each section acted independently of the other with the result that the Irish peasant passed through a

season which for many of them was characterised by rapidly
alternating periods of scarcity and abundance.[33]

Lessons were learned from the experience of 1879–81. The practice of placing responsibility for the establishment of relief
works in a number of different hands had not worked well, and
was not repeated. Landlords had failed to rise to the challenge
presented by the crisis, and were never again given a leading
role in relief operations. Events had also reinforced the suspicions of Irish officials regarding the likelihood of relief measures
being abused, and of Irish nationalists regarding the innate
hostility of British ministers towards Ireland. While ministers
had intervened to prevent starvation, they had done so grudg-
ingly and with excessive caution. The *Freeman's Journal* had
complained in February 1880 that the action of the government
'was like that of a man who is afraid of being swindled'.[34] At the
same time, stories of the widespread abuse of relief became a
staple element of anti-nationalist propaganda. Famine in
Ireland, it was claimed, had become a profitable business. As
one writer observed caustically in 1880, if 'without a death from
starvation or a strain upon the poor rates, over three millions
can be secured in hard cash by an inexpensive agitation, there
are few ventures in political warfare that offer results so
substantial as the producing of a famine to order'.[35]

The return of distress 1882–83

During 1881 the situation improved sufficiently to allow relief
works to cease. The power to extend the provision of outdoor
relief expired on 1 March 1881, and in April 1882 the Local
Government Board reported that 'all ... temporary measures
have ceased to be necessary, and that the relief administered in
the ordinary manner has been found sufficient to meet the
wants of the poor during the past winter'.[36] Towards the end
of 1882 serious distress was reported to have returned to the
west. The potato crop yielded less than half the average return
and grain crops were also deficient following a bad storm at
the beginning of October 1882. In November, a number of poor
law boards from the south and west of the country passed
resolutions calling on the government to establish relief

works.[37] This, the government was very reluctant to do. The newly appointed under-secretary, Sir Robert Hamilton, fully concurred with the Local Government Board in thinking that the succession of overlapping relief measures introduced since the winter of 1879 had had a very demoralising effect, and that the people of the west must be weaned off their reliance on emergency relief.[38]

On 9 December 1882, Hamilton issued a public statement of government policy with regard to exceptional distress. The government, he explained, had 'determined to rely solely upon the administration of relief through the ordinary channel provided by the law, viz., the boards of guardians'. The only concession made was to assure boards of guardians that should they find themselves in financial difficulties due to the distress, they would be allowed to borrow money to meet their liabilities. Acknowledging 'the great objection entertained by many people to entering the workhouse', Hamilton observed that, 'persons who are unable to procure for themselves the necessaries of life', were hardly in a position 'to determine the manner in which public relief is afforded, nor can any just ground of complaint exist if to every destitute person the means shall be readily accessible of obtaining effectual relief'.[39] When some boards of guardians continued to lobby for relief works, they were curtly reminded that responsibility for the administration of relief rested not with the executive government, but with the guardians, 'and it is not competent for them to divest themselves of the obligations imposed upon them by law to provide relief for the destitute poor in their unions'.[40]

Irish nationalists were outraged by the government's approach. *United Ireland* described the December statement as 'a hateful and miserable failure', and printed a cartoon attacking the Liberal lord lieutenant, Lord Spencer, for his heartlessness.[41] In the Commons, Justin McCarthy complained that the Irish people had 'asked for bread and the Lord Lieutenant gave them a sneer'. The Chief Secretary, G.O. Trevelyan, defended the government's policy, claiming that distress only existed in areas where holdings were 'too small' and where 'the people could not live on the land without running into debt'. It was not a matter of money, but of social morality. It would, he insisted, 'be a cruel kindness to go on expending the public money upon a system which was neither advantageous to the Exchequer nor to Ireland ... They would do much better by encouraging in the Irish people greater self-reliance at home, and if they gave assistance, without exercising compulsion, to those who wished to go elsewhere to seek a home.'[42] Trevelyan's argument reflected official thinking. The view that the nature and extent of Irish poverty made it both impractical and irresponsible to attempt to relieve 'distress' was consistently advanced by Local Government Board inspectors, and by H.A. Robinson in particular. Reporting from Ballina in County Mayo in March 1883, Robinson described the people in the locality as 'living in the hope that government interference will come to their aid and prop them up in their untenable position a little longer, and they seem also to have formed the opinion that the government can take the place of private enterprise, and speculate in schemes of possible and impossible desirability'.

Robinson believed that economic conditions in the west were basically unsustainable. Distress, he predicted, would 'only be felt by that class of persons who live in a state of chronic poverty on holdings, the gross produce of which could not maintain them, at the best of times, from harvest to harvest'. If extraordinary measures of relief were adopted, he warned, 'the discontinuance of them at any time hereafter must invariably leave this class of small tenants in the same state that they are at present'.[43] Robinson and his colleagues believed that while central government had a responsibility to prevent starvation and encourage economic development within the distressed districts, the immediate responsibility for improving the quality of people's lives lay in their own hands and in those of the local authorities. Within the Catholic community, this view was regarded as both inhumane and counter-productive. The Catholic hierarchy in Connaught had sought to convince the Lord Lieutenant in January 1883 that effective relief measures would be 'taken by the people as evidence of good-will and sympathy', and would thus be indispensable in 'remedying the chronic discontent and destitution from which all classes in the country are suffering'. As those affected by distress were 'in no way accountable' for their plight, and since the people could not relieve themselves, it was evident 'that to save the health and lives of the destitute the Government must interfere'. In doing so, moreover, government needed to rethink its normal approach. Any measure adopted should be 'prompt and general [and] it should be such as the destitute will accept'.[44] In other words, the aim should be not to minimise but to maximise relief.

Having persuaded ministers to resist all pleas for government intervention in 1882–83, the Local Government Board took much satisfaction in reporting in 1884 that although the numbers receiving both indoor and outdoor relief had risen during the spring and summer of 1883, 'all who were really destitute had the means of obtaining needful aid and support'.[45] Board officials, and H.A. Robinson in particular, believed this episode to have demonstrated that the poor law remained the best test of destitution. Irish nationalists and Catholic clergy disagreed, insisting that the people had a right to look for assistance from both public and private charity during periods of distress. By the time that distress returned to the west in 1885–86, the issue of home rule dominated the political agenda and the Local Government Board was to find it far more difficult to persuade ministers to rely on the poor law alone to provide relief.

John Morley and the Relief of Distress Act 1886[46]

The Local Government Board had been receiving reports of serious crop failures in the west, coupled with warnings of widespread destitution, since the summer of 1885. On his arrival in Dublin in February 1886, the new Chief Secretary, John Morley, found himself under great pressure to act on these reports for, as Robinson cynically observed, 'with a Government pledged to govern according to Irish ideas and supported and advised by the Irish members who wanted to see English gold circulating in Ireland', the Chief Secretary was in no position to resist the 'assurances of his political supporters to the effect that the resources of the Poor Law must be supplemented to meet distress'.[47] Morley's decision to make money available to boards of guardians in the west, and to allow them to distribute it as they thought fit, was to be interpreted as an early application of home rule principles.

The Relief of Distress Act relaxed the restrictions on outdoor relief and made available £20,000 in grants to supplement poor law resources in six western unions (Belmullet, Clifden, Galway, Oughterard, Swinford and Westport.) At the same time, a further £20,000 was set aside for the construction and repair of roads and piers in the distressed districts.[48] Robinson was later to claim that the Local Government Board had warned Morley against allowing boards of guardians to distribute relief money without any test of destitution, but that he had 'considered the board were out of date in their ideas'.[49] By abandoning the minimalist approach favoured by the Local Government Board, Morley seemed to be embracing the kind of inclusive relief policy that had been advocated by the Connaught bishops in 1883, when they had called for a measure that would be prompt, general and acceptable.

In administering the act, boards of guardians and their relieving officers adopted a much looser definition of destitution than that normally applied. The chair of the Belmullet Board of Guardians, for example, was to justify the granting of relief to people who owned livestock on the grounds that 'the markets were bad – there were no prices. They could not sell at any price ... and they were as much in need of relief as people with nothing at all'.[50] Within five weeks, the total number of people receiving relief in the distressed unions had jumped from under 2,000 to over 96,000. Conscious of the escalating cost of relief, the Local Government Board wrote to the six boards of guardians to warn them that any expenditure above the amount of the parliamentary grant would have to be met out of the rates. This led to the summary removal of large numbers of people from the relief lists. Despite this belated attempt to economise, over £36,000 was spent on outdoor relief in the distressed unions during the late spring and early summer of 1886 of which only £19,400 was judged by the Local Government Board to be covered by grants under the act. The boards of guardians were thus left facing considerable debts. While the Local Government Board held the guardians entirely responsible for this situation, the guardians argued that the Board was at fault for allowing them to believe that the cost of relief would be borne by central government.[51] Morley left Ireland in the summer of 1886 following the defeat of the home rule bill.

With the return of the Conservatives to office, political priorities within government changed. Home rule was off the
agenda. Irish nationalists were no longer to be conciliated but
were rather to be taught the benefits of firm government.
Having originated as a goodwill gesture and an expression of
confidence in Irish local administrators, Morley's relief act now
became an object lesson in the dangers of self-government.
Reporting from Ireland in the autumn of 1886, a special correspondent of the London *Times* described the act as 'the worst
instance of abuse ... in connection with Boards of Guardians',
and made a direct link between maladministration and the political allegiance of the guardians. In the poorer unions, it was
explained, 'almost the entire poor-rate falls on the landlords...
and the elected guardians, who are almost invariably
Nationalists, can afford to be reckless in their expenditure'.
Morley had been warned of the consequences of entrusting
public money to the boards, 'but the charm of allowing people
to manage their own affairs was too great'.[52]

A commission of inquiry was appointed to investigate the
administration of the Relief of Distress Act, and the financial
condition of the scheduled unions. In their report, the two
commissioners, H.A. Robinson and C. T. Reddington, were
highly critical of the guardians' administration of the act, noting
that they had 'practically surrendered the entire control of the
relief to the Relieving Officers and their assistants'. They did,
however, acknowledge that it would be impossible to levy the
full amount of rates necessary to meet the guardians' debts,
'without great hardship to all classes of ratepayers', and recommended that the government consider making a loan available
to the boards of guardians to be spread over a number of years.[53]
While the Local Government Board was prepared to accept the
commissioners' recommendations, Balfour was not. He was
convinced that the guardians had proved themselves incapable
of effective administration. Brushing aside the reservations of
Sir Henry Robinson, Balfour determined to dissolve the insolvent boards of guardians permanently and appoint paid
commissioners to administer the unions.[54] Acting on protests
from the guardians, Irish MPs blocked the dissolution bill[55] and
it was subsequently dropped. Left to manage as best they could,
the guardians of Clifden, Oughterard and Westport struggled to

pay off their debts from the rates. The Belmullet and Swinford Boards sank deeper into debt and were dissolved in October 1887 and February 1888 respectively.[56] Both unions remained under the control of vice-guardians until March 1889. Despite finding itself at odds with Morley and Balfour, the Local Government Board had nevertheless managed to achieve its objectives, first by limiting excessive expenditure in the scheduled unions and then by avoiding the permanent dissolution of the boards of guardians.

Nationalist newspapers that had initially supported the boards of guardians in their administration of the relief act had mostly turned against them following the publication of the inquiry commission report. The *Freeman's Journal*, which in September 1886 had argued that the conduct of the guardians 'needs no justification', subsequently concluded that it was 'impossible on the evidence presented ... to acquit the local bodies of the grievous charges which are brought against them'. Public money had been 'jobbed away in the most iniquitous fashion'.[57] The events of 1886–87 reinforced the association in many people's minds between emergency relief and large-scale fraud. As the *Dublin Evening Mail* gleefully noted in 1888, the report of the commission of inquiry provided 'a golden text for the Unionist platform', demonstrating 'the people's capacity for spending without caring a rap out of whose pocket the money comes'.[58] It was left to local newspapers to question the official version of events, just as it had been left to the local Catholic clergy to defend the actions of the boards of guardians to the inquiry commissioners. The *Mayo Examiner* reminded its readers of the beneficial effects of the relief measures adopted, observing that if 'hunger, disease and death were averted by the outlay of a few thousands or more, in each union, that is a matter of administrative congratulation'.[59] But such arguments carried little weight outside the distressed districts. The highly politicised nature of the debate over the 1886 act made any serious discussion of the relative merits of different approaches to relief policy, or of how best to fund relief measures, impossible.

Arthur Balfour and the centralisation of relief 1889–91

Morley declined to accept any responsibility for what had occurred in 1886. Yet, whilst disassociating himself from the boards of guardians, he remained committed to local autonomy and publicly defended the record of local authorities in general.[60] Balfour, on the other hand, was confirmed in his hostility to local authorities. Perceiving the chronic poverty of the west as a serious threat to the stability of British rule in Ireland, he regarded the relief of distress as much a political as a welfare issue and thus as too important to be left to local representatives. Under Balfour, emergency relief was to be a central rather than a local responsibility. Following a second successive failure of the potato harvest in 1890, distress was apprehended all along the western seaboard from Donegal down to Cork.[61] Contemplating the likely need for relief measures, Balfour concluded that the best course of action 'would be rigidly to enforce the workhouse test and to deal with the distress through the existing machinery of the Poor Law and through that alone'. But, as he acknowledged to Tuke, this 'may be a counsel of perfection, which it may prove impossible to follow'. If so, he was determined not to repeat the mistakes of the past: 'The history of 1879 and 1886 is full of lessons as to the gross abuses which have accompanied the distribution of Public Funds by the Local Authorities, and as at present advised, I think that if we are driven to the construction of Relief Works ... we should work absolutely independently of the corrupt Boards of Guardians.'[62]

Relief operations in 1890–91 were kept under tight central control. The Chief Secretary had decided, Ridgeway later recalled, 'that the Executive Government itself should be solely responsible for and have complete control over the measures to be adopted'. Operations were co-ordinated in the Chief Secretary's Office, 'under the personal superintendence of the Under-secretary', and were administered in the localities by a variety of government officials. Railway construction schemes were already underway in some parts of the distressed districts under the light railways act of 1889. Local government inspectors were directed to identify areas where it was necessary to supplement the poor law and available sources of employment

by opening relief works. They were also responsible for selecting those eligible for employment. The works themselves were
conducted under the supervision of officers and men from the
Royal Engineers with members of the Royal Irish Constabulary
acting as timekeepers and paymasters. Relief works were
intended to assist only those people suffering from 'chronic'
distress. Distress not materially differing in amount 'from the
annually recurring condition of destitution in which the people
find themselves', was to be relieved by the poor law.[63] Boards of
guardians were authorised to borrow money from the Board of
Works for the purchase and supply of seed potatoes, subject to
the approval of specially appointed seed inspectors.[64] Anyone
incapable of working could apply to a charitable fund established by the Irish government. Administered by the police with
the cooperation of local government inspectors and poor law
authorities, the fund raised just over £50,000. This was used to
assist 12,594 families, comprising over 50,000 individuals, in ten
counties.[65]

In the months from December 1890 to August 1891, relief
works were opened in 23 unions at a total cost of nearly
£240,000.[66] On 23 May 1891, the works were employing 15,529
people, the largest number employed on any one day. In addition between 7,000 and 8,000 people were employed on the two
lines of light railway being constructed from Mulranny to Achill
and Collooney to Claremorris.[67] Wages on the relief works were
kept at a low level in order to encourage people to take up other
employment, and to act as a test of destitution.[68] This policy had
only limited success. Many people preferred to apply to local
relief works, rather than take up employment away from home.
A number of men from Swinford Poor Law Union, for example,
refused an offer of work at 12s a week with free lodging on the
Claremorris to Collooney railway line, despite being said by
their priest to be 'in dire distress and bordering on starvation'.[69]
(The rate of pay on relief works was rarely more than 7s a week.)
The low rate of wages also failed to act as a deterrent to the
extent expected. Reporting on the relief works in November
1891, the officer in charge of their execution, Major W. Peacocke,
observed that low wages had not deterred 'even notoriously
well-to-do people from availing themselves of the employment
along with their poorer brethren'.[70] To check this, local govern-

ment inspectors were asked to compile lists of people whose circumstances justified their employment. The inspectors were thus required not only to diagnose distress but also to discriminate between real and simulated destitution. Recognising the onerous nature of their responsibilities, the government approved the appointment of seven additional, temporary inspectors.[71]

The relief measures were broadly welcomed in Ireland. Boards of guardians were delighted to be relieved of the responsibility and the cost of assisting the distressed, having long argued that this was not a task that they could perform effectively without bankrupting their unions. In August 1890, the Swinford Guardians had passed a resolution calling on the government to establish public works in the union, declaring that 'the system of out-door relief, no matter how well administered, is most demoralising, and that is it only by employing the working classes on a line of railway … that the coming crisis can be met'. In January 1891, the guardians expressed their gratitude to Balfour for 'grappling with the demon of famine which threatened to desolate the congested districts of this and neighbouring unions'.[72] Relief works opened in Swinford in March 1891.[73] Where there were complaints regarding the relief measures, these emanated from districts in which it had not been thought necessary to start works. Micks made himself very unpopular in the Rosses district of Donegal by reporting favourably on the state of the district and refusing to endorse the case for relief works being advanced by local people.[74]

Balfour publicly congratulated himself in March 1891 for having resisted the temptation to earn 'cheap popularity in Ireland by a lavish assent to the applications made to me, irrespective of the interests of the British taxpayer'. He had, he declared, 'succeeded in relieving the distress with the minimum of demoralisation to the people'.[75] This statement is a good example of what Alvin Jackson has described as Balfour's 'characteristic disingenuousness'.[76] Through the provision of employment on railway construction and relief works, and the distribution of charitable funds, Balfour had met very many of the demands for assistance made on him, and had done so largely at the taxpayer's expense. His objective was to build on the success of his pacification policy.

As Colonel Alfred Turner, the district magistrate responsible for the southwest, had assured him in November 1890, 'spend money on works extensively through this winter in the parts where the crop has failed [and] the battle will be won'.[77] Balfour was quick to brand the boards of guardians as corrupt for allowing politics to influence the manner in which they expended public money, but his own measures were just as much influenced by political considerations.

The relief operation of 1890–91 was judged a success. Ridgeway noted there was gratification felt within government that the plan adopted had 'worked so well and so smoothly, and has been productive of such good results'. The Local Government Board declared itself in no doubt that 'in point of efficiency and economy these measures compared favourably with any which had been hitherto adopted to meet exceptional distress, and that the wants of the destitute poor were fully provided for'.[78] It was true that the amount expended by government in 1890–91 was much less than in 1879–81 – around £0.52m compared to £2.2m – but such comparisons were misleading, not least because distress was less extensive and less prolonged in 1890–91 than it had been in 1879–81.[79] Balfour had conceived his relief policy in a spirit of beneficence tempered by mistrust. Yet far from resenting this mistrust, Irish local authorities enthusiastically embraced his policy, welcoming the fact that central government had finally acknowledged its responsibility to those living in poverty-stricken areas. Poor law guardians, ratepayers and the recipients of relief all benefited from the employment of public money to fund relief measures and of government officials to administer them. Determining who should and should not receive assistance when almost everyone was affected by distress to some degree was an invidious task. Government officials were, however, in a less invidious position than were local functionaries required to pass judgement on their neighbours.

Morley and the reintroduction of relief works 1894–95

Local Government Board officials shared the satisfaction felt by Balfour and Ridgeway regarding the success of the relief operation. They did not, however, wholly share Balfour's confidence that this success had been achieved 'with the minimum demoralisation'. The provision of any government aid was regarded as demoralising. In its annual report for 1890–91, the Board sought solace in the attempts being made to promote economic development, expressing the hope that these might 'give an impetus to the industry and resources of the country, and, ultimately, be the means of diminishing that sense of dependence on extraneous help which unhappily exists throughout the west of Ireland in times of scarcity, and which is so prejudicial to habits of thrift and industry'.[80]

Long experience of exceptional distress had convinced senior Local Government Board officials that the provision of emergency relief yielded long-term problems for short-term gains. When serious distress once again threatened the west coast in November 1894, H.A. Robinson sought to persuade Morley to consider both the long-term and short-term consequences when assessing the need for relief measures. Robinson acknowledged that it might be difficult to resist the cry for relief works, but warned that 'if the Government admit their obligation to make up to the people for a partial loss of the potato crop, it is greatly to be feared that ameliorative measures in the West of Ireland must ultimately become more or less of a permanent character as a year seldom passes when the people have not some cause for complaint'.

What ministers should be asking themselves, Robinson suggested, was not whether assistance was needed, since assistance was always needed, but whether it was absolutely essential. Commenting on the observation of one inspector that there were 1,000 families in Connemara who required assistance, Robinson noted that 'he does not however predict what the result would be of not assisting them'. If government did decide to introduce special measures, Robinson recommended the introduction of 'relief works on Mr Balfour's system'.[81]

With local government inspectors forecasting that around 5,400 families would require relief the following year, Morley was not prepared to gamble with people's lives, and relief works on the Balfourian model were opened in January 1895.[82] These were supplemented not by a charitable fund as in 1890–91, but by an extension of outdoor relief. Morley thus reversed the policy by which local authorities were almost entirely superseded in the distribution of emergency relief, whilst maintaining central government's responsibility for the organisation and financing of relief works. A limit of £80,000 was set for the expenditure on the works. From January to May 1895, relief works were opened in eleven unions in counties Donegal, Cavan, Mayo and Galway, at a total cost of £80,000. Of this, £68,000 was charged to the distress fund and £12,000 to other government services. A seed supply act was also passed under which a little over £62,000 was advanced to boards of guardians across the country for the supply of seed.[83]

Boards of guardians welcomed the opening of relief works and forwarded numerous requests regarding the location and nature of the works to be undertaken.[84] As in 1890–91, guardians had no objections to central government taking control of relief works. They did, however, object to interference in their administration of outdoor relief. The root cause of friction between central and local authorities lay in a disagreement over the relationship between different forms of relief. The guardians thought relief works should be the primary form of relief; the Local Government Board insisted that the poor law remained primary and that relief works were supplemental. When the Swinford guardians directed their relieving officers to issue each applicant for relief with an order for employment on the relief works, the Local Government Board wrote to remind them that that the works were only intended to assist the operation of the ordinary poor law, they were not being introduced 'to remove from the Guardians' shoulders the responsibility of relieving the destitute poor'. Boards of Guardians, and the distressed, regarded the opening of relief works as a signal that central government had assumed responsibility for relief. If relief works were in prospect, therefore, indoor relief was discounted as an option. In April 1895, Dillon forwarded a letter to Morley from five tenants from Kilbeagh, County Mayo, complaining about the delay in the starting a relief works in the district. People in the village were starving for want of food, and if works were not started soon, they warned, 'there will be many who will have no alternative but starvation or the workhouse'.[85]

Gerald Balfour and the devolution of responsibility

The appointment of Gerald Balfour as Chief Secretary in 1896 might have been expected to mark a return to the policies adopted by his brother earlier in the decade. But while many historians have seen Gerald Balfour's period of office as representing the 'second phase of constructive unionism',[86] his approach to Irish policy differed from that of his brother in means if not in ends. Both aimed to anchor Ireland more firmly within the United Kingdom by redressing social and economic grievances, but where Arthur sought to do this through state action, Gerald Balfour sought to promote social and economic development through an extension of local power and responsibilities. It is no surprise, therefore, that in confronting the economic crisis of 1897–98, Balfour sought to reduce the role of central government and to return responsibility for emergency relief to the boards of guardians.

As in 1879, the crisis was the culmination of a number of bad years and credit was virtually exhausted. The area affected was wider than in 1895 and in Connemara and Mayo the distress was more intense than in either 1895 or 1891. If the scale of the crisis recalled that of 1879–80, so did the official reaction to it. For most of 1897, ministers and officials denied the existence of serious distress and insisted that people could be adequately relieved under the poor law. Talk of famine and demands for government intervention were regarded as political propaganda, just as they had been in 1879. Distress, the under-secretary, Sir David Harrel, warned Balfour in December 1897, was 'being run in the west on political lines for all its worth'.[87] With government refusing to act, a charitable fund was established at a public meeting in Manchester Town Hall on 30 December 1897. Operating through an organising committee based in Dublin the fund distributed a little over £20,000 mostly in the form of seed, sprays, tools and grants of money to establish relief works. A further £11,000 was raised by the Mansion

House Fund, which was opened in Dublin on 24 February 1898.[88]

Balfour had accepted by the beginning of November 1897 that special relief measures would be necessary but, as he explained to his cabinet colleagues, he was determined not to follow the course adopted in 1890–91 and 1895. By assuming responsibility for dealing with distress, the government had taught the people 'to imagine that they have a right to dip their hands in the public purse every time the harvest is a little worse than the average, and whose motive for exerting themselves is proportionately weakened'. In order to combat this tendency he proposed to throw 'the primary responsibility and at least a proportion of the cost on the local authorities themselves'. Boards of guardians would be authorised to give outdoor relief subject to a labour test. Government would contribute part of the cost, according to the financial state of the union. This was, in essence, a return to the system adopted in 1886, except that in 1898 the government declined to reveal how much money was available in government grants, and provision was made for much closer supervision of the boards of guardians in devising schemes of work and selecting those to be employed on them. The advantages of this plan, Balfour maintained, was that 'while adequate relief would be given to the rate-payers, sufficient safeguards are ... provided against the reckless and wasteful expenditure of public money'.[89]

The Local Government Board claimed to have had 'considerable misgivings' about Balfour's scheme that the Chief Secretary had overruled.[90] Having previously endorsed Arthur Balfour's centralised model of emergency relief, it was this that H.A. Robinson had recommended to Morley in 1894. It is clear, however, that Robinson was quickly persuaded of the merits of the new scheme. Indeed, he later asserted that it was the Local Government Board that had 'suggested that the guardians themselves should start the relief works', and that Balfour had 'adopted this plan'.[91] Robinson's appropriation of the policy is an indication of the degree to which he came to identify with it. Under Gerald Balfour, the relationship between the Chief Secretary's Office and the Local Government Board became closer and more harmonious than it had been under either his brother or John Morley. This was due partly to ideological and partly to personal factors. In placing so much emphasis on local responsibility while also attempting to keep expenditure to a minimum, Balfour's priorities corresponded closely with those of the Board. Furthermore, from mid-1897 Balfour had been working closely with Robinson on the local government bill and the two men had developed a strong mutual respect. Balfour's confidence in Robinson, who was the Board's recognised expert on emergency relief, was reflected in his decision to trust the implementation of his relief policy to the Local Government Board.

Reaction to the government's relief measures in Ireland was almost universally hostile. 'It is the same old story of fifty years ago', the *Connaught Telegraph* complained in February 1898, 'when the cruel and callous government of the day allowed the people to be decimated by famine'. Declaring the ratepayers in the distressed districts to be too poor to support the higher taxes necessary for effective relief, the *Freeman's Journal* condemned the government's failure to intervene: 'There never was in the history of the nations a more shameful spectacle than the rich country letting the poor country, which she annually plunders of millions, suffer in famine for the lack of a few thousand pounds judiciously spent in relief.'[92]

Set up shortly after Balfour's announcement of relief measures, the Mansion House Fund was an implicit condemnation of the course adopted. There would have been no need to appeal to the public for money had the government been prepared to do its duty. Much of the energy of the Fund's organising committee was devoted to publicity. Around 30,000 pamphlets containing detailed accounts, and illustrations, of the distress were circulated in Ireland, Britain and America in an effort to raise public awareness and thereby funds, and to shame the government.[93]

Irish MPs denounced the relief measures as inadequate and inappropriate, arguing that the government was morally obliged to relieve distress, first, because the British state had the resources to do so while Irish people themselves did not, and, secondly, because the root cause of distress lay in centuries of misgovernment.[94] In May 1898, John Dillon moved a motion to censure the Chief Secretary for his handling of the crisis. On no other occasion, Dillon claimed, had the starving population of the west been treated more harshly or in a more unsatisfactory manner. The Chief Secretary had failed to recognise 'the responsibility which this condition of affairs throws upon him in the government of Ireland'. Balfour was unapologetic, and infuriated Irish MPs by continuing to deny that the situation was as bad as they claimed. He was not trying to save money he insisted, 'but by throwing the responsibility upon the local authorities, I think I may say I have ensured a condition of things which will render the temptation to exaggerate distress in the future much less than it has hitherto been'.[95] This was the real reason, Robinson believed, for Irish hostility to the measures. In his twenty years of experience of distress debates he told Balfour, he had 'never known the Irish members make such a desperate and determined effort to smash up a Government relief measure ... [T]hey feel you have beaten them and have at length hit upon a plan which brings relief only to those in need and which makes famine-mongering cease to be a profitable occupation to the rate-payers'.[96]

Poor law guardians were equally critical of Balfour's scheme, believing that they were being required to take on a task that rightfully belonged to central government. In July 1897, the chair of the Belmullet Board of Guardians, together with a number of his colleagues, had resigned in protest at 'the repeated refusals of the Government to come to the aid of the starving poor', forcing the Local Government Board to appoint vice-guardians. The *Freeman's Journal* had approved the guardians' action declaring, 'Let responsibility be placed on those who are really responsible'.[97] Many boards of guardians refused to implement the relief measures unless government met the entire cost. Others hoped to persuade or manoeuvre the government into taking responsibility for relief. The Westport Board of Guardians threatened to cancel works that had been started in the union in the hope that government would step in. The guardians backed down after being reminded that relieving officers would be obliged to give provisional relief to all those struck off the works. The Board would thus be depriving itself of any government assistance but would still have to provide relief.[98]

Eleven unions (Ballinrobe, Bawnboy, Belmullet, Caherciveen, Clifden, Dunfanaghy, Galway, Killala, Oughterard, Swinford, and Westport) eventually adopted the relief measures in the period from January to July 1898, and relief works were approved in 98 electoral divisions. The works provided employment for 6,375 heads of households thus providing support for around 32,000 people. Interest-free loans for the purchase of seed potatoes were obtained by 75 boards and, in a new departure, boards were also authorised to borrow money to purchase seed oats and spraying machines. In total, guardians borrowed nearly £78,000. The Local Government Board arranged for the free distribution of 500 tons of seed potatoes to people engaged on relief works at a cost of around £3,800. Total government expenditure on the relief measures was £45,460, considerably less than the £70,000 voted by parliament.[99]

The Local Government Board kept close watch on the situation in the distressed districts. When guardians in the County Galway unions of Oughterard and Clifden proved unduly cautious in approving applications for relief, relieving officers were directed to give any applicant for relief the benefit of the doubt 'pending further inquiries'.[100] In March 1898 an inspector was sent to report on the sufficiency of relief operations on the Carraroe peninsula, following complaints from the local Catholic priest. Robinson reassured Balfour that the inspector had found no evidence of the Oughterard guardians 'having refused relief to a really necessitous family properly eligible for relief'. He acknowledged, however, that union relief operations, 'which only undertake to keep the people out of the workhouse', often appeared harsh in comparison those to of charitable associations. The guardians, he explained, 'have the ratepayers to think of which the distributors of private charity have not – and the Guardians will not give relief to persons who have a few head of live stock in a saleable condition whereas private charity will relieve those who are on the border land between destitution and comparatively fair circumstances – and can do so without drying up the sources of supply'.[101]

Robinson judged the relief operations a success. The measures were working admirably, he informed Balfour at the end of March; 'we have struck the minimum level of abuse'. He was far less enthusiastic about the work of the charitable funds. Not only were the organisers fostering the impression that the government was doing nothing, but they were distributing aid in a way that would do more harm than good. It was, he lamented,

> the old story – the personally conducted visits of philanthropic Englishmen to 'show' houses – the abominable lying and the absence of any shame when misrepresentations are exposed – the neglect of ordinary work, the well-to-do begging and cringing for a share in the spoil, the record Easter collections in the churches, the envy, rivalry and ill-feeling engendered, the complete loss of independence and self respect.[102]

As in 1879–81, the perceived failure of government to act stimulated both charitable and political activity. William O'Brien, whose concern for the plight of western small holders comprised a central theme of his political career, seized the opportunity to establish a popular organisation that could provide both a focus for agrarian discontent and a means of bringing together the fractured sections of the nationalist movement. Distress and evictions in the west provided the backdrop to the emergence of the United Irish League in 1898, as they had done for the establishment of the Land League in 1879. But instead of rent reductions and the abolition of landlordism, the League sought compulsory purchase and land redistribution. Its constitution called tellingly for 'the suppression of famine ... by compulsory purchase of the grazing lands of Connaught'.[103] Thus while Balfour and the Local Government Board were correct in believing that cutting back on state aid would not result in deaths from starvation, the political cost to government was considerable.[104]

A confidential memorandum on the relief of distress operations 1897–8 complied by the Local Government Board concluded that the people had been 'brought through a very trying period without undue hardship, and at a very small cost to the Government and to the ratepayers of the Unions concerned'. The course adopted had 'proved that if the Guardians of Unions are given a direct incentive to economy and to a judicious administration of relief, it is better to give them the responsibility and control of anything in the shape of works opened for the relief of exceptional distress'.[105] The success of the experiment persuaded Balfour to include relief of distress among the responsibilities of Ireland's new local authorities. Under the 1898 Local Government Act, county councils were empowered to declare a state of exceptional distress to exist in their county and then to apply to the Local Government Board for permission to extend outdoor relief for up to two months 'to poor persons of any description'.[106] This provision was fiercely opposed by nationalist MPs such as Dillon, who argued that the object was 'to transfer for all future time the whole responsibility and the entire burden of dealing with any exceptional distress in the west of Ireland from the shoulders of the British Government to the shoulders of the ratepayers of the poorest counties of Ireland'. The only concession that Balfour was prepared to offer, however, was to place a limit on the contribution that any county council could be called upon to make.[107]

Conclusion

The avoidance of famine-related deaths in the second half of the nineteenth century has been attributed to a combination of relief measures, public investment in economic development, improvements in public health, and a change in public attitudes.[108] Mindful that public opinion would not tolerate starvation in Ireland, politicians responded more promptly and more effectually to the threat of famine in the 1880s and 1890s than they had in the 1840s. The declining cost of relief measures reflected improvements in the efficiency of the operations, a decline in the numbers affected by distress, and a growing reluctance to finance what was increasingly coming to be seen as poor relief rather than emergency relief. In material terms, emergency relief was effective. As T.P. O'Neill has observed, government relief in the 1890s 'prevented deaths, provided employment, improved the seed supply, and while it added to the rates burden in certain areas it also poured substantial amounts into these same areas as free grants'.[109] But emergency relief was never just a question of material concerns; it was always was closely bound up with politics. Thus in judging the effectiveness of government relief we also need to consider ministerial objectives, and these were by no means consistent. Every chief secretary wished to prevent people dying from starvation but beyond that their agendas were different. John

Morley wanted to demonstrate the government's responsiveness to local demands and its faith in local self-government.
Arthur Balfour sought to pacify Ireland while his brother sought
to promote local responsibility and a self-help ethic. All
achieved their objectives to a greater or lesser extent though the
consequences of doing so were not always what they had anticipated.

Emergency relief enabled the population of the distressed
districts to survive successive economic crises, but it did little to
improve their long-term prospects or to address the problem of
chronic poverty. While ministers and officials condemned the
dependency culture in the west, they failed to acknowledge the
extent to which they were responsible for this. Since there was
no consistency in the administration of emergency relief, with
different criteria being applied at different times, the only way
of ensuring access to aid was to exaggerate the extent to which
it was required. Equally, since people never knew whether or
not they were going to be judged eligible for relief, they
accepted whatever they could get irrespective of their actual
needs at the time. Local Government Board officials sought to
discourage the resort to emergency relief but were sufficiently
pragmatic to realise that the convergence of humanitarian and
political objectives often made resistance pointless. In this event,
the Board attempted to ensure that aid reached those who
needed it, and only those who needed it, thus preventing excessive expenditure.

Poor law guardians believed emergency relief to be the
responsibility of the state. This belief was based on both principled and practical considerations. Relief measures were difficult
to administer without causing resentment among ratepayers, or
the distressed, or both, and they disrupted the ordinary administration of the poor law. Periodically relaxing the restrictions on
outdoor relief stimulated demand for this form of assistance,
and increased popular aversion to the workhouse. If it was
appropriate for government to intervene to prevent people
being forced into the workhouse at times of economic crisis,
why was it inappropriate for guardians to use outdoor relief to
achieve the same objective at other times? As Robinson had
warned Morley in 1894, the practical effect of almost continuous
ameliorative measures 'would be to finally supersede the

system of Workhouse relief for the Western peasantry'.[110] Morley was not alone in disregarding the wider implications of government intervention. During the second half of the nineteenth century the Irish poor law system increasingly diverged from the English system. Modification was judged necessary to meet Irish conditions and to allow for the incorporation of new functions. The relief of distress acts are one example of this process; the labourers acts, which form the subject of the next chapter, are another.

Notes

1 In 1873, for example, approx. 3 per cent of the population was in receipt of poor relief in Connaught compared to 8 per cent in Leinster. *Return showing the Area, Population, Pauperism and Expenditure for the Relief of the Poor in Ireland*, PP, 1874 (409), lvi, 933–1043.

2 For the government response to distress during these years, see the papers of Thomas Larcom (under-secretary 1853–68): NLI, Ms 7783–5.

3 Cormac Ó Gráda, *Ireland: A New Economic History 1780–1939* (Oxford, Clarendon Press, 1994), p. 253.

4 Robinson to Harrel, 13 Nov 1894; note by Morley, 14 Nov. 1894: NAI, CSORP, 1896/14603.

5 Relief measures introduced during this period are discussed in more detail in Virginia Crossman, '"With the experience of 1846 and 1847 before them": The Politics of Emergency Relief, 1879–84', in Peter Gray (ed.), *Victoria's Ireland? Irishness and Britishness, 1837–1901* (Dublin, Four Courts Press, 2004), pp. 167–81.

6 Sir Henry Robinson, *Memories*, p. 22.

7 Report of H.A. Robinson, 12 Mar. 1880: NAI, CSORP, 1880/7070. See also report of A. Bourke, 13 Jan. 1880: *Annual Report of the Local Government Board for Ireland*, PP, 1880 [C.2603], xxviii, 155.

8 Ibid., 7–11.

9 See remarks of the Home Secretary, R.A. Cross, *Hansard 3*, ccl, 445 (10 Feb. 1880).

10 *Hansard 3*, ccl, 1011 (19 Feb. 1880).

11 *Freeman's Journal*, 21 Feb. 1880.

12 *Hansard 3*, ccl, 1012 (19 Feb. 1880).

13 43 Vict., c. 4, s. 21.

14 Report on Relief Measures in 1880–81, 23 June 1891: NAI, CSORP, 1891/17944.

15 *Hansard 3*, cclii, 1806 (11 June 1880).
16 James H. Tuke, *Irish Distress and its Remedies... A Visit to Donegal and Connaught in the Spring of 1880* (London, W. Ridgway, 1880), p. 55.
17 *Freeman's Journal*, 7 Feb. 1880.
18 43 & 44 Vict., c. 14. The rate of interest was reduced from 3.5 per cent to 1 per cent, and payment postponed for two years without incurring any interest.
19 *Annual Report of the Local Government Board for Ireland*, PP, 1880 [C.2603], xxviii, 11.
20 Robinson, *Memories*, p. 12. Tuke commended Robinson's 'zeal and ability'. See Tuke, *Irish Distress and its Remedies*, p. 78.
21 *Annual Report of the Local Government Board for Ireland*, PP, 1881 [C.2926], xlvii, 363–5.
22 Belmullet Board of Guardians Minutes (hereafter BBGM), 30 Oct. 1879; 20 Nov. 1879; 15 Jan. 1880: NLI, MS 12349, 266, 325–6, 448.
23 BBGM, 18 Dec. 1879: ibid., 409; *Annual Report of the Local Government Board for Ireland*, PP, 1881, [C.2926], xlvii, 364.
24 BBGM, 7 July 1881: NLI, MS 12350, 187–8.
25 Robinson, *Memories*, p. 29; BBGM, 5 May 1881: NLI, MS 12350, 66.
26 *Annual Report of the Local Government Board for Ireland*, PP, 1881 [C.2926], xlvii, 279.
27 Report of Capt. Dorwood, 14 Sept. 1880: CSORP 1880/26726. See also Report of Capt. Dorwood, 13 Aug. 1880: ibid.
28 Resolution of Mohill Board of Guardians, 19 June 1880: ibid; Report on Relief Measures in 1880–81, 23 June 1891: NAI, CSORP, 1891/17944.
29 Expenditure on Relief of Distress in 1879 and 1890, 13 July 1891: ibid. See also Papers collected by Mr Balfour in the Autumn of 1890 to show the nature and results of steps taken in former years of failure of the potato crop for the purpose of relief of distress: BL, Balfour Papers, Add MS 49822, ff 126–32.
30 Cited in Ó Gráda, *Ireland: A New Economic History*, p. 252.
31 Gerald Moran, *A Radical Priest in Mayo: Fr Patrick Lavelle: The Rise and Fall of an Irish Nationalist 1825–86* (Dublin, Four Courts Press, 1994), p. 169.
32 R.V. Comerford, 'The Politics of Distress, 1877–82', in Vaughan (ed.) *A New History of Ireland*, p. 38.
33 Report on Relief Measures in 1880–81, 23 June 1891: NAI, CSORP, 1891/17944.
34 *Freeman's Journal*, 7 Feb. 1880.
35 Terence McGrath, *Pictures from Ireland* (London, C. Keegan Paul and Co., 1880), p. 206.

36 *Annual Report of the Local Government Board for Ireland*, PP, 1882 [C.3311] xxxi, 12.

37 *United Ireland*, 18 Nov. 1882.

38 Robinson, *Memories*, pp. 43–5

39 Printed letter, 9 Dec. 1882: PP, 1883 (92), lix, 30.

40 Circular signed by R.G.C. Hamilton, 2 Jan. 1883: ibid., 31.

41 *United Ireland*, 30 Dec. 1882. The cartoon appeared 23 Dec. 1882. Spencer is depicted saying 'Starving are you? Well, go to the work-house or turn informer, or be hanged!'

42 *Hansard 3*, cclxxvi, 1051 (27 February 1883); ibid., 1066, 1073 (27 Feb 1883). The Arrears Act of 1882 empowered boards of guardians to borrow money from the board of works to assist people to emigrate. Around 25,000 emigrants received help under this provision in 1883–84. See R.B. McDowell, 'Administration and the public services, 1870–1921', in Vaughan (ed.), *A New History of Ireland: VI*, p. 582.

43 Report from Mr Robinson, 12 Mar. 1883: PP, 1883 (92), lix, 16–18.

44 *Memoranda of Statement made to His Excellency the Lord Lieutenant of Ireland, on the 9th January 1883, by the Catholic Prelates of Connaught, relative to the Destitution apprehended in their respective dioceses*, PP, 1883 (92), lix, 49–51.

45 *Annual Report of the Local Government Board for Ireland*, PP, 1884, [C.4051], xxxviii, 13. Grants totalling a little over £10,000 were made to five western unions (Belmullet, Clifden, Newport, Galway, and Swinford) to relieve ratepayers of the financial burden of the relief provided. See, ibid., 14.

46 This episode is discussed in more detail in Virginia Crossman, '"The Charm of Allowing People to Manage their own Affairs": political perspectives on emergency relief in late nineteenth-century Ireland', in D. George Boyce and Alan O'Day (eds), *Ireland in Transition, 1867–1921* (London, Routledge, 2004), pp. 193–208.

47 Robinson, *Memories*, pp. 78–9.

48 49 Vict., c. 17.

49 Robinson, *Memories*, p. 79.

50 Evidence of Peter O'Malley, *Poor Relief (Ireland) Inquiry Commission*, PP, 1887, xxxviii [C.5043], 44.

51 Robinson to Hamilton, 12 Oct. 1886; J.J. Louden (Chair of Westport Board of Guardians) to Lord Chancellor of Ireland, 9 Sept. 1886: NAI, CSORP, 1887/10224.

52 'Letters from Ireland', xiv, *The Times*, 18 Nov. 1886.

53 *Poor Relief (Ireland) Inquiry Commission*, 7, 10–11. Redington had chaired the commission appointed earlier in the year to oversee the establishment of public works under the Relief Act.

54 Buller to Balfour, 14 May 1887: BL, Balfour Papers, Add MS 49807, f. 100; Balfour to Buller, 12 May 1887: ibid., Add MS 49826, f. 68.

55 PP, 1887, ii, 175. Galway was not included in the bill as it was thought it would be able to raise enough money from the rates to meet its liabilities of just over £850.

56 *Annual Report of the Local Government Board for Ireland*, PP, 1888 [C.5455], 1, 13, 77–9. See also BBGM, 6 Oct. 1887: NLI, MS 12,354, 669; 20 Oct. 1887: ibid., 712.

57 *Freeman's Journal*, 1 Sept. 1886; quoted in *Mayo Examiner*, 4 June 1887.

58 [*Dublin Evening*] *Mail*, 15 June 1888, reprinted in *Notes from Ireland*, 23 June 1888.

59 *Mayo Examiner*, 4 June 1887. For the evidence of Catholic priests see, *Poor Relief (Ireland) Inquiry Commission*, 73–4, 202–3.

60 See, for example, the report of Morley's speech at Hull: *The Times*, 26 Nov. 1887.

61 See, for example, Micks to Browning, 16 Aug. 1890: BL, Balfour Papers, Add MS 49817, f. 137; Tuke to Balfour, 5 Aug. 1890: ibid., f. 242.

62 Balfour to Tuke, 25 Aug. 1890: ibid., f. 248.

63 Sir West Ridgeway, Draft Report on Relief of Distress 1890–91, Jan. 1892: ibid., Add MS 49823, ff. 180–236. See also Constabulary Circulars, 24 Jan. 18981: NA, Home Office Papers, HO184/117.

64 Memorandum as to Seed, Dec. 1891: NAI, CSORP, 1891/26481. During 1890–91 loans amounting to £282,830 were sanctioned for advancement to the boards of guardians of 111 unions. The actual amount advanced was £274,520. See, Appendix to Memorandum on the Relief of Distress in Ireland, 2 Nov. 1897: NA, Cabinet Papers, CAB 37/45/41.

65 George Morris, Memorandum on the Operations for the Relief of Distress, 1 Dec. 1891: NAI, CSORP, 1891/26481; Ridgeway, Draft Report on Relief of Distress 1890–91, f. 188.

66 *Return of Particulars of Relief Works Undertaken in Certain Parts of Ireland in the Latter Part of 1890 and in 1891*, PP, 1892 (85), lxiv, 655–85; Appendix to Memorandum on the Relief of Distress in Ireland, 2 Nov. 1897.

67 Ridgeway, Draft Report on Relief of Distress 1890–91, f. 186; *Hansard 3*, cccli, 780–82 (12 Mar. 1891); Expenditure on Relief of Distress 1879 and 1890, 13 July, 1891: NAI, CSORP, 1891/17944.

68 Relief Works (Ireland), 1890–91, Report of Major W. Peacocke, 21 Nov. 1891: BL, Balfour Papers, Add MS 49823, f. 196; Micks to Browning, 26 Nov. 1890, ibid., Add MS 49817, f. 148.

69 Strikes and refusals to accept employment on the Claremorris to Collooney Railway, Jan.–Mar. 1891, Papers on Relief of Distress 1890–91: NA, Balfour Papers, PRO 30/60/9.

70 Relief Works (Ireland), 1890–91, Report of Major Peacocke, f. 196.

71 Morris, Memorandum on the Operations for the Relief of Distress.

72 Swinford Board of Guardians Minutes, 6 January 1891: NLI, MS 12594, 81. Similar resolutions passed by Westport Board of Guardians on 16 July 1891 and by the Clifden Board on 28 October 1891. See, Papers on Relief of Distress 1890–91: BL, Balfour Papers, PRO 30/60/9.

73 Ridgeway, Draft Report on Relief of Distress 1890–91, f. 186.

74 Micks to Browning, 3 May 1891: BL, Balfour Papers, Add MS 49817, f. 189.

75 *Hansard 3*, cccli, 787 (12 Mar. 1891).

76 Alvin Jackson, *The Ulster Party: Irish Unionists in the House of Commons, 1884–1911* (Oxford, Oxford University Press, 1989), p. 212.

77 Turner to Balfour, 27 November 1890: BL, Balfour Papers, Add MS 49689, f. 106.

78 Ridgeway, Draft Report on Relief of Distress 1890–91, f. 191; Morris, Memorandum on the Operations for the Relief of Distress.

79 Expenditure on Relief of Distress 1879 and 1890, 13 July, 1891; Notes by Mr Browning on the Relief of Distress Report, 28 Apr. 1892: BL, Balfour Papers, Add MS 49812, ff. 227–30.

80 *Annual Report of the Local Government Board for Ireland*, PP, 1890–91 [C.6439], xxxv, 18.

81 H.A. Robinson, Failure of the Potato Crop in the Western Union (Confidential Memorandum), 7 Nov. 1894: Bodleian Library, Oxford, Uncatalogued papers of John Morley; Robinson to Morley, 8 Nov. 1894: ibid.

82 Distress, Ireland, 1895, Special reports made to Government by the Local Government Board for Ireland, respecting the state of the Potato and other Crops in the districts in which distress is likely to be felt among the small land-holders, 3 Jan. 1895: ibid.

83 *Return of Particulars of Relief Works opened in Certain Portions of Ireland up to the 1st day of May 1895*, PP 1895 (287), lxxx, 345–63; Appendix to Memorandum on the Relief of Distress in Ireland, 2 Nov. 1897; Loans under Seed Supply Acts as to 31st March 1897: NA, Cabinet Papers, CAB 37/45/41.

84 See, for example, Resolution and correspondence, Swinford Union, Feb. 1895: NLI, Dillon papers, MS 6803, ff 24–43.

85 Local Government Board to Clerk of Swinford Union, 2 Mar. 1895: ibid., f. 44; Dillon to Morley (with enclosure), 4 Apr. 1895: ibid., MS

6798, f. 88.

86 Euan O'Halpin, *The Decline of the Union: British Government in Ireland 1892–1920* (Dublin, Gill and Macmillan, 1987), p. 14.

87 Quoted in Andrew Gailey, *Ireland and the Death of Kindness: The experience of constructive unionism 1890–1905* (Cork, Cork University Press, 1987), p. 53.

88 T.P. O'Neill, 'The Food Crisis of the 1890s', in E. Margaret Crawford (ed.), *Famine: The Irish Experience 900–1900. Subsistence Crises and Famines in Ireland* (Edinburgh, John Donald, 1989), pp. 186–7. See also *Distress in the West of Ireland, 1898* (Manchester, 1898); Daniel Tallon, *Distress in the West and South and Ireland, 1898. Report of the Work of the Mansion House Committee* (Dublin, Dollard Printing House, 1898).

89 Memorandum on the Relief of Distress in Ireland, 2 Nov. 1897. See also H.A. Robinson, *[Confidential] Memorandum as to Relief of Distress Operations, 1897–8* (Dublin, 1899).

90 Ibid., pp. 1–2.

91 Robinson, *Memories*, p. 111.

92 *Connaught Telegraph*, 19 Feb. 1898; *Freeman's Journal*, 16 Apr. 1898.

93 Tallon, *Distress in the West and South and Ireland, 1898*, p. 8.

94 *Hansard 4*, liii, [Healy] 197–8, [M'Hugh] 219 (9 Feb. 1898).

95 *Hansard 4*, lvii, 1232 (13 May 1898); ibid., 1268.

96 Robinson to Balfour, n.d. (Feb. 1898): Scottish Record Office, Balfour Papers, GD 433/2/114/14.

97 *Independent*, 16 July 1897: NAI, CSORP, 1897/12744; *Freeman's Journal*, 19 July 1897.

98 Robinson to Balfour, n.d. (Feb. 1898): Scottish Record Office, Balfour Papers, GD 433/2/114/14.

99 *[Confidential] Memorandum as to Relief of Distress Operations, 1897–8*.

100 Robinson to Balfour, n.d. (Feb. 1898): Scottish Record Office, Balfour Papers, GD 433/2/114/14.

101 Robinson to Balfour, 18 Mar. 1898: NA, Balfour Papers, PRO 30/60/15.

102 Robinson to Balfour, 30 Mar. 1898: ibid.; Robinson to Balfour, 17 Apr. 1898: Scottish Record Office, Balfour Papers, GD 433/2/114/1.

103 Cited in Paul Bew, *Conflict and Conciliation in Ireland 1890–1910: Parnellites and Radical Agrarians* (Oxford, Oxford University Press, 1987), p. 55. See also Philip Bull, *Land, Politics and Nationalism: A Study of the Irish Land Question* (Dublin, Gill and Macmillan, 1996), pp. 109–15.

104 Fergus Campbell, 'Irish Popular Politics and the Making of the Wyndham Land Act, 1901–3', *Historical Journal*, 45, 4 (2002) and,

Land and Revolution: Nationalist Politics in the West of Ireland 1891–1921 (Oxford, Oxford University Press, 2005).
105 *[Confidential] Memorandum as to Relief of Distress Operations, 1897–8*, p. 9.
106 61 & 62 Vict., c. 37, Part I, s. 13.1.
107 *Hansard 4*, lvii, 312 (4 May 1898); ibid., 451 (5 May 1898).
108 Ó Gráda, *Ireland: A New Economic History*, pp. 253–4.
109 O'Neill, 'The Food Crisis of the 1890s', p. 190.
110 Robinson to Morley, 7 Nov. 1894: Bodleian Library, Oxford, Uncatalogued papers of John Morley.

5

Labourers' cottages: the poor law system as an engine of social change

> One sequel of the land settlement, scarcely less wonder-working than the abolition of landlordism itself, has been the establishment of an entire rural labouring class in cosy cottages with allotments of one acre apiece ... where only a few years ago they were huddled landless in some foetid room in a town slum, at a crushing rent to starve for half the year.[1]

William O'Brien's rosy account, published in 1910, exaggerated the speed but not the significance of the revolution that had taken place in rural housing. Since the 1880s a total of around 30,000 cottages had been built by Irish local authorities and let to rural labourers at modest rents. By 1914 the total had increased to over 45,000. This was the result of a series of acts known as the labourers acts (1883–1906) that empowered boards of guardians, and later local councils, to undertake improvement schemes where housing for labourers was deficient or unsanitary. O'Brien was not alone among Irish nationalists in heralding the success the legislation and in seeking to take credit for it.[2] According to its leaders, the acts provided solid evidence of the national movement's commitment to the cause of labour.

Whilst questioning the strength of that commitment, historians have largely accepted O'Brien's linkage of the labourers acts with land reform. Generally seen as a by-product of the land agitation, the acts have been described as the result of 'a trade off between land for farmers and housing for agricultural labourers'.[3] But if the role of nationalist politicians as originators of the legislation is acknowledged, that of the local authorities as the administrators of it has received little attention. Boards of guardians are generally believed to have made no real effort to put the acts into operation until spurred into action by the introduction of state subsidies and the presence of labour representatives on local councils following the 1898 Local Government Act. Where boards were active it is thought to be for the wrong reasons. Thus James Donnelly describes guardians in County Cork as seldom acting 'unless under pressure, with the notable exception of their frequent attempts to harass landlords by selecting sites for dwellings on evicted farms'.[4] Such comments echo the complaints of contemporary critics whose accounts of maladministration by elected guardians invariably included examples of labourers' cottages irregularly sited or allocated.

A more nuanced analysis of the labourers acts is provided here encompassing their origin, reception and operation. As in other areas of local administration, the relationship between local authorities and the Local Government Board was a crucial factor in determining the extent and rate of progress. Boards of guardians found themselves both looking to the Local Government Board for advice and assistance in implementing the acts, and chaffing against its attempts to regulate their activities. As the body responsible for sanctioning and overseeing improvement schemes, the Local Government Board came into conflict with both nationalist and unionist-controlled boards of guardians, attempting to prevent the former from using the acts as a form of outdoor relief and as a means of attacking landlords, whilst endeavouring to persuade the latter to discharge their responsibilities under the legislation. At issue was the nature of individual and public responsibility for the state of labourers' housing, and the appropriate role of local authorities. Questions of entitlement and respectability, previously discussed in relation to the distribution of poor relief, are also relevant here. As we shall see, decisions regarding the provision and allocation of cottages involved a complex interaction of social and political considerations.

The condition of agricultural labourers

The condition of agricultural labourers had formed a particular focus of concern in Ireland from before the Famine. The Whately Commission had found in the mid-1830s that a great portion of the labouring poor lacked even the 'commonest necessaries of life', and had advocated the replacement of the 'wretched hovels' in which they lived with new cottages funded jointly by the landlord and the locality.[5] As the most economically vulnerable section of the population, labourers were badly hit by the Famine and numbers had declined dramatically as death and emigration eroded their former predominance within the rural population. The agricultural labour force fell by 20 per cent between 1841 and 1851 and continued to decline in subsequent decades. Clark estimates that the proportion of labourers within the male agricultural labour force as a whole fell from 56 per cent in 1841 to 38 per cent in 1881, while that of farmers and farmers' sons rose from 42 per cent to 60 per cent.[6] The decline was most evident in areas where smallholdings remained common, particularly in Connaught. Fitzpatrick notes that the post-Famine period saw an increasing divergence between those parts of the country specialising in commercial farming and those dominated by small-holdings, with labourers concentrated in the former areas.[7] Despite the decline in their numbers, the circumstances of agricultural labourers appear to have improved less quickly and less noticeably than those of farmers, for although wage levels increased so did living expenses. Similarly while housing conditions were generally better than they had been before the Famine, they remained poor and a major source of grievance amongst labourers.[8]

The hardships experienced by agricultural labourers were attested to by a variety of witnesses from government officials to foreign visitors. Giving evidence to a select committee in 1884, a sanitary officer from County Limerick, described labourers' houses as being of a very inferior character. They were, he said, 'wretched; you would not put pigs to live in some of them'.[9] Within rural communities, however, there seemed to be little interest in addressing the situation. Local government inspector Richard Bourke, commented in 1872 that neither landlords nor tenants 'were alive to the considerable advantages, social and economic, arising from the improved condition of the labourer'. Even labourers were said to be unconcerned about ameliorating their surroundings. Houses that had been built for them were, according to another inspector, often kept in a 'filthy and disgusting condition', the occupants being 'but little sensible of the benefits to be derived from healthful and comfortable dwellings'.[10]

Tenant farmers justified their failure to provide adequate accommodation for labourers by insisting that they could not afford to do so.[11] This argument was subsequently incorporated into Land League rhetoric as way of maintaining vital cross-class alliances within the national movement. The farmer, Parnell claimed in 1881, was 'compelled by rack-rents to starve both himself and his labourers'. As the American academic, D.B. King, noted in 1882, 'while the tenant farmers are often responsible for not a little of the distress [among labourers], there is a great effort to place the whole responsibility for it on the landlords.'[12] For their part, Irish landlords took every opportunity to emphasise the culpability of farmers. Thus William Bence Jones from Clonakilty told the Cowper Commission in 1881 that 'if the landlords treated their tenants with half the hardness that the farmers treat their labourers, there would be a rebellion tomorrow. It is the most utter screwing.' The Revd Thomas Meagher from Newport in Tipperary implicitly confirmed this analysis when he informed the Commission that he would like to see labourers independent: 'I would allow no slavery if I could'.[13]

The making of the labourers act

What was needed, many observers agreed, was an adequate supply of habitable cottages, preferably with gardens attached so that labourers could supplement their wages.[14] How to achieve this was more problematic. Acknowledging that the 'lamentable condition of the Irish labourer moves the compassion of all observers', *The Times* in 1881 warned that it was easier to acknowledge this than 'to discern how that condition is to be directly improved by legislation'. The best way to improve the labourers' condition, *The Times* concluded, was to improve the condition of the country generally.[15] British ministers largely shared this view, believing that the most the state could do was to encourage and facilitate private enterprise. The land act of 1870 had allowed landlords to provide cottage accommodation for labourers on tenanted land without paying compensation for disturbance. The 1881 land act empowered the Land Commission to order either landlords or tenants to provide such accommodation. By the end of January 1882, 42 orders had been made requiring tenants to erect or improve cottages, or to provide cottages with gardens. By May 1883 this had increased to 350 orders but many of these had not been acted upon and the enforcement procedure was slow and cumbersome.[16] It was becoming increasingly clear to politicians from all parties that a more radical approach to the problem was necessary.

Such an approach was only feasible in Ireland because of a particular combination of social and political circumstances. There was growing concern within government and society regarding the link between dirt and disease and an acceptance of the need for state intervention. Under the public health acts of 1874 and 1878, poor law boards had been constituted rural sanitary authorities and empowered to monitor and, if necessary, enforce basic standards of hygiene and cleanliness. Following lobbying by the Dublin Sanitary Association, which had been established in 1872 to raise public awareness on sanitary matters generally, the artisans and labourers dwellings act of 1875 had been extended to Ireland allowing the major urban authorities to borrow money in order to demolish unsanitary dwellings and provide for their replacement. The labourers acts can, therefore, as Frank Cullen has suggested, be seen as 'a logical progression' of public health legislation.[17] The problem of rural housing was acknowledged to be general and acute, and to have public health implications, and previous attempts to find a solution had proved unsuccessful. It is unlikely, however, that these considerations alone would have been sufficient to prompt government action. Similar conditions, as Murray Fraser notes, prevailed in parts of Britain. 'What was different about rural Ireland', he argues, 'was the determination of the Irish Party to win the landless labourers over to constitutional Nationalism through the offer of better housing', and the willingness of the Liberal government 'to concede this social improvement so as to mediate the conflict between farmers and labourers'.[18]

Most historians have seen the incorporation of labourers' concerns into the programme of the Land League as a somewhat cynical exercise prompted by the need to maintain a united front against Irish landlords and the British government.[19] Speaking at the national land convention in September 1881, Parnell called on Irish farmers to promote better housing and working conditions for labourers and advocated legislation to achieve these ends. The following summer Parnell again appealed to Irish farmers to recognise the 'urgent and acknowledged' claims of labourers, arguing that their co-operation was indispensable to any further measure of agrarian reform.[20] Parnell realised that the national movement needed to secure tangible benefits for labourers if it was to retain their support. His appeals to farmers notwithstanding, Parnell was well aware that it was unwise to rely on any sense of social obligation to effect real improvements in labourers' conditions. Some element of external stimulus was necessary. Speaking in the Commons in 1881, he had recommended giving the Land Commission responsibility for re-housing labourers, arguing that if the labourer were made independent of landlords and farmers, 'the quality of his labour would be much improved, and he would be contented with his lot'.[21] The labourers act of 1883 was intended to achieve this end by a slightly different route, by giving responsibility not to the Land Commission but to boards of guardians.

The Labourers (Ireland) Act 1883

Introduced in February 1883, the Labourers (Ireland) Bill empowered rural sanitary authorities to implement housing schemes on behalf of agricultural labourers on the representation of twelve ratepayers. Any scheme requiring the compulsory purchase of land had to be approved first by the Local Government Board, and then by parliament. Parliamentary confirmation was not required for schemes involving land acquired by agreement. Such schemes could, however, be blocked by a petition signed by three ratepayers. Once a scheme was approved, the board of guardians could borrow money on the security of the rates in order to carry out the scheme. Every cottage built under the act was to have a half-acre of land attached as a means of supplementing the occupant's income. Introducing the bill in the Commons on 30 May 1883, T.P. O'Connor presented it as an uncontroversial and moderate measure that merely extended the same powers to rural sanitary authorities that the Artisans Dwelling Act had given to urban authorities. Parnell took a similar line whilst reiterating his belief that the state had a responsibility 'to place the labourer in an independent position'.[22] The bill met with little direct opposition, although a number of MPs doubted whether any use would be made of the measure. Boards of guardians, the Conservative MP for Dublin County, Colonel E.R. King-Harman, observed were mainly composed of farmers of small means, and 'they had not shown themselves very careful of the labourers' condition during the past two years'. Faced with this relative unanimity, the chief secretary, G.O. Trevelyan, felt he had no option but to support the second reading of the bill whilst warning that Treasury approval would have to be obtained.[23]

Prior to the debate, the lord lieutenant, Lord Spencer, had warned Trevelyan that while anything that would improve the condition of labourers' cottages was 'extremely desirable and should receive the support of the Government', the details would have 'to be very carefully considered with the view of securing that private rights are not unnecessarily interfered with'. Interfering with property rights could only be justified, he explained, 'where it can be shown that interference is necessary to secure the health or public interests of some portion of the community'. Henry Robinson, he added revealingly, 'doubts whether if passed much will come of the measure'.[24] Both Spencer and his under-secretary, Hamilton, were firmly convinced that improving social and economic conditions in Ireland would do much to undermine support for nationalism. Hamilton was also a keen advocate of local government reform. The introduction of representative local government, he argued, would allow local affairs to 'rest where they ought to rest, with local authorities, and the state would be relieved from the almost impossible duty of looking efficiently after local interests'.[25] Spencer was, therefore, disposed to be sympathetic towards a measure that would empower the existing local authorities to address an acknowledged social evil.

Having accepted the principle of the bill, Trevelyan believed that the only practical course now open to the government was to reconstruct it, 'by means of amendments'. Great care would have to be taken, he warned Spencer, 'to avoid private injustice and public disadvantage. We must not make it a bill for endowing farmers' sons'.[26] As Irish officials got to work on drafting amendments, Trevelyan began to have second thoughts. He was, he confessed to Spencer on 4 June, 'very much afraid of the Labourers Bill in anything like its present shape'. Spencer declined to share his alarm. He agreed that even in an amended form the bill was a substantial piece of legislation 'to swallow', but observed that given the support the measure had received, he saw 'no other course than to go on'.[27] Shortly before the bill was due to be considered in committee, Trevelyan alerted Spencer that English Conservatives such as Goschen and Peel were planning to attack the bill as 'socialistic'. Spencer saw no reason for concern. If the labourers bill was socialistic, he reminded his Chief Secretary, this was 'equally true to the Artisans Dwelling Bill which was a Conservative production'.[28]

In the event English Conservatives took no part in the debate. Irish Conservatives such as Edward Gibson, MP for Dublin University, moved a number of amendments intended to protect the interests of landowners.[29] Amongst those accepted was a provision preventing improvement schemes from interfering with any landowner's demesne or home farm. The bill that emerged from committee was a more limited measure than it had been when first introduced. Most significantly, accommodation was only to be provided for agricultural labourers narrowly defined. But it was still a radical departure in housing legislation. As a correspondent to *The Times* noted, it went much further than the Artisans Dwelling Act that enabled urban sanitary authorities to replace houses that had been condemned as unsanitary. The labourers bill allowed rural sanitary authorities to build cottages merely on the representation of ratepayers that existing accommodation was deficient. This power he pointed out, 'is entirely new to the statute-book, and yet it has been given by the House of Commons without any discussion whatever'.[30]

It was left to members of the lords to raise substantive objections to the bill. Condemning the measure as a 'wild scheme',

the Earl of Wemyss remarked that if the state built houses for the
working classes, 'he did not see why they should not undertake
to clothe them also'. The Duke of Argyll described the bill as
'full of objection and danger', only taking comfort from the fact
that it would be 'wholly unworkable, owing to the great
complexity of its machinery'. Yet even in the lords, the bill was
able to secure significant cross-party support. Salisbury
defended the principle of advancing government money for the
benefit of a private individual pointing out that this had been
done under Tory administrations to enable Irish landowners to
drain their estates. In order to protect the Irish ratepayer, he
proposed that there should be a maximum limit on the amount
of rate that could be levied, and that the duration of the bill
should also be limited. The government accepted these suggestions, and the bill was amended. Any rate was not to exceed one
shilling in the pound in any one year, and the duration of the act
was limited to five years.[31] It is clear from the foregoing that the
role of the Irish party in formulating the labourers act has been
exaggerated. The act would never have passed, even in its
substantially amended form, if it had not commanded genuine
all-party support among Irish MPs and if Spencer and Trevelyan
had not been prepared, however nervously, to adopt it as what
was in effect a government bill. Despite its limitations, the act
constituted, as Daly notes, 'a landmark in Irish housing legislation because it provided for rents to be subsidised by the rates'.[32]
Irish local authorities were given powers to provide social
housing that their equivalents in the rest of the United Kingdom
were not to obtain until after the First World War.

Implementing the act

The link between levels of poverty and the conditions in which
labourers lived was generally acknowledged. Workhouse
numbers and applications for outdoor relief regularly rose in the
winter months when there was less agricultural employment
available. There were, however, deep divisions amongst poor
law guardians and ratepayers over the exact relationship
between labourers' circumstances and pauperism. Some
guardians saw the wretchedness of labourers' houses as a direct

cause of pauperism. As the Limerick MP, William O'Sullivan, explained in the Commons in 1884, in his experience as a guardian of the Kilmallock Union one quarter of those entering the workhouse did so 'for want of good houses to live in and for no other reason'. Providing housing for the labouring population would, he argued, be a 'very great step towards the extinction of pauperism'.[33] Others believed that where there were labourers, there would inevitably be pauperism. One reason why so few landlords and farmers were prepared to provide accommodation for labourers was that the presence of labourers in a district was seen as a potential burden on the rates, since they were likely to enter the workhouse, or apply for outdoor relief, for two or three months out of every year. Landowners were further discouraged by having to pay the poor rate on labourers' holdings.[34] The Marquis of Drogheda was to petition against the erection of 44 cottages on his property in Athy Union in February 1887, on the grounds that 'their erection would create a fresh pauper class in the district'.[35] The way in which poor law guardians and ratepayers perceived pauperism was to be a crucial factor in determining how the labourers act was received, and the extent to which it was utilised.

Shortly after the labourers act became law in late August 1883, the Local Government Board forwarded a copy of the act to each sanitary authority in the country together with an explanatory memorandum. Within weeks, a number of boards of guardians were considering representations.[36] At the end of October, *United Ireland* welcomed the decision of the Limerick Board to prepare a scheme for 1,000 cottages, noting that if the project met opposition from local landlords or the Local Government Board, the labourers would know whom to blame.[37] By the end of March 1884, 70 boards had inaugurated over 700 schemes under the act for the erection of around 6,000 cottages. Some of these schemes fell through at an early stage. The Local Government Board rejected others. In its annual report for 1883–84, the Board estimated that it would be able to confirm schemes for a total of around 2,800 dwellings; less than half those originally applied for. Tipperary Union obtained the largest number of houses, gaining approval for 29 schemes and authorisation for 376 houses.[38]

Boards in Connaught and Ulster showed little interest in the
act. Of the 60 boards that submitted schemes to the Local
Government Board for approval, 33 were from Munster, 25 from
Leinster, two were from Connaught, and none were from Ulster.
There were various reasons for this regional disparity, which
was to remain a feature of the legislation. Wage labourers were
concentrated in Leinster and Munster, and while many small-
holders in Connaught and Ulster occupied sub-standard
housing they did not qualify for assistance under the act.
Moreover, few unions in the western parts of Connaught and
Ulster could afford to undertake such schemes. Resistance to the
act across much of Ulster reflected the greater influence of
landowners on poor law boards throughout the province. Ulster
guardians regularly rejected representations by ratepayers for
the initiation of improvement schemes on the grounds that
labourers were already well provided for by landlords.[39] As
Padraig Lane has noted, Ulster's record in this regard was held
up as an example of thrift and austerity, in contrast to the profli-
gacy of guardians in other parts of the country. Private
enterprise, it was claimed, provided adequately for labourers'
needs.[40]

Reviewing the act in 1884, the Local Government Board
presented the progress made as satisfactory. Representations
had been freely signed by ratepayers, improvement schemes
had been drawn up and provisional orders made and
confirmed. Moreover, the act had been the means of drawing
attention to the defective sanitary state of labourers' dwellings
in many localities and improvements had been 'voluntarily
effected', although no indication was given of the number of
houses thus improved.[41] This remained the official line.
Appearing before a select committee to investigate the working
of the act in 1884, Henry Robinson claimed that it had worked
'wonderfully well', commenting that the authorisation of 3,000
cottages 'is very good work for a few months'. He did, however,
admit that there was a danger that schemes that had been
approved would not be built because of the expense involved.[42]
Robinson's favourable assessment of the act was not widely
shared and has been dismissed by historians. In her study of
agricultural tenure, Elizabeth Hooker stated that 'no action' was
taken in the twelve months after the passage of the 1883 act.[43]

This is to overstate the case. There was considerable activity and while it is true that no cottages were actually built, this would have been impossible under the procedures laid down in the act. Nevertheless, the rate of progress was slow and gave little grounds for complacency. Labourers criticised the legislation as defective and condemned the reluctance of many boards to initiate schemes. Many doubted whether poor law guardians could be trusted to administer the act properly. Labourers from Kilmichael, near Macroom in County Cork, addressed a memorial to Gladstone in February 1884 calling for the allocation of cottages to be left to a government officer rather than the board of guardians. This, they argued, would be the most effective means of saving the labourer from starvation.[44]

Amending the act

There was general agreement amongst guardians and labourers that procedures under the act were too complicated and too expensive. Speaking in the Commons in 1884, H.W. Villiers-Stuart, Liberal MP for Waterford County, revealed that his own board had been defeated by 'the intricate technicalities of the Act'. If boards with MPs on them could not work the act, what hope was there, the Home Rule MP, A.J. Moore, wondered for ordinary guardians, 'men very often in humble positions in life, to understand and administrate it'? Even Robinson's colleagues were said to be doubtful about the efficacy of the act. William Shaw, Home Rule MP for County Cork, told the Commons that 'every official of the Irish Local Government Board that he had met admitted it to be unworkable'. It imposed too great a financial burden on unions and its machinery was too elaborate.[45] In order to address these problems, Irish nationalist MPs introduced an amendment bill to speed up procedure and reduce expense. They further proposed that the Local Government Board should be empowered to put a scheme into operation if a sanitary authority failed to do so. Trevelyan was wary of agreeing to further legislation, arguing that the existing act had not been given a chance to work. He also rejected the idea of giving the Local Government Board the power to impose a scheme on the grounds that it would be 'most unfortunate' to give the

central authority power to override local authorities: 'If the local
bodies did not do their duty in the matter, the ratepayers had
their remedy, in their own hands'. He did accept that there were
a number of areas in which the legislation could be improved
and proposed that the matter be referred to a select committee.[46]

The select committee on agricultural labourers reported in
December 1884, and recommended various measures to
simplify procedure and reduce the cost of improvement
schemes. Sanitary authorities should be able to acquire land on
a long lease as well as by purchase, and the Irish Privy Council
or Land Commission, rather than parliament, should be made
the final authority in the confirmation of schemes. The committee also recommended that authorities should be empowered to
repair existing cottages and to acquire gardens for them, and
that any rate levied under the act should be levied on the union
at large. Early in 1885, the Liberal government produced a bill
incorporating virtually all of the committee's recommendations,
the most notable omission being union rating. Boards of
guardians anxious to utilise the legislation welcomed the publication of the bill, but regretted that it did not go further.
Following a meeting on 7 February 1885, the Wexford Board of
Guardians recommended a number of amendments that were
subsequently endorsed by other boards including those of Sligo
and Bawnboy. These included the introduction of a national rate
to subsidise the cost of erecting cottages, and the transfer of the
duty of confirming provisional orders to the Land Commission
rather than the Privy Council.[47] Rejected by the Local
Government Board, the Wexford proposals are interesting as
evidence both of the commitment of some boards of guardians
to the implementation of the labourers act, and of the divergence
between local and central government over the purpose of the
act.

Local Government Board officials regarded the act primarily
as a means of improving rural housing, and thus public health,
and were anxious to keep its administration separate from the
administration of relief as far as possible. They were also
committed to the principle of local accountability for the implementation and funding of improvement schemes. The Board
opposed the idea of a national rate on the grounds that it was
unreasonable to expect that a union in which there were hardly

any labourers or where labourers were properly housed, 'should have to contribute for houses in some other union, or that an urban union, like Belfast, should have to pay for agricultural labourers while themselves unable to take advantage of the act'.[48] Many boards of guardians, on the other hand, perceived the labourers act as an integral part of the relief system. Thus the Wexford guardians called for the introduction of a clause permitting boards of guardians to grant the occupants of labourers' cottages outdoor relief. (Since the tenant of a labourers' cottage held more than a quarter acre of land, he could only receive relief within the workhouse.) Robinson opposed this, arguing that it was not desirable 'to afford special facilities to the occupants of labourers cottages'. He could see 'no valid reason for exempting such persons from the operation of a clause affecting all occupiers of land in Ireland'.[49]

The Liberal government fell in June 1885, but the amending bill was taken up by the succeeding Conservative administration and passed into law in August.[50] Speaking on behalf of the government, the Marquess of Waterford admitted that the 1883 act had been found to be 'almost inoperative'.[51] The new act removed the main obstacles to the operation of the legislation and extended its duration from five to seven years. In addition, loan terms were made more favourable. Interest rates were reduced and the maximum term extended to fifty years.[52] Further amendments were made the following year, when a bill introduced by Irish nationalist MPs extended the definition of an agricultural labourer to include women, and those who combined agricultural labouring with other forms of work such as fishing or weaving.[53] In their annual report for 1885–86, the Local Government Board noted increased activity on the part of boards of guardians. Some boards that had suspended operations in anticipation of fresh legislation were now moving ahead, whilst others were taking their first steps to put the acts into operation. A total of 3,401 houses had been authorised, of which 610 had been built and 479 let to labourers. Since the 1885 act had been passed, new improvement schemes had been prepared to provide another 10,899 cottages.[54] The accommodation provided generally consisted of a one-storied cottage containing a kitchen, and two bedrooms, with a yard and privy. In some cases the cottages were two-storied, having a third bedroom; in others a storeroom was provided. A piggery was a common addition.[55]

Perceptions of the acts

Comments made on the progress of the acts reveal a striking disparity between perceptions at the centre and in the localities. While ministers and officials continually stressed how much was being done under the acts,[56] Irish MPs and labourers' representatives lamented how little had been achieved. The difference was one of perspective. The most immediate concern for those in the centre was the increased workload resulting from the acts. The Local Government Board had to appoint extra staff including four temporary inspectors to assist with the work of holding inquiries, as well as extra clerks and copyists.[57] Unaware of the extra cogs being added to the bureaucratic machine, those in the localities looked for visible signs of progress in the form of actual cottages. Resolutions passed by the Ballinsaloe Board of Guardians in 1889 and 1891 were typical in their criticism of the labourers acts as 'cumbrous, unwieldy and far too expensive to admit even of building cottages on the land we have purchased'.[58] Within government, however, the complexity and expense of the acts came to be seen as a positive feature that prevented guardians both from abusing their powers and from utilising them on too grand a scale.

Local Government Board officials had been taken aback by the enthusiasm with which some guardians had embraced the acts. Far from having a problem with apathetic local authorities, one official recalled in 1906, the 'difficulty in the beginning was to restrain them'.[59] Responding to the Ballinsaloe resolutions, Robinson observed that it was difficult to see how the acts could be worked with much greater economy, 'having due regard to the interests of the ratepayers, and the protection of persons whose lands are taken compulsorily'.[60] As he had explained to Ridgeway, in March 1889, complaints about the 'cumbrous officialism' of the acts were misplaced; 'the measure takes property compulsorily from the owners and occupiers of land, and it is necessary for the protection of such persons that much care and attention should be given to the details and working of the Act'. Everything that could be done to simplify and cheapen procedure, 'consistent with the rights of the owners and occupiers of the property concerned', had, he claimed, been done in 1885.[61]

By the late 1880s, public attention had shifted from the inadequacies of the legislation to the manner in which it was being applied. It became an article of faith amongst representatives of the landed interest that elected guardians were abusing their powers under the acts. In January 1888, *The Times* informed its readers that nationalist boards had,

> in the most flagrant manner worked the [Labourers] Act for the advancement of their own political aims. For example, farmers who are members of the National League were protected, while the land of their political opponents was compulsorily acquired for building purposes. In other cases the small farms of Unionists were selected to the exclusion of large holdings in the hands of Nationalists. Labourers who joined the League were promised new houses and told they would have them rent free, and those who wanted them badly were denied them because they did not 'throw in their lot with the people'.[62]

Visiting Ireland in 1887, the Suffolk barrister, George Pellew, was fed similar stories. Nationalist unions in County Clare he was told were 'miserably mismanaged'. These included the Tulla Union where the number of labourers' cottages was said to be 'enormous, most of them built only to spite the landlords'. Such occurrences, it was claimed, had reinforced opposition to Home Rule by showing 'that the people cannot yet be trusted'.[63] Nationalist politicians and commentators concentrated on publicising the achievements of boards of guardians in executing the acts, whilst taking every opportunity to highlight the comparative lack of progress in unions under landlord control.[64] In January 1886, *United Ireland* noted that 'where the elected guardians are the ruling power, the Labourers Act is being almost universally put into practice, while in Ulster, where the landlord influence predominates, the Act remains an absolute dead-letter'. The refusal of boards in Ulster to put the act in force, the paper declared, exposed landlords' pretensions 'to pose as champions of the labourers'. At the same time, however, labourers were warned not to advance their claims for cottages too aggressively. Labourers who attempted to overawe boards of guardians by crowding into the boardroom and refusing to leave 'do injury rather than service to their cause'.[65]

Some local newspapers were critical of the level of activity among elected guardians. The *Leinster Leader*, for example, condemned the guardians of Mountmellick Union in February 1888 for their 'unwonted coolness and inexplicable apathy' in relation to the acts. More frequently, the limited success of the acts was blamed on the obstacles placed in the way of boards of guardians by landlords, the Local Government Board and the Privy Council. *United Ireland* had warned in January 1887 that the Privy Council threatened 'to be the death of the Labourers Act. Without the ghost of a consultation they are throwing out every scheme for cottages that comes before them.' Recent cases had shown that 'all the evidence of engineers, sanitary inspectors and guardians, and all the pleading of the ablest advocates the friends of the labourer can command, count for nothing against the uncorroborated assertion of a landlord or his bailiff'. Later that year the *Leinster Leader* noted that the Privy Council had acted 'as if their duty under the Act was to defeat and destroy'.[66]

The role of the Privy Council

There was some justification for such complaints. It is clear from reports of the proceedings of the judicial committee of the Privy Council that councillors paid greater heed to the evidence of landowners than to that of poor law guardians, or even local government inspectors. In September 1887, for example, Thomas Cusack petitioned against the erection of four cottages on his land in Ballymahon Union, County Longford, on the grounds that they 'were not put on his land to carry out the provisions of the Act, but to injure him', the object of the guardians being to accommodate evicted tenants. Evidence was produced regarding the unsanitary condition of existing cottages, and the lack of accommodation for labourers in the district. The judicial committee nevertheless concluded that 'the project of erecting the cottages was not to meet a general want but to meet the wishes of persons antagonistic to the person on whose land they were to be built. They, therefore, allowed the petition'. Official returns show that between May 1886 and April 1887, of 65 objections to provisional orders heard by the judicial committee, 57 were allowed. It is hard not to sympathise with Francis Nally, architect to the Mullingar Board of Guardians, who, when asked what he thought the Privy Council would believe, exclaimed, 'Anything against the poor, I think, would be believed very well'.[67]

Local government inspectors found themselves in an unusual position in these proceedings, being aligned with boards of guardians and against landlords. Every improvement scheme was subject to a local inquiry conducted by an inspector, and could not proceed without his approval. Inspectors spent a considerable amount of their time on such inquiries, and it struck many observers as strange that their judgement could be so easily discounted. Touring the south west of Ireland in September 1891, Sir John Gorst, secretary to the Royal Commission on labour, expressed surprise that an improvement scheme sanctioned by a local government inspector and approved by the Local Government Board could be thrown out by the Privy Council. How, he wondered, could the local knowledge of the Privy Council be compared to that of a local government board official and the board of guardians?[68] It is difficult to know to what extent these temporary alliances affected the relationships between individual inspectors and the boards of guardians under their supervision. Their efforts did, however, earn inspectors praise from some unlikely quarters. Having represented a number of boards of guardians in cases before the Privy Council, T.M. Healy, concluded that local government inspectors were 'really and truly anxious to promote the interests of labourers', despite the efforts of privy councillors to intimidate them.[69]

Within government, the Privy Council was seen to be performing a vital function. Whilst stressing that the number of cases that went before the Privy Council were 'small compared with the entire number of cottages applied for', Robinson claimed that it was evident from the hearings, 'that the grossest injustice would have been done to owners and occupiers in certain districts except for the appeal'.[70] Balfour endorsed this view, observing that 'it has only been for the intervention of the P[rivy] C[ouncil] that the [labourers] acts have been prevented from being used as engines of oppression against unpopular persons'.[71] A memorandum on local administration produced by the Local Government Board in 1892, at Balfour's request, provided examples of 26 unions where attempts had been made 'to build cottages upon boycotted farms for evicted tenants'. These attempts were unsuccessful only because the cottages had been 'excluded from the schemes either by the Inspectors of the Local Government Board or the Privy Council'.[72] So long as Privy Councillors were drawn almost exclusively from the landed class, the judicial committee was always going to give a sympathetic hearing to landowners. As the *Leinster Leader* noted in March 1887, one leading Privy Councillor who sat regularly on the judicial committee was Arthur M'Murrough Kavanagh. This was a man who had opposed the erection of cottages on his own property in Carlow Union the previous year, declaring that 'men would be much more usefully employed helping some of the labourers to emigrate than building new dwellings for them'.[73] It was not until the appointment of John Morley as Liberal Chief Secretary in 1892 that the composition of the Privy Council came under critical scrutiny. In September 1892, Morley alerted Gladstone to the need 'to infuse a popular element into the Privy Council', given the importance of its appellate work in connection with the labourers acts, and other legislation. Gladstone subsequently approved three names proposed by Morley including that of the Parnellite Joseph Meade, who had served as Lord Mayor of Dublin 1891–92.[74]

Extending the acts

By the late 1880s the first wave of construction under the labourers acts was nearing completion. Yet it was clear that the number of cottages authorised – 9,552 by 31 March 1888[75] – would by no means satisfy demand. Some kind of impetus was necessary if boards of guardians were to be persuaded to undertake new schemes. In May 1890, Irish nationalist MPs proposed to provide a financial incentive by making available £1.5 million from the Irish Church Surplus Fund. Boards of guardians would be able to apply for up to half the cost of schemes already undertaken and of new schemes.[76] Balfour promptly dismissed this proposal as an attempt to undermine his land purchase scheme that drew on the same fund.[77] Unionist MPs such as Ellison Macartney (Antrim South) supported the principle of a subsidy but argued that a carrot would be ineffectual without a stick. Macartney and his colleagues had long lamented the fact that the labourers acts were practically a 'dead letter' throughout the whole of Ulster, and had come to the conclusion that an element of compulsion was necessary if Ulster labourers were to gain any benefit from the acts. The inactivity of Ulster guardians was blamed on inertia and political differences, though the strongest criticism was reserved for elected guardians. These were drawn mainly from the farming class, Sir Charles Lewis (Antrim North) explained to the Commons in August 1889, 'and the farmers are even more out of sympathy with the labourers than are the land-lords'.[78] In November 1890, Unionists introduced their own bill to amend the labourers acts. This appropriated the idea of a subsidy, proposing that the Land Commission should be able to provide up to half the amount of any improvement scheme, with the proviso that the total subsidy should not exceed £250,000. Labourers themselves would be enabled to make representations under the acts, while the Local Government Board would be required to enforce approved schemes where the board of guardians had failed to act. Not to be outdone, the following year Irish nationalists introduced an allotments bill to increase the maximum size of a cottage garden from half an acre to an acre.[79] Neither bill was opposed by the government, though the former, more radical, measure only reached the statute book in an emasculated state: the Local Government Board was empowered but no longer required to intervene in cases where boards of guardians refused to proceed, and the subsidy provision was dropped.[80]

The labourers acts amendment bill presented an opportunity for unionists, and the government, to outflank nationalists in the battle for labourers' support, and Balfour's acceptance of it should be understood in this context. Pressure to amend the acts came from without rather than within. The Local Government Board had expressed no dissatisfaction with either the acts or their implementation. Commenting on a parliamentary question tabled by Sir Charles Lewis in June 1889, Robinson had acknowledged that improvement schemes had been authorised in only 3 of Ulster's 43 unions (in Bailieborough, Cavan and Ballymena), with a further one (in Ballycastle) under consideration, but had denied that this was any cause for concern. It did not appear he concluded blandly, that 'any legislation is required with the view of coercing Boards of Guardians to put the provisions of the Labourers Acts into operation'.[81]

Balfour was not averse to the idea of subsidising the construction of labourers' cottages, but he had his own ideas about how this should be done. In August 1890 it had been announced that £40,000 from the Probate Fund was to be distributed amongst boards of guardians in aid of liabilities incurred under the labourers acts.[82] Balfour proposed to continue this subsidy under the land purchase act of 1891 in the form of an annual exchequer grant of £40,000. The money was to be used in the first instance as a loan guarantee fund, but if not required for this purpose the bulk of the grant was to be divided amongst Irish counties and applied towards the cost of providing cottages.[83] Balfour wished to secure maximum political advantage for the government and its supporters, and he had no desire to see most of the money disappear into the coffers of nationalist boards of guardians. In order to prevent this, the land purchase act provided that the grant was to be allocated to the various counties in proportion not to the number of cottages built, but to the expenditure on roads in the year 1887.[84] Historians of the labourers acts have overlooked the significance of this provision.[85] Roads expenditure was the responsibility of landlord-dominated grand juries. By linking his subsidy to expenditure on roads, Balfour was ensuring that he protected the interests of the landed class, and his own political supporters, whilst at the same time being able to present himself as a friend to the labourers.[86] The grant appears to have had little effect in persuading boards that had not previously done so to utilise the acts. All that happened was that a significant proportion of the money remained unspent. In 1898, almost £23,000 from the exchequer grant for 1896–97 and 1897–98 was unissued and was being held in reserve.[87] This situation was eventually acknowledged to be unsatisfactory, and in 1907 the system was altered so that the money was divided in proportion to the number of cottages built.[88] Although the sums made available in this way were relatively small, amounting in most cases to no more than a few hundred pounds each year, the principle was important. As Fraser observes, the original grant 'qualifies as the first direct housing subsidy from central government'.[89]

Following the 1891 act, inquiries were held in a number of Ulster unions in which boards had refused to act on representations made to them. In the vast majority of cases, the inspector recommended that improvement schemes should be carried out. While a number of boards agreed to carry out the recommended schemes, others refused. In its annual report for 1894–95, the Local Government Board noted that it had been required to initiate schemes in the unions of Strabane, Stranorlar and Cootehill, 'the boards of guardians of those unions having declined to carry out improvement schemes as recommended by the Inspector after due local inquiry'.[90] Such cases did little to alter the determination of most Ulster boards of guardians to ignore the acts, and the number of cottages built in the province remained significantly lower than in the rest of the country. By 31 March 1895, the total number of cottages approved in Ulster stood at 111 compared with 5,513 in Leinster. Three years later these totals had risen to 267 and 6,405.[91] The main disincentive amongst Ulster guardians, elected and ex-officio alike was their reluctance to increase local taxation.[92]

Across the country as whole, the 1890s saw renewed activity under the acts, although the rise in the number of cottages being built each year was hardly spectacular. The average yearly total grew from 700 in the years 1891–95 to just 800 in the years 1895–99.[93] A more significant increase was evident following the passage of the Local Government Act. This enfranchised labourers as residents, allowing many to vote and stand in local elections for the first time.[94] The first elections held under the act in 1899 saw significant successes for labour candidates. The under-secretary, Sir David Harrel, estimated that labour representatives formed one sixth of the elected councillors in urban areas, having taken votes mainly from the various nationalist factions. Significantly, many nationalist candidates, including those standing in rural districts, pledged themselves to support the interests of labourers.[95] In its annual report for 1900–01 the Local Government Board noted the 'very general revival throughout Ireland of operations under the Labourers Acts'. New schemes had been received from 82 rural district councils, proposing to erect 5,891 new cottages.[96] This surge in activity peaked in 1904–05 with the completion of 1750 cottages, bringing the cumulative total to just over 19,000.[97]

The acts in operation

The labourers acts altered the terms of social and political relationships in rural Ireland. Having been partially responsible for the original legislation, the nationalist movement both locally and nationally had an interest in its successful implementation. Nationalist MPs sought ways to improve and develop the acts, while nationalist guardians in Leinster and Munster endeavoured to put them into operation. Correlation between numbers of cottages erected and the political complexion of boards of guardians suggests that tenant-dominated boards built more cottages more quickly than those controlled by landlords. By the end of March 1888 only ten unions had succeeded in erecting 100 or more cottages. All were tenant-controlled.[98] Furthermore, unions that had built no cottages were more likely to be landlord-dominated or to have boards on which landlords maintained a significant presence. Every tenant-controlled board of guardians in Leinster, for example, had managed to build some cottages by 1888 with the exceptions of Granard, New Ross and Urlingford.[99]

In some areas, local branches of the National League incorporated support for the acts into their political programmes. The Kilmallock branch was reported to have passed a resolution in September 1890 calling on people to boycott 'any landlord, agent, or farmer who tries to change the site fixed by the engineer or delay the building of any labourers cottage in our division under the present scheme'.[100] Progress under the acts became a measure of achievement for nationalist guardians in areas where there were concentrations of labourers. At a meeting of the Ballincollig National League held in February 1888 to select a candidate for the forthcoming poor law elections, the sitting candidate was roundly condemned for his failure to get any cottages erected, and was accused by labourers of leaving them to 'live in our old hovels'. Nationalists emphasised the commonality of interests within rural society, and dismissed reports of divisions between the National League and labourers. The labourers' question, *United Ireland* declared in 1890, was 'regarded in the popular mind as just as much a National topic as the land question. To suggest that the farmers are the enemies of the labourers in the matter is simply an absurdity'.[101] This unity was, however, a precarious one. By providing a test of guardians' interest in and commitment to the well being of labourers, the acts had the potential to widen class divisions as well as bridge them.

Agitation by labourers was often necessary both to initiate improvement schemes and to maintain pressure on guardians to execute schemes once approved. In January 1887, for example, labourers in Tipperary Union were reported to have invaded a meeting called to consider the labourers act, and to have protested at the delay in providing them with houses.[102] Inquiries into proposed schemes revealed the extent to which such schemes could divide local communities. Local government inspector, W.L. Micks, was obliged to adjourn a public inquiry in Kilmallock in May 1887, when labourers attempted to prevent local farmers from opposing a scheme for the erection of 477 cottages in the union. The labourers were said to have behaved 'in a very noisy manner, and persons who were expected to be hostile to the erection of the cottages were vigorously hooted by them'. Efforts were made to prevent people from entering the courthouse where the inquiry was being held, and to eject others from the building.[103] Such demonstrations merely confirmed the view among many farmers that labourers were a class apart. One local farmer described those agitating for cottages in Kilmallock as 'roughs – like labourers'.[104]

It would be wrong to exaggerate the influence or activism of labourers. Rural labourers in Connaught showed little interest in the acts even after 1891 when labourers could apply for cottages themselves.[105] In areas where labourers were numerous and more assertive, agitation alone was rarely enough to ensure the implementation of the acts. Without the active support of influential figures within the locality, be they landowners, poor law guardians, or local clergy, labourers could expect little from the acts. James O'Shea has demonstrated the significant role that Catholic priests played in County Tipperary in encouraging guardians to develop improvement schemes, and in persuading

farmers to provide land for them. Assessing the record of two of
the most active unions in the county, Tipperary and Nenagh,
O'Shea notes that not alone did these two unions 'experience the
most extensive clerical involvement, but they contained strong
nuclei of highly politicised and determined priests'.[106] But just
as poor law guardians and farmers were divided in their
responses to the acts, so too were Catholic priests. While some
championed the cause of labourers, others were more concerned
about ratepayers. A parish priest in the Skibbereen Union criticised the erection of cottages in the union, declaring that
although he was 'a Nationalist and a Home Ruler', he judged the
scheme to be 'most ill-considered'. It had been 'brought forward
by a few people who wanted to get a little cheap popularity at
other people's expense'.[107] O'Shea concludes that a number of
factors influenced the rate of construction of labourers' cottages.
Union size and population, levels of clerical activity, guardian
diligence, National League influence, and labour militancy all
played a part.[108]

The allocation of cottages

Local influence was important not only in getting schemes
underway but also in the allocation of the cottages once erected.
It was commonly claimed that in unions where nationalist
guardians predominated labourers could only acquire a cottage
though the influence of the National League.[109] Branch officials
undoubtedly sought a role in the selection process. The Catholic
curate of Hollyford, County Tipperary pressed the claims of
National League members on the Tipperary Board of Guardians
in 1886, informing the clerk of the union that it had be unanimously agreed that members of the local branch 'should get a
preference of the labourers cottages'. But since his letter was
prompted by the allocation of a cottage to a non-member, it
would appear that such injunctions did not always carry much
weight with boards. When the unionist MP, Edward
Saunderson, brought the curate's letter to the attention of the
government, the Chief Secretary, John Morley, reassured MPs
that boards of guardians were well aware that they had
'absolute control' over the erection and allocation of cottages,

and that there was no reason to believe that such interventions would have any effect.[110]

There were frequent claims of cottages being built to accommodate evicted tenants. An official memorandum from 1892 cited the example of the Tulla guardians who had erected a labourers' cottage 'for Michael Dwyer on a farm from which he was evicted'.[111] Other boards were said to have given evicted tenants preference over labourers. The Castlecomer guardians were reported to have granted the tenancy of a labourers' cottage 'to the occupant of a land league hut, named Tyndall, who had been evicted from a farm of 121 acres leaving the labourer for whom the cottage had originally been approved in a condemned cabin.[112] As with outdoor relief, cottages could be used both to reward and to punish. The Killarney guardians were said to have refused a cottage to a man named Denis Sullivan, 'because he was caretaker of evicted farms at Ballyoughton'.[113] The attention focused on such cases helped to create the impression that evicted tenants occupied large numbers of labourers' cottages. Had this been the case it would have been a serious abuse of the acts since few evicted tenants would have qualified under the legal definition of an agricultural labourer. In reality, however, such instances were rare. An official return produced in November 1888, revealed that of 3,359 cottages then completed, only 27 were let to evicted tenants.[114]

Whatever role politics played in the allocation of cottages, it is clear that need was not the primary qualification. Character and contacts were more important. When asked in 1884 how the Wexford Board would allocate cottages, the clerk of the union, James O'Connor, replied that the board would

> ask for a character of the labourer from respectable men in the electoral division in which he resided, or from ex officio guardians who lived in the division ... clergymen both Protestant and Catholic who knew the parties would have something to say to it, and respectable ratepayers also; everything would be taken into consideration by the guardians before they gave a house to anybody.

Following this procedure, O'Connor maintained, would have a good effect in encouraging labourers to be more industrious.[115] The selection of tenants was seen as a local matter and decisions were expected to reflect local sentiment. Indeed, one Tipperary priest, Patrick O'Donnell, argued that since the National League was a more representative assembly, and better informed about the character of applicants, than the board of guardians, it was a more appropriate body to select tenants.[116] Where particular local interests were not consulted, this was usually intended as a sign of disrespect or disapproval. In March 1887, for example, the Tulla Board of Guardians in County Clare was said to have let a number of cottages sited on an evicted farm to 'women of a low reputation' in order to 'further annoy' the man who had taken the farm.[117]

In most cases, the guardian representing the division in which the cottage was sited seems to have had a major say in the selection of a tenant. He was, however, expected to consult with local ratepayers before making a recommendation. In 1887, a farmer, William Deady, wrote to the Thomastown Board of Guardians to complain that a cottage erected on his land had not been given to the labourer he had recommended. Responding to Deady's complaint, the guardian for the division explained that two men had been selected as tenants for this cottage and another one nearby at the request of local ratepayers. The two men selected were said to be 'very good working-men'. Deady's labourer had been passed over for 'many reasons ... The neighbours did not like him ... [They] preferred these two men, and they are men of good, honest character.'[118] Such decisions, Marilyn Silverman suggests, 'made clear [to labourers] that local power hierarchies, patronage, and political sentiments affected their access to decent housing along with their personal traits and the good will and material priorities of farmers'.[119] The determining factors in the allocation of labourers' cottages – reputation, industriousness and political allegiance – were the same as those in the distribution of outdoor relief. As a consequence, those most in need were not necessarily those selected. Questioned about the working of the labourers acts in 1888, a number of inspectors noted that the occupants of unsanitary and condemned houses were frequently passed over in the selection process.[120]

Investigations by the Local Government Board revealed that guardians were sometimes ignoring the letter of the law in their selection of tenants. In 1890, ex-officio guardians of Rathkeale

Union in County Limerick put together a detailed complaint regarding abuses of the labourers acts in the union. Cottages were being given to 'old couples without children, to unmarried men, and while intended exclusively for agricultural labourers, are given to tradesmen of all kinds'. Having investigated the allegations, local government inspector Edmund Bourke reported that of the eleven cases enumerated, six were not open to objection. In the other five, he concluded that the guardians had acted improperly in selecting tenants. Two cottages were held by men who did not live in them but rented them simply for the land. A widow in receipt of outdoor relief occupied another together with her 17 children. The guardians explained that this cottage had originally been let to James Griffin, an agricultural labourer. He died and his widow applied for outdoor relief. The guardians had refused to grant relief while she occupied the cottage, whereupon she had surrendered the cottage to her brother, Michael Wall, an agricultural labourer. Bourke doubted this version of events, concluding that 'although Mrs Griffin was in reality the occupier of the cottage, Wall was named as the tenant so as to admit of his sister being given the 5s a week outdoor relief that she at present receives'.[121]

There was little the Local Government Board could do in such cases. As Robinson had explained to the under-secretary, Redvers Buller, in 1887, although 'numerous complaints' had been received 'regarding the letting of cottages generally', the Local Government Board had no power to interfere. It was, however, open to local ratepayers to challenge the guardians' decision in any particular case.[122] Ratepayers who attempted this often found themselves frustrated. Lord Annaly sought to prevent the Ballymahon guardians from letting a cottage to an evicted tenant, only to be informed that there was no point in taking out an injunction against the guardians since even if the man were put out of the cottage the guardians could simply reinstate him.[123] In response to the complaint about the Rathkeale guardians, the Local Government Board reiterated the fact that it had 'no power to control the actions of the Guardians in this respect', but pledged to take the complaint into consideration in the event of the guardians applying for additional cottages.[124]

Like the emergency relief acts, the labourers acts represented a dilution of poor law principles. They provided boards of guardians with the power to relieve the ordinary poor as well as the destitute. Indeed, many guardians appear to have regarded the acts as a way of providing cheap housing for people who would otherwise require outdoor relief, or support within the workhouse. It was common practice, for example, to allow the widow of a deceased labourer to take over the tenancy of a cottage.[125] The Limerick Board went one step further when it attempted to let a cottage to the widow of a deceased labourer at a nominal rent of 1d a week.[126] In such cases, the acts were being used as an extension the relief system rather than a means of re-housing agricultural labourers.

Landlord–tenant relations

Once a labourer had been allocated a cottage his or her relationship with the local board of guardians changed from that of supplicant and potential pauper to that of tenant. Labourers found it easier than guardians to negotiate this transition. Many elected guardians clearly felt uncomfortable in the role of landlord, and the idea of evicting people made them particularly uneasy. Their concern was not only for the welfare of the individuals involved, but for their own reputations also. In 1887 the Kilmallock Board prosecuted a tenant who had been in his cottage for two years and had refused to pay any rent. Having been sentenced to a week's imprisonment, which was not enforced, the man agreed to pay £2. Horrified by the board's action, one guardian protested that the money had been 'extorted ... under the threat of eviction', and accused his colleagues of 'becoming tyrants'.[127] Some boards of guardians allowed tenants to get behind with their rent, and then sought to write off the arrears. Others reduced rent levels, or delayed collection during periods of distress. The Ballymahon guardians, for example, decided not to press for rents during the winter of 1887–88, 'as there was little employment for labourers during the winter'.[128] Such decisions might be regarded as good practice within the rural community but could be construed as maladministration within government. A report compiled by the Local Government Board in 1892 concluded that many boards of guardians had exhibited 'a want of firmness in dealing with the tenants', noting that it had been necessary to remind the guardians of a number of unions that they were neglecting their duty to the ratepayers in failing to enforce regular payment or to recover arrears.[129] Generally speaking, landlord-controlled boards were more active in enforcing rent payments than those controlled by tenants, but the latter were capable of firm action. In 1888, a number of labourers were summoned for non-payment of rent in the Tralee Union, for example, and six were subsequently evicted.[130]

As tenants, labourers were prepared to protest against poor standards in the construction or maintenance of their homes, and to combine together to demand improvements. In 1888, the occupants of cottages in Youghal, County Cork, were reported to be refusing to pay rent 'on the grounds that their cottages were uncomfortable and not worth the rent they were called upon to pay'. Nothing could be 'more natural', the *Daily Express* commented gleefully, than that labourers 'should follow the example of the farmers, and resort to their practices, but it is not very encouraging to find the generous action of the Legislature taken advantage of to promote dishonest practices'. On investigation, local government inspector Edmund Bourke rejected talk of a strike but confirmed that a number of labourers were in arrears with their rent. The 'reason why the labourers refuse to pay', he explained, 'is that the cottages, according to them, let in the rain. This, I fear, is true, and the Sanitary Authority are only waiting for suitable weather to commence the necessary repairs'.[131] Tenants of cottages in Clondalkin village in County Dublin refused to pay their rents in 1890, 'because the manager of the adjacent [paper] mill had kept some straw in their gardens'.[132]

Conclusion

The way in which housing policy developed in Ireland, Fraser concludes, was the result of a 'tripartite mediation between Irish Nationalists, the British Government and the Castle Administration'.[133] This, however, is to ignore the role of the local authorities responsible for executing the acts, and of labourers themselves. Boards of guardians helped to shape the legislation, lobbying government for amendments and suggesting improvements. They also helped to shape policy through their operation of the acts. The tendency of nationalist guardians to use their powers to promote their own agenda, be that social or political, reinforced the determination within government to proceed cautiously, and to rely on internal checks to slow down the rate of construction. At the same time, the inactivity of boards of guardians in Ulster persuaded ministers to invest the Local Government Board with compulsory powers. Pressure from labourers helped to determine where and when the acts were utilised. By validating labourers' claims to decent housing, the acts empowered labourers and promoted negotiation between them and boards of guardians. The MP for Londonderry North, H.L. Mulholland, told the Commons in 1886 that labourers in his constituency considered that the Acts 'had conferred certain legal rights on them to acquire a cottage and half-an-acre of land at a certain rent', and were consequently aggrieved if guardians failed to provide this.[134]

Appearing before a Commons select committee in 1906, Local Government Board official Michael O'Sullivan, stated that the object of the labourers acts had been 'to make the labourer independent of the farmer'. As one Tipperary labourer had declared in 1893, a 'Union cottage gives independence – no-one can put you out while you pay your rent'.[135] Independence carried great significance in rural society and was a crucial factor in distinguishing landholders from labourers. Even though the former were often little better off in material terms, they enjoyed a higher social standing.[136] But not all labourers sought independence. Labourers in Cork told Sir John Gorst that it was better to be tied to one farmer than to be an independent labourer, 'and probably have nothing to do all year round, and in the end to go to the town, and perhaps to the workhouse'.[137] Possession of a cottage was no guarantee of work, but it did place the occupant on a more secure social footing. This, as Cullen observes, was not simply a case of no longer having 'to play second fiddle to the small farmers'. Occupants of cottages 'found themselves in a stronger social position when it came to dealings with those above them in the social pyramid'.[138] Through their occupancy of union cottages, labourers acquired a more secure position within the local community and within rural society as a whole. Ironically, however, labourers may have gained status but lost influence. Fitzpatrick has suggested that the weakness of collective action by labourers in pursuit of their own sectional interests can be attributed to their numerical decline and to the increasingly blurred line between the labourer and small tenant farmer.[139] The provision of labourers' cottages that transformed landless labourers into small holders accelerated this process.

Initially, the labourers acts did help to maximise support for, and promote unity within, the nationalist movement. National League candidates in the general election of 1885, for example, both sought the support of labourers, and generally received it.[140] By the end of the century, however, over twenty years' experience of the operation of the acts had helped to convince labourers that without direct representation on local government bodies, their claims to assistance would struggle to be heard over those of other interest groups. While the nationalist movement was remarkably successful in reconciling the competing demands of sectional interests, it did so by maintaining not challenging existing class and gender inequalities. Like labourers, women were encouraged to support nationalist campaigns but not to lead them, and were urged to subordinate their own interests to those of nation. As we shall see in the next chapter, pressure to reform the poor law to enable women to act as poor law guardians came not from nationalists, but from social reformers and suffrage campaigners the majority of whom were unionists.

Notes

1 William O'Brien, *An Olive Branch in Ireland and its History* (London, Macmillan and Co., 1910), pp. 388–9.
2 See, for example, Michael Davitt, *The Fall of Feudalism in Ireland* (London, Harper and Brothers, 1904), p. 464.
3 Tony Fahey, 'Housing and Local Government', in Mary E. Daly (ed.), *County and Town: One Hundred Years of Local Government in Ireland* (Dublin, Institute of Public Administration, 2001), p. 121.
4 James S. Donnelly, jr., *The Land and People of Nineteenth-Century Cork: The Rural Economy and the Land Question* (London, Routledge, 1975), p. 242.

5 *Third Report of the Commissioners for Inquiring into the Condition of the Poorer Classes in Ireland*, PP, 1836 (43), xxx, 3, 21.

6 Samuel Clark, *Social Origins of the Irish Land War* (Princeton, Princeton University Press, 1979), p. 113.

7 David Fitzpatrick, 'The Disappearance of the Irish Agricultural Labourer, 1841–1912', *Irish Economic and Social History*, vii (1980), 76.

8 Donnelly, *The Land and People of Nineteenth-Century Cork*, pp. 240–3.

9 *Report from the Select Committee on Agricultural Labourers (Ireland)*, PP, 1884 (317), viii, 330.

10 *Reports from Poor Law Inspectors in Ireland... [on] Labourers' Dwellings in that Country*, PP, 1873 [C.764], xxii, 708, 694.

11 See, for example, evidence of Edmond Fitzgerald, *Report of Her Majesty's Commissioners of Inquiry into the Working of the Landlord and Tenant (Ireland) Act, 1870, and the Acts Amending the Same*, PP, 1881 [C.2779], xix, 145.

12 Cited in Liam Kennedy, 'The Economic Thought of the Nation's Lost Leader', in D.G. Boyce and Alan O'Day (eds), *Parnell in Perspective* (London, Routledge, 1991), p. 189; D.B. King, *The Irish Question* (London, W.H. Allen and Co., 1882), pp. 274–5.

13 *Report of Her Majesty's Commissioners of Inquiry into the Working of the Landlord and Tenant (Ireland) Act, 1870, and the Acts Amending the Same*, PP, 1881 [C.2779], xix, 86; ibid., xviii, 299.

14 For a discussion of the cottage as a remedy for poverty in England, see Sarah Lloyd, 'Cottage conversations: poverty and manly independence in eighteenth-century England', *Past and Present*, 184 (2004), 69–108.

15 *The Times*, 7 May 1881.

16 *Return of the Nature of the Provision made for Labourers in Each of the Cases Reported by the Land Commission on the 28th day of January 1882...*, PP, 1882 (211), lv, 315–22; *Hansard 3*, cclxxix, 1261–2 (30 May 1883).

17 Frank Cullen, *Cleansing Rural Dublin: Public Health and Housing Initiatives in the South Dublin Poor Law Union, 1880–1920* (Dublin, Irish Academic Press, 2001), p. 35.

18 Murray Fraser, *John Bull's Other Homes: State Housing and British Policy in Ireland, 1883–1922* (Liverpool, Liverpool University Press, 1996), p. 27. See also Padraig Lane, 'Agricultural Labourers and the Land Question', in Carla King (ed.), *Famine, Land and Culture in Ireland* (Dublin, University College Dublin Press, 2000), pp 106–7; F.H.A. Aalen, 'The Rehousing of Rural Labourers in Ireland under the Labourers (Ireland) Acts, 1883–1919', *Journal of Historical Geography*, 12, 3 (1986), 291.

19 See, for example, Donnelly, *The Land and People of Nineteenth-Century Cork*, pp. 238–9; Bew, *Land and the National Question in Ireland 1858–82* (Dublin, Gill and Macmillan, 1978), pp. 142, 175; Lane, 'Agricultural Labourers and the Land Question', p. 108; T.W. Moody, *Davitt and the Irish Revolution 1846–82* (Oxford, Clarendon Press, 1982), pp. 423–4; John W. Boyle, 'A Marginal Figure: the Irish Rural Labourer', in Samuel Clark and J.S. Donnelly, jr. (eds), *Irish Peasants: Violence and Political Unrest, 1780–1914* (Manchester, Manchester University Press, 1983), pp. 329–30.

20 Clark, *Social Origins of the Irish Land War*, p. 299; Moody, *Davitt and the Irish Revolution*, p. 494; D.B. King, *The Irish Question*, p. 275.

21 *Hansard 3*, cclxi, 895 (19 May 1881).

22 Ibid., cclxxix, 1240–41, 1247–8 (30 May 1883).

23 Ibid., 1244; 1252–3.

24 Spencer to Trevelyan, 30 May 1883: BL, Althorp Papers (uncatalogued), Add MS 76956.

25 Hamilton to Spencer, 7 July 1883: ibid., Add MS 77057.

26 Trevelyan to Spencer, 31 May 1883: ibid., Add MS 76956.

27 Trevelyan to Spencer, 4 June 1883: ibid.; Spencer to Trevelyan, 6 June 1883: ibid.

28 Trevelyan to Spencer, 27 June 1883: ibid., Add MS 76957; Spencer to Trevelyan, 28 June 1883: ibid.

29 *Hansard 3*, cclxxxii, 1772–6 (6 Aug. 1883).

30 Letter from John P. Thomasson, *The Times*, 13 Aug. 1883.

31 *Hansard 3*, cclxxxiii, 927–10 (17 Aug. 1883); ibid., 1485–6 (21 August 1883); 46 &47 Vict., c. 60.

32 Daly, *Buffer State*, p. 203.

33 *Hansard 3*, cclxxxviii, 955 (21 May 1884). See also Villiers Stuart, ibid., 943–4.

34 See, evidence of Thomas Shillington, *Report of Her Majesty's Commissioners of Inquiry into the Working of the Landlord and Tenant (Ireland) Act*, PP, 1881 [C.2779], xviii, 417; Revd Charles Davis, ibid., xix, 152–31; Daniel Leahy, ibid., xix, 98. See also D.B. King, *The Irish Question*, p. 269.

35 Newspaper cutting (*Express?*), 25 Feb. 1887: NAI, CSORP, 1892/4813.

36 See, *The Times*, 18 Oct. 1883, for references to the Middleton and Clonakilty Boards of Guardians.

37 Quoted in *The Times*, 26 Oct. 1883.

38 *Annual Report of the Local Government Board for Ireland*, PP, 1884 [C.4051], xxxviii, 16–17, 25–6; evidence of Henry Robinson, *Report from the Select Committee on Agricultural Labourers (Ireland)*, PP, 1884 (317), viii, 271; evidence of Horace Townsend, ibid., PP, 1884–85

(32), vii, 612. The Tipperary guardians had applied for 677 cottages.

39 See, for example, the report of a special meeting of the Cookstown Board of Guardians: *Belfast Newsletter*, 12 Apr. 1886.

40 Lane, 'Agricultural labourers and the Land Question', p. 142; *Ireland's Gazette*, 19 Aug. 1899.

41 *Annual Report of the Local Government Board for Ireland*, PP, 1884 [C. 4051], xxxviii, 17.

42 *Report from the Select Committee on Agricultural Labourers (Ireland)*, PP, 1884 (317), viii, 271. Loans under the act carried a relatively high rate of interest (4 per cent) and had to be repaid within 35 years. Furthermore substantial legal expenses were incurred in carrying the schemes into effect.

43 Elizabeth R. Hooker, *Readjustments of Agricultural Tenure in Ireland* (Chapel Hill, University of North Carolina Press, 1938), p. 178.

44 *The Times*, 19 Feb. 1884. See also 3 Mar. 1884.

45 *Hansard 3*, cclxxxviii, 941, 953, 973 (21 May 1884).

46 Ibid., 955–65, 976.

47 Suggestions for the Amendment of the Bill now before Parliament, made by the Wexford Board of Guardians at their meeting held on Saturday, the 7th of February, 1885: NAI, CSORP, 1885/15229.

48 Notes by Cullinan on Bawnboy Union, Labourers (Ireland) Act 1885, Suggestions for Amendment of the Bill now before Parliament ..., 16 March 1885: ibid.

49 Robinson to Campbell-Bannerman, 1 Apr. 1885: ibid.

50 48 & 49 Vict., c. 77.

51 *Hansard 3*, ccc, 1436 (7 Aug. 1885).

52 Boards were given a choice of loans: 3.25 per cent over 35 years, 3.5 per cent over 40 years or 3.75 per cent over 50 years.

53 49 & 50 Vict., c. 59.

54 *Annual Report of the Local Government Board for Ireland*, PP, 1886 [c 4728], xxxii, 15–16.

55 Robinson to Ridgeway, 13 Apr. 1888: NAI, CSORP, 1892/4813.

56 See, for example, John Morley's comment that 'timid persons may think that [the working of the acts] have been so rapid as almost to be alarming': *Hansard 3*, cccii, 1815 (3 Mar. 1886).

57 *Annual Report of the Local Government Board for Ireland*, PP, 1884 [c. 4051] xxxviii, 40; Under-Secretary to Secretary of Treasury, 16 Oct. 1886: NAI, Chief Secretary's Office Letter Books, v. 285 (Oct. 1886–Nov. 1887), 39. See also Under-Secretary to Secretary of Treasury, 11 Jan. 1887: ibid., 151.

58 Resolutions of Ballinsaloe Board of Guardians, 21 Aug. 1889, 15 Apr. 1891: NAI, CSORP, 1891/11049.

59 Evidence of Michael O'Sullivan: *Report and Special Report from the Select Committee on Housing of the Working Classes Act Amendment Bill* ..., PP, 1906 (376), ix, 238.

60 Robinson to Balfour, 30 Aug. 1889: NAI, CSORP, 1891/11049.

61 Robinson to Ridgeway, 11 Mar. 1889: ibid., 1892/4813.

62 *The Times*, 6 Jan. 1888.

63 George Pellew, *In Castle and Cabin or Talks in Ireland in 1887* (London, The Knickerbocker Press, 1888), pp. 182–3. The number of cottages erected in the Tulla Union to March 1887 was in fact 68, which was higher than average but hardly enormous. See, *Return showing the Working of the Labourers Act (Ireland), and the number of cottages erected, and the expenses connected therewith, to 31st March 1887*, PP, 1887 (202) lxviii, 493.

64 See, for example, the comments of Parnell and Sheehy: *Hansard 3*, cclxxxviii, 969 (21 May 1884); ibid., cccii, 1818 (3 Mar. 1886).

65 *United Ireland*, 2 Jan. 1886; 16 Jan. 1886.

66 *Leinster Leader*, 11 Feb. 1888; *United Ireland*, 1 Jan. 1887; *Leinster Leader*, 5 Mar. 1888.

67 Unidentified newspaper cutting, 15 Sept. 1887, in Abuses of the Labourers Cottages Act: NAI, CSORP, 1892/4813; unidentified newspaper cutting, 5 Apr. 1887: ibid.; *Return of Cases in which Objections were Lodged against Provisional Orders issued by the Local Government Board for Ireland...*, PP 1887 (139), lxvii, 399–419.

68 *Cork Examiner*, 21 Sept. 1891.

69 *Hansard 3*, cccxx, 698 (31 Aug. 1887).

70 Note by Robinson to Ridgeway, 15 March 1888: NAI, CSORP, 1892/4813.

71 Note by Balfour, 18 Apr. 1888, on Robinson to Ridgeway, 13 Apr. 1888, in Abuses of the Labourers Cottages Act: NAI, CSORP, 1892/4813.

72 Memorandum as to administration by Local Governing bodies in Ireland, 2 Apr. 1892: ibid.

73 *Leinster Leader*, 5 Mar. 1887.

74 Morley to Gladstone, 22 Sept. 1892: BL, Gladstone Papers, Add MS 44256, f. 245; Gladstone to Morley, 23 September: ibid., f. 250.

75 *Return of Operations under the Labourers (Ireland) Acts up to the 31st March 1888...*, PP 1888 (133), lxxxiii, 531.

76 A Bill to Amend the Law relating to Agricultural Labourers in Ireland, 12 Feb. 1890: PP, 1890, i, 35.

77 *Hansard 3*, cccxliv, 902–5 (14 May 1890).

78 *Hansard 3*, ccxl, 152 (22 Aug. 1889). See also O'Doherty: ibid., 160; Mulholland: cccxliv, 887 (14 May 1890); Macartney: ibid., 885.

79 A Bill to Amend the Labourers (Ireland) Acts, 26 Nov. 1890: PP,

1890–91, v, 171; A Bill to Amend the law Relating to Allotments for Labourers in Ireland, 9 June 1891: ibid., 159.

80 54 & 55 Vict., c. 71; 55 Vict., c.7.

81 Robinson to Balfour, 7 June 1889: NAI, CSORP, 1889/17661.

82 *The Times*, 5 Aug. 1890.

83 The counties were to get £37,000, the remaining £6,000 going to six municipal boroughs.

84 Each county share was then sub-divided among rural sanitary authorities in proportion to their expenditure upon cottages since 1891. See, *Annual Report of the Local Government Board for Ireland*, PP, 1897 [C.8599], xxxvii, 456–7; evidence of Michael O'Sullivan, *Report and Special Report from the Select Committee on Housing of the Working Classes Act Amendment Bill...*, 238.

85 See, for example, Aalen, 'The Rehousing of Rural Labourers in Ireland under the Labourers (Ireland) Acts, p. 295; Fraser, *John Bull's Other Homes*, p. 34.

86 See, for example, *Hansard 3*, cccxlii, 1714 (24 Mar. 1890).

87 *Annual Report of the Local Government Board for Ireland*, PP, 1898 [C.8958], xli, 62–3.

88 Evidence of Michael O'Sullivan, *Report and Special Report from the Select Committee on Housing of the Working Classes Act Amendment Bill ...*, 232.

89 Fraser, *John Bull's Other Homes*, p. 34. Loans under the labourers acts were made available at slightly lower rates of interest from 1895. The following year, a bill introduced by the Chief Secretary, Gerald Balfour, removed various technical problems in the administration of the acts and enabled sanitary authorities to sell cottages that were no longer required for labourers: Treasury Minute, 23 Sept. 1895: NAI, CSORP, 1896/4264; 50 & 60 Vict., c. 53.

90 *Annual Report of the Local Government Board for Ireland*, PP, 1895 [C.7818] liii, 53.

91 Map of Ireland Showing the Working of the Labourers (Ireland) Acts to 31st March 1895: *Annual Report of the Local Government Board for Ireland*, PP, 1895 [C.7818], liii; Map of Ireland Showing the Working of the Labourers (Ireland) Acts to 31st March, 1898: *Annual report of the Local Government Board for Ireland*, PP, 1898 [C.8958], xli.

92 See, comments of T.W Russell, *Hansard 3*, cccxliv, 890–1 (14 May 1890).

93 Fraser, *John Bull's Other Homes*, p. 308.

94 For discussions of the impact of the Local Government Act see, Fraser, *John Bull's Other Homes*, p. 35; Daly, *Buffer State*, 204; Enda McKay, 'The Housing of the Rural Labourer, 1881–1916', *Saothar*, 17 (1992), 30–33.

95 Note by Harrell on the Recent Elections, 27 Jan. 1899: NA, Balfour Papers, PRO 30/60/28; Précis of files relating to the forthcoming elections under the Local Government Act of 1898, Jan. 1899: NAI, Crime Branch Special, CBS/1898, 18000/S.

96 *Annual Report of the Local Government Board for Ireland*, PP, 1902 [C.1259] xxxvii, 45–6.

97 Fraser, *John Bull's Other Homes*, pp. 35, 308.

98 The ten were Cashel, 108; Kanturk, 156; Kilmallock, 240; Limerick, 181; Mullingar, 110; Nenagh, 115; Newcastle, 100; Tralee, 128; Tipperary, 165; Wexford, 190.

99 *Return of Operations under the Labourers (Ireland) Acts up to the 31st March 1888...*, PP 1888 (133), lxxxiii, 527–31.

100 *The Times*, 7 Oct. 1890.

101 *Cork Examiner*, 27 Feb. 1888; *United Ireland*, 11 Jan. 1890.

102 *The Times*, 21 Jan. 1887.

103 *Freeman's Journal*, 3 May 1887.

104 Ibid., 12 Nov. 1888.

105 John Cunningham, *Labour in the West of Ireland: Working Life and Struggle 1890–1914* (Belfast, Athol Books, 1995), p. 39.

106 James O'Shea, *Priest, Politics and Society in Post-Famine Ireland: A Study of County Tipperary 1850–1891* (Dublin, Wolfhound Press, 1983), p. 132.

107 *Royal Commission on Labour: The Agricultural Labourer: Ireland*, PP, 1893 [C.6894–xviii], xxxvii, Part I, 452.

108 O'Shea, *Priest, Politics and Society in Post-Famine Ireland*, p. 132.

109 See, for example, *Hansard 3*, cccii, 1833–4 (3 Mar. 1886); *Express*, 25 Feb. 1887.

110 *Hansard 3*, cccii, 1527 (1 Mar. 1886).

111 Intelligence Department Memorandum, Particulars of known cases of oppression on the part of public bodies such as Corporations and Boards of Guardians, 1 Mar. 1892: NAI, CSORP, 1892/4813.

112 Memorandum as to administration by Local Governing bodies in Ireland.

113 Intelligence Dept. Memo., Particulars of known cases of oppression on the part of public bodies.

114 *Return showing the Working of the Labourers (Ireland) Acts up to the 31st day of May 1888...*, PP, HL, 1888 (288), xix, 203–7. See also *Hansard 3*, cccxxix, 626–7 (27 July 1888).

115 *Report from the Select Committee on Agricultural Labourers (Ireland)*, PP, 1884 (317) viii, 345.

116 O'Shea, *Priest, Politics and Society in Post-Famine Ireland*, p. 130.

117 Hector Vandaleur to Balfour, 21 Mar. 1887: NAI, CSORP, 1887/5313.

118 Quoted in Marilyn Silverman, *An Irish Working Class: explorations in*

political economy and hegemony, 1800–1950 (Toronto, University of Toronto Press, 2001), pp. 212–14.

119 Ibid., p. 215.

120 Queries to inspectors regarding labourers' cottages, 13 Apr. 1888, Abuses of the Labourers Cottages Acts, Apr. 1888: NAI, CSORP, 1892/4813.

121 J.B. Hewson to W. Kenny Q.C., 10 Dec. 1890: NAI, CSORP, 1891/20488; Report of E. Bourke, 4 Mar. 1891: ibid.; Extract from Rathkeale Board of Guardians Minutes, 15 Apr. 1891: ibid.

122 Robinson to Buller, 26 Mar. 1887: 1887/5313.

123 Memorandum as to administration by Local Governing bodies in Ireland.

124 Morris to Ridgeway, 6 Aug. 1891: ibid., 1891/20488.

125 See, for example, Bandon Board of Guardians Labourers Acts Ledger, 1886–1896: Cork Archives Institute, BG42/SA1.

126 Note on Limerick Union, Rents of Labourers' Cottages, 6 May 1892: NAI, CSORP, 1892/4813.

127 *Munster News*, 3 Dec. 1887; 10 Dec. 1887.

128 Comment of A. Bourke in answer to query 4, ibid. See also Resolution of Macroom Guardians, 7 Sept. 1889: Cork Archives Institute, Macroom Board of Guardians Minutes, BG115/A4, 57.

129 Rents of Labourers' Cottages, 6 May 1892: NAI, CSORP, 1892/4813.

130 *Kerry Sentinel*, 6 June 1888.

131 *Express*, 18 Feb. 1888, cutting in Abuses of the Labourers Cottages Acts, Apr. 1888: NAI, CSORP, 1892/4813; Report by E. Bourke, Mar. 1888: ibid. See also *Cork Examiner*, 20 Feb. 1888.

132 Quoted in Cullen, *Cleansing Rural Dublin*, p. 48.

133 Fraser, *John Bull's Other Homes*, p. 292.

134 *Hansard 3*, cccii, 1821 (3 Mar. 1886).

135 *Report and Special Report from the Select Committee on Housing of the Working Classes Act Amendment Bill*, 230; evidence of John Ryan: *Royal Commission on Labour: The Agricultural Labourer: Ireland*, PP, 1893–94 [C.6894–xviii], xxxvii, 196.

136 Clark, *Social Origins of the Irish Land War*, p. 39.

137 *Cork Examiner*, 21 Sept. 1891.

138 Cullen, *Cleansing Rural Dublin*, p. 52.

139 Fitzpatrick, 'The Disappearance of the Irish Agricultural Labourer', 83.

140 K. Theodore Hoppen, *Elections, Politics and Society in Ireland 1832–1885* (Oxford, Clarendon Press, 1984), pp. 478–9.

6

Domestic politics: women and poor law administration

Having looked at the way in which nationalist ideology influenced the selection and conduct of poor law guardians, we turn now to the impact of gender ideology. Prevailing assumptions about gender roles both restricted the contribution of women to poor law administration, and provided motivation and justification for their involvement. By the end of the nineteenth century women had won the right to act as poor law guardians, an achievement hailed as an important milestone on the road to women's suffrage. The evolution of the campaign for women guardians is examined here together with public responses to it. The focus then shifts from the general to the particular. In 1898 a dispute arose between the Clogher Board of Guardians and the Local Government Board over the appointment of Ann Magill as a rate collector. In appointing Magill and refusing to accept a male collector imposed by the Local Government Board, the Clogher guardians posed as champions of women's rights. Closer investigation of the case, however, reveals more ambivalent attitudes both to women and to central authority on the part of the Clogher guardians. As in previous conflicts between boards of guardians and the Local Government Board, this dispute involved both local and national issues and was played out against the backdrop of national political campaigns. And, once again, the ensuing controversy raised important questions concerning the operation of the poor law system, and the bounds of local autonomy.

The employment of women within the poor law system

The poor law system catered predominantly for women,[1] but was administered and staffed predominantly by men. Until 1896, Irish poor law guardians were exclusively male, as were most poor law officials. Women were employed as workhouse matrons, schoolmistresses and nurses, but other posts were closed to them. There were no women relieving officers or rate collectors in the nineteenth century, although, as we shall see, the Clogher Board fought a long and ultimately unsuccessful campaign to appoint a woman rate collector in 1898–99. Official policy on the employment of women reflected prevailing social attitudes. Consequently, the opportunities available to women in either local or central government were severely limited. Marie Dickie was the first woman to join the ranks of the local government inspectorate when she was appointed as a temporary inspector with specific responsibility for boarded-out children in May 1902. Four years later her salary was still considerably lower than those of more recently appointed male colleagues.[2]

Appearing before the Royal Commission on the Civil Service in 1913, H.A. Robinson was asked about the relative capabilities of male and female inspectors. He acknowledged that in some respects, such as in 'the inspection of female wards of workhouses', women inspectors performed 'as well, and perhaps better, than men'. There were, however, other duties that were beyond them. The holding of inquiries, Robinson explained, was in Ireland, 'rather a troublesome business. You have a noisy turbulent people sometimes, and sharp solicitors, and it is not the sort of task that you would like to set a lady to.' He went on to question a woman's physical capacity for the work of a general inspector, considering the amount of travelling they were required to do. His experience of women working in the Local Government Board office, he observed, was that they were 'knocked up much more easily than men; there are more casual absences, and more complaints of headache, and so forth. Also when faced with very great pressure of work, they are inclined to lose their heads and not to get on so quickly'.[3] With such attitudes permeating central and local government, it is hardly surprising that where women did make advances in poor law administration in the later part of the nineteenth century, they did so primarily by subverting rather than challenging gender ideology.

Informal involvement

Middle-class women had long been involved in poor law administration on an informal basis. Activities such as arranging Christmas treats and organising summer outings for workhouse children formed part of the charitable work performed by middle-class women of all religious denominations. As Maria Luddy has noted, religious teaching 'gave middle-class women the excuse to organise voluntarily, to enter the public domain and engage in work which was considered socially useful'.[4] Women philanthropists focused their attention primarily on poor women and children, groups for whom they were assumed to have a natural and innate concern. Many middle-class women became involved in voluntary work linked to the workhouse through male relatives. The wife of Morgan John O'Connell, for example, was to recall in 1880 that she had first become interested in the poor, 'because my husband was a workhouse chairman in a district where we had a shooting lodge which we visited occasionally, and on those sporadic visits he worked hard at the board, and took an interest in the effort to do his duty'. O'Connell described herself as 'a country lady, widow and daughter of energetic ex-officio guardians ... who, as land-owner, employer of labour, and signer of red tickets [for medical relief], has an intimate knowledge of her poor neighbours'. In this capacity, she read a paper to the Statistical and Social Inquiry Society of Ireland on the treatment of women and children under the poor laws. Those who concerned themselves with the poor law, she pointed out, rarely considered 'the simple, domestic aspects of the question'. It was on these matters and on these matters only, that she felt qualified to comment.[5]

O'Connell sought to draw the attention of poor law guardians and others to the needs of women and children and thus to exercise an indirect influence over poor law administration. She expressed no desire to exert a more direct influence or to assume any responsibility for that administration. There were others, however, who believed that women needed to be more directly involved. Addressing the Social Science Congress in 1881, Isabella Tod observed that the

> subjects with which the guardians of the poor have to deal are almost all what are acknowledged to be 'women's subjects' some of them emphatically so. The care of the poor generally – and especially of women – the care of children ... the prevention no less than the cure of sickness – these are the principal objects for which boards of guardians exist, and they are all women's duties on a large scale no less than a small.

It was not enough for women to be involved informally, they must be able to exercise 'authoritative supervision ...Only those ladies who know they have the support of the ratepayers who elected them will venture to criticise efficiently, to insist on troublesome work being done, to go where officials may not want them, and where often it would be quite unsuitable for men to go, and to urge new plans which they see to be wanted.' Tod maintained that she felt able to 'speak boldly on this question, because I know that I carry with me the entire sympathy of many Chairmen and Members of Boards'. This claim reflected her Ulster location.[6] Guardians in other provinces where traditions of lay female philanthropy were less strong were far less sympathetic.

In many unions, guardians were reluctant to allow women any role in union affairs, however limited. Even the establishment of visiting committees to supervise the treatment of women and children within the workhouse proved problematic.[7] Gaining access to the workhouse required the support of local guardians and this often proved difficult to obtain. Questioned about the establishment of ladies visiting committees in 1861, the Catholic philanthropist Ellen Woodlock observed that she had heard that guardians had 'expressed themselves rather against it ... And I need not say that ladies will be always very chary of intruding into any establishment where they think they will not be perfectly welcome.'[8] Reluctance to grant women access to workhouses was compounded by religious feeling and the fear of proselytism. The Cork guardians only granted permission for a ladies visiting committee on the condition that it contained an equal number of Catholic and Protestant women.[9] Members of the Workhouse Visiting Society established in the South Dublin Union in 1861 were confined to visiting the relatively small number of Protestant inmates since all 24 members of the Society were Protestants.[10]

The poor law authorities neither encouraged nor discouraged the involvement of women in workhouse management, declaring that this was a matter for boards of guardians.[11] Intervention was only thought necessary when the authority of poor law officials appeared under threat. Chief Commissioner Alfred Power explained in 1861 that nuns had been refused permission to visit children in the Cork workhouse because they were coming between the children and the workhouse matron and teachers who 'were responsible for the proper training of those children'.[12] Similar concerns had prompted the opposition of the poor law commissioners to the introduction of nuns to workhouse hospitals.

The employment of nuns as nurses

Until the end of the nineteenth century, most boards of guardians employed workhouse inmates as infirmary nurses. These women were not paid but received extra rations. Concerns about poor standards of hygiene and of patient care in the Limerick workhouse infirmary in 1860 had led the Board of Guardians to investigate the possibility of handing the management of the infirmary over to the Sisters of Mercy. The poor law commissioners were unhappy about this idea, questioning the advisability of appointing untrained women religious as workhouse staff. Their main concern was the impact that the introduction of nuns would have on staff relationships within the workhouse. Was it expedient, they inquired of the Limerick guardians, 'that ladies whose social position may be regarded as placing them above the ordinary motives which render responsibility practical, should be selected for the performance of the official duties of nurses and assistants to the Master and Matron of a workhouse?'[13] The commissioners were clearly concerned that nuns would find it difficult to acknowledge the authority of the lay officials responsible for the day-to-day operation of the workhouse. Despite continuing objections from the commissioners, the Limerick guardians proceeded to appoint three Mercy nuns as nurses the following year.

The number of boards of guardians opting to follow Limerick's example increased significantly during the 1880s and 1890s. By 1903, nuns staffed 84 of the 159 workhouse infirmaries. This increase, Luddy suggests, 'had much to do with the take-over of boards of guardians by Catholic nationalists in decades after 1870'.[14] Nationalist-controlled boards were attracted by the financial as well as the religious benefits of employing nuns. Nuns were willing to work for low salaries and often provided more staff than they were contracted to provide. In the early 1870s, for example, there were between eight and ten Sisters of Mercy nursing in the Limerick workhouse hospital, only three of whom were paid.[15]

As the providers of care in a range of welfare institutions, female religious orders were seen as ideally equipped to provide medical care within the workhouse since they could minister to the spiritual as well as the physical needs of workhouse inmates. The results were hailed as fully justifying the arrangement. The English philanthropist, Fanny Taylor, described her impression of Limerick infirmary in the late 1860s in the following terms: 'floors clean and fresh, beds with spotless linen and white coverings; the medicines, books and little comforts the patients require close at their side; the Sisters of Mercy with pleasant faces and kind words moving about in lieu of the pauper nurses; an indescribable air of comfort and repose in the whole place'.[16] Twenty years later, the American, William Hurlbert, attributed the well-ordered state of Portumna workhouse to 'the influence of the Sisters who have charge of the hospital, but whose spirit shows itself not only in the flower-garden which they have called into being, but in many details of the administration beyond their special control'.[17] Despite the fears of the poor law authorities, nuns usually avoided coming into conflict with other workhouse staff, or with poor law officials. This was probably less because of any spirit of co-operation and more because nuns were reluctant to enter a workhouse unless they had complete control over the staff of the infirmary. Relations between male poor law officials, such as

medical officers and poor law inspectors, and the nuns nomi-
nally under their charge were often prickly, but both sides were
generally careful to avoid public disagreements.[18]

The poor law authorities were gradually reconciled to the
presence of nuns within workhouse infirmaries, but they
remained anxious to promote the appointment of trained staff.
In 1898 the Local Government Board adopted a recommendation of the Irish Workhouse Association that one trained nurse
should be appointed in every union, their salary to be paid
jointly by the board of guardians and the government.[19]
Responding to an inquiry from the Catholic hierarchy regarding
the implications of this development for hospitals under the
charge of nuns, H.A. Robinson reassured the Bishop of Limerick
that the intention was not to supersede nuns but to give them
'skilled instead of unskilled assistance'. The Local Government
Board, he observed, was 'fully sensible to the excellent work of
reform which has been effected by the nuns in the workhouses
which have been placed under their charge. The cleanliness,
good order and comfort, and the improved moral tone which
seems invariably to follow upon the introduction of nuns is very
striking' Furthermore, their presence had been found to go 'a
long way towards removing the objections that the sick poor
have to entering these institutions'.[20] But if nuns were now
acknowledged to be preferable to pauper nurses, their lack of
medical training still precluded them from holding certain positions. Robinson refused to sanction the appointment of a Mercy
nun as matron of Galway hospital in 1899. As he explained to
Gerald Balfour, 'a nun makes an excellent matron in a general
workhouse where there are children and ablebodied women
and feeble old people to look after as well as the sick', but this
was not the case in a hospital such as Galway, 'where everything
is purely a medical question and where the matron's chief duty
is to see that the nurses properly carry out the Doctors' orders'.
Here it was necessary to have 'a qualified person' in charge.[21]

Robinson was suspicious of the motivation of religious orders
in undertaking workhouse nursing, seeing this as rooted less in
their sense of religious mission than in their desire to maintain
their power and influence within the Catholic community. Their
supporters emphasised the personal sacrifices made by nuns in
undertaking workhouse nursing duties. Thus Fanny Taylor

noted how the Sisters of Mercy assigned to the Galway workhouse lived in a set of small rooms adjoining the sick wards. 'It
would be far better', she observed, 'if they had large airy rooms
at a greater distance from the sick; but it is of no use to talk to
the Sisters of Mercy about their own comfort and conven-
ience'.[22] Robinson, on the other hand, portrayed the Mercy nuns
as more concerned with their own welfare than with that of
workhouse inmates. Apprising Balfour of the actions of the
Mercy nuns appointed to Glenties workhouse in 1898, he
described how, on coming to a workhouse, nuns generally gave
an

> indication of the privations they endure in the cause of humanity
> by taking possession of the best of everything in the way of
> accommodation and making the Guardians spend any amount of
> money in putting up oratory, refractory, cells, etc. I do not care
> how comfortable they are made – the more so the better – but
> these Glenties ladies have actually taken possession of the poor
> little children's yard; and turned the girls in among the adult
> women. They won't give up the yard and want to turn it into a
> private garden for themselves. So classification may go to the
> dogs, and little innocent children may spend their childhood
> among foul-mouthed women because the 'Sisters of Mercy' want
> a garden with a southern aspect.

As Robinson was all too uncomfortably aware, there could
hardly be a more graphic demonstration of the standing enjoyed
by nuns within the workhouse, not only in relation to the
inmates but also to the board of guardians. Anxious to remind
the nuns that they were answerable to a higher authority, he
sent the local inspector to speak to them 'privately and explain
that this can't be allowed, and to point out to them what a
profound feeling it would create against them in England, if
they showed so little concern for the children placed under their
care'.[23]

By the later part of the nineteenth century, nuns provided the
most significant female presence within a majority of Irish
workhouses. As far as many guardians were concerned, if
women were to be involved in workhouse management, this
was the arrangement that offered the most advantages for the
least disruption. Nuns were hardworking, economical and
unobtrusive. And while they undoubtedly influenced the char-

acter and ethos of workhouse administration in unions where they were employed, nuns had no direct input into union affairs. Those campaigning for women to be accepted as active partners in union management were thus not only challenging convention, they were also competing against what many believed to be an ideal form of womanhood and of gender relations.

The campaign for women poor law guardians

The campaign for women poor law guardians was established and conducted as an adjunct to the women's suffrage movement. Leading members of the campaign, such as Isabella Tod and Anna Haslam, were active suffragists who saw the poor law as one of the many aspects of public life that would be improved by women's involvement. Responses to the campaign reflected this broader political context. Both supporters and opponents tended to regard the issue of women guardians as inextricably linked to the achievement of the parliamentary franchise. Unlike other local franchises, the poor law franchise already included women. But while women ratepayers were entitled to vote in poor law elections, they were explicitly excluded from standing for election.[24] The enfranchisement of women under the 1838 poor law act appears to have caused little comment or concern. This may have been partly because the voting system did not require women to venture out to exercise their vote since voting papers were delivered to and collected from the ratepayer's home. Indeed, one of the arguments put forward against the introduction of voting by ballot was that this would discourage women from participating. Women, one official warned in 1878, 'would not submit to what they would have to submit to in the case of ballot'.[25]

It was widely assumed that women took little interest in poor law elections. Writing in 1898, Anna Haslam attributed this to the fact that prior to 1896, elections were 'so commonly carried out upon exclusively party lines, and with so little regard to the well being of our destitute poor'.[26] While it was not unusual for male relatives to fill in the voting papers of women ratepayers, it is clear that some women took a keen interest in poor law elections. Appearing before the 1878 select committee, Thomas Mayne, a Dublin woollen merchant, recounted how 'a respectable old lady of strong Conservative notions', had filled in and returned 400 voting papers that had been delivered to her house by mistake. (The votes were declared invalid.) Furthermore, around 250 members of the Sisters of Charity were said to have applied to be registered as voters in both the North and South Dublin unions claiming that the congregation owned property in various electoral divisions that was held in common by its members.[27] This application reflects the anxiety within the Catholic Church regarding the management of the Dublin unions and the desire to secure the election of Catholic guardians. It also calls into question the conventional image of female religious congregations as having no involvement or interest in politics.

A campaign to allow women to stand in poor law elections was underway from the early 1880s. The South Dublin Union, for example, passed a resolution in favour of women guardians in June 1882.[28] But it was not until the 1890s, when developments in England encouraged Irish campaigners to press the claims of Irish women more vigorously, that the campaign really gathered momentum. The democratisation of poor law elections in England in 1894, and the abolition of plural voting, saw the number of women guardians rise from 50 in 1887 to over 800 in 1895.[29] MPs supportive of women guardians in Ireland attempted to amend the Irish poor law in 1892 and 1894, before finally succeeding in 1896.

The advocates of women guardians based their case on traditional conceptions of gender difference. Women, it was argued, would bring particular qualities to poor law administration and would take a particular interest in those aspects of it, such as hygiene and diet that men were ill-equipped to address. They would thus complement not replace male guardians. As Emily Dickson explained to an audience of fellow medics in 1895, 'I believe in the co-operation of men and women here as elsewhere; what I wish to urge is the very great need for one or two women on each Board to assist and give advice in matters concerning women and children and domestic affairs.'[30] MPs and peers who supported the 1896 bill did so on this basis. Dr Kenny, MP for Dublin College Green, explained that as a visiting surgeon to a large poor law union, he 'knew well the amount of good that women guardians would be able to do. The wants of women in unions must be better understood by members of their own sex than by men'.[31] Kenny was unusual amongst Irish nationalist MPs in giving the bill his full support. Most of his colleagues were either lukewarm towards it or openly hostile. Tim Harrington objected to the measure on the grounds that 'no general desire had been expressed in Ireland for such a change', adding that 'he considered the presence of ladies on boards of guardians instead of tending to facilitate, would rather have the effect of embarrassing the proceedings of those bodies'. If there was to be reform of the poor law franchise in Ireland it should be a general one such as had taken place in England. Even Tim Healy, who claimed to be a supporter of women poor law guardians, argued that it would be better to introduce a general measure of reform.[32]

Whatever their personal views on the issue, Irish nationalists regarded the women's suffrage movement as at best a diversion from the fight for home rule, and at worst a threat to it. They were also suspicious of a movement that included so many staunch unionists. William Johnston, the sponsor of the 1896 bill, was not merely a unionist but a leading member of the Orange Order. As Kenny confessed, it was not often he found himself in agreement with Johnston and in disagreement with Harrington.[33] By stating that the main aim of the bill was to extend the same privileges to women in Ireland that were enjoyed by their sisters in England and Wales, Johnston did little to win over Irish nationalists. Harrington was quick to reject the idea that what was appropriate for England was appropriate for Ireland.[34]

Women seek election

The Poor Law Guardians (Ireland) (Women) Bill became law on 31 March 1896.[35] This was too late to allow women to stand in the poor law elections of that year. A by-election in Lisnaskea Union in County Fermanagh in September led to the unopposed election of the first woman guardian in Ireland, Miss E. Martin, the daughter of the local Presbyterian minister. Suffrage

campaigners set to work to publicise the act and to encourage
women to stand for election. The Dublin Women's Suffrage and
Local Government Association (DWSLGA) distributed
hundreds of copies of a leaflet entitled 'Suggestions for
Intending Lady Guardians', which explained the legal qualification for candidates and the procedure for securing a nomination.
Prospective candidates were encouraged to take advantage of
by-elections as they would 'not then be entering into competition with men who have already had some experience as
Guardians', and they would thus stand a good chance of being
returned unopposed. Aware of the politicised nature of Irish
poor law elections, suffragists endeavoured to involve women
of all political persuasions in the campaign to get women
elected. The DWSLGA leaflet urged the formation of committees
'consisting of influential men and women of all shades of political opinion, and of all religious denominations – to promote the
election of two or more capable, judicious women ... in all the
more important Unions in Ireland'.[36]

The campaign did succeed in bridging political and religious
divisions. Reports of a public meeting held in Tralee in July
1896, noted that: 'the principal speakers were Miss Rowan of the
Primrose League, and Mrs E. Harrington, wife of the Nationalist
ex-M.P.; in fact, men and women of all political and religious
parties met on common ground, and unanimously agreed on the
value of women taking their share in the work of the Poor
Law'.[37]

Despite this, the poor law elections held in 1897 and 1898
produced only moderate successes for women candidates, 13
women being returned in 11 unions in 1897, and 22 women in 18
unions in 1898.[38] Public reaction to the elections highlighted the
ambivalence many people felt about women taking any kind of
public role. *United Ireland* gave the election of a few women
guardians in 1897 a cautious welcome, observing that women
'who are really true to the best characteristics of their sex should
be able to bring into the proceedings of these bodies much of
that feeling of love and pity at the sufferings of the poor that
nowadays does not excite the least throb or pulse of sympathy
in the hearts of nine guardians out of ten'.

At the same time, the paper hoped that the women had not
put themselves forward out of a 'desire for popularity'. A few

days later an incident at the Monaghan Board of Guardians when Margaret M'Manus had to be removed from the board-room by force after her election was declared invalid, strengthened the paper's 'conviction that women anxious to mind their own domestic affairs are unwise in trying to shove themselves too prominently into public positions'.[39]

It took the establishment of local democracy before English women were elected as poor law guardians in any significant numbers.[40] Local government reform provided an equally important catalyst in Ireland even if the numbers subsequently elected were more modest. The Irish Local Government Act of 1898 created a two-tier system of county and district councils elected triennially on a parliamentary franchise with the inclusion of women and peers. Plural voting was abolished, as were ex-officio guardians. In rural areas, district councillors also acted as poor law guardians. In urban areas, separate boards of guardians were retained, elected on the same franchise as councillors. The act enfranchised women householders, leaseholders, lodgers and ratepayers. Vigorous lobbying by suffrage societies had secured two important amendments to the act, a residential qualification for candidates for rural district councils and two-member constituencies for district councils. The first meant that women who were not qualified to vote in their own right could stand for election provided that they had resided in the district for at least twelve months. The second increased the chance of women being elected since 'according to the views of women guardians in Ireland, the electors of a constituency would desire to elect a man to represent them in religion and politics, and only after that would they elect a woman to see to the sick poor'.[41]

Haslam predicted that the first elections under the Local Government Act in 1899 would 'excite an unexampled interest amongst our women in almost every district; and the circumstance that the electors will have the option of voting for whatever candidates of their own sex may present themselves will intensify the excitement'.[42] Others took a different view. Reporting on the election for the Nenagh urban district council, the *Nenagh Guardian* commented on the number of female voters. Attributing their 'somewhat bashful and diffident manner' to the fact that 'they were out of their element in the turmoil and excitement of the contested election', the *Guardian* concluded that 'it is outside the region of a woman's sphere to exercise the franchise. And we are sure many of the dear old souls that recorded their votes would much prefer to remain at home by the firesides and only came out in response to friendly pressure.'[43]

Women candidates and their supporters appealed to the social conscience of voters. Pointing out that it was 'generally admitted' that women possessed special qualities that recommended them for discharging the duties of ministering to the destitute and infirm, one Tyrone voter argued that it was, therefore, the duty of everyone interested in social progress to 'use their best endeavour to obtain for the ladies recognition of the privileges they can now exercise with so much advantage to all concerned'.[44] Women's 'special mission to look after homes and children and food', could, it was suggested, usefully be extended to include the 'home sphere' of the workhouse. Sarah Persse, who stood in Galway's West Ward in 1899, undertook to do 'her utmost to watch over the interests and well-being of the suffering and the needy'. Letters that appeared in the local press supporting Persse and another candidate, Esther Jesson, stressed the women's records as philanthropists.[45]

Few women candidates stood on a party political platform. An exception was the trade unionist, Mary Galway, who stood in Belfast in 1899 as the official candidate of the Belfast United Trades and Labour Council.[46] With most women presenting themselves as non-political, the ability of successful candidates to win support across party and denominational lines was a source of particular satisfaction to their advocates. Assessing the impact of the Local Government Act, Mrs Maurice Dockrell noted that whilst the act had generally resulted in power passing from 'the Unionists to the Nationalists, from Protestants to Catholics, from the educated, cultured, leisured classes to the traders, small farmers, and, in many cases, even to the labourers ... the women who have been elected nearly all belong to the highly-educated class, and some of them are Unionists and Protestants'.[47] One of Isabella Tod's arguments in favour of women guardians had been that this would lead to the election of a better class of guardian. Permitting the election of 'ladies as well as gentlemen', she had maintained, would 'greatly increase

the range of satisfactory choice'.[48] Tod would have welcomed
the fact that women poor law guardians in Ulster were
frequently 'of a higher social status than their male counter-
parts'.[49]

In other provinces, however, the social status, and more
particularly the religion, of women candidates could prove an
electoral liability. The *Galway Pilot*, for example, objected to the
candidature of 'two Protestant ladies', in a city whose poor were
'almost 99 per cent Catholic'. Since the women's wards of the
workhouse were in the charge of nuns, the *Pilot* argued, there
was no need for 'lady guardians'. According to a letter in the
Galway Observer this was also the reason why no Catholic
women had come forward as candidates.[50] One of the results of
the advancement of female religious in Ireland was 'to remove,
almost totally, the lay Catholic woman from engaging in public
philanthropy'.[51] Lacking a background in philanthropy,
Catholic women may have felt less qualified and possibly less
motivated to act as poor law guardians. Catholic women did
stand for election in 1899, but judging from the names of
successful women candidates those elected would appear to
have been in the minority, not, as Dockrell implied, the majority.[52]

The election results in 1899 confirmed Haslam's optimistic
predictions regarding the interest that women candidates would
arouse. A total of 85 women were elected in 33 unions. The
DWSLGA hailed the results 'as a manifestation of the growing
interest which our women are taking in public affairs', and thus
as 'one of the most encouraging incidents of our time'. In many
unions where there were already women guardians, the
DWSLGA noted happily, 'so highly have their services been
appreciated by the Rate-payers that the number of women
elected has been largely increased'. In Dublin the number of
women guardians had increased from two to thirteen, in Belfast
from two to five.[53] The DWSLGA was determined to stress the
positive outcome of the elections. The Women's Local
Government Society, on the other hand, lamented the loss of
'several ladies who have been doing most excellent work in their
respective Unions during the past year – more particularly in
Belfast and Co. Dublin', attributing this to the fact that the elections had been 'run very largely upon Party lines'.[54] The losses

included Sarah Thompson and Kate Megahy in Belfast, and Mrs Lawrenson and Miss J.K. Burton in County Dublin. Lawrenson and Burton failed to secure re-election despite having being publicly thanked for their contribution to the management of Rathdown Union by the chair of the board of guardians the previous year.[55]

Unions in Leinster elected the highest number of women guardians with a total of 40, followed by those in Ulster that returned 30 women. Numbers dropped considerably in Munster and Connaught. Ten women were elected in Munster and five in Connaught.[56] This regional disparity largely reflected the rate of political activism among women. This was strongest in urban areas where poverty and related social problems such as illegitimacy, were more in evidence. Some, though by no means all, voters appear to have shared the view of the *Galway Pilot* that women guardians were unnecessary in unions where nuns were employed in the workhouse. Out of the eight unions that had the longest history of employing nuns, five (Ballinsaloe, Cork, Galway, Kilmacthomas and Tullamore) elected no women guardians in 1899. The other three unions (Wexford, Limerick and Killarney) elected two women each, the majority of whom appear to have been Protestant. In Ulster, where few boards of guardians employed nuns, there were disproportionately high numbers of women guardians. The success of women candidates appears to have depended on local traditions of female philanthropy, the willingness of local women to put themselves forward, and the readiness of voters to support non-party, female candidates.

Diane Urquhart has noted that the election of women to poor law boards in Ulster was followed by 'an immediate division of poor law work amongst guardians on gender lines'. Women were engaged in matters relating to 'the diet and clothing of [workhouse inmates], the appointment of female staff, illegitimacy, orphans, education and workhouse visiting'. She further observes that a majority of women guardians 'identified the office as an end in itself and not as an apprenticeship to a wider political career'.[57] Even those guardians who were suffragists did not use their position to promote women's suffrage. But it is difficult to see how women guardians could have promoted suffrage given that most Ulster boards refused to permit discussion of any matter extraneous to the poor law. Moreover, there is little evidence that Irish suffragists envisaged such a role for women guardians. They were more concerned with the indirect influence they could exert and the example they provided. The elections of 1899 were hailed by DWSLGA as furnishing 'a conclusive answer to those who affirm that Irish women are too exclusively wrapped up in their family concerns to take their rightful share in the duties of local government; and it also conclusively proves that they will be well qualified worthily to perform their duties as intelligent electors when the Parliamentary vote has been conferred upon them'.[58]

Irish local government reform had been presented to parliament as the natural consequence of reform in Britain, and the Irish act followed the English model as closely as was deemed practicable.[59] Irish landowners bitterly opposed the act, arguing that councils would be dominated by Irish nationalists and would be characterised by the extravagance, jobbery and maladministration that were alleged to characterise poor law administration. The first prediction proved accurate. The local elections of 1899 saw nationalists increase their total representation on poor law boards from around 50 per cent to 78 per cent, while that of unionists dropped from 50 per cent to 18 per cent.[60] It was against this background that the Clogher Board of Guardians decided to make a stand over the appointment of Ann Magill as rate-collector for the Aughnacloy district.

The Clogher Board of Guardians and Miss Magill

In May 1898, Ann Eliza Magill applied to the Clogher Board of Guardians to be allowed to complete the rate collection of her late father, Thomas Magill, explaining that she had 'practically performed all the duties in connection with the collection' for the previous five years.[61] On seeking the sanction of the Local Government Board to appoint Miss Magill, the guardians were informed that being a woman Miss Magill was not eligible for the post. Adverts were duly issued for the appointment of a new rate collector and on 11 June the board proceeded to consider the applications received. There were three candidates: Ann Magill, Peter Duffy, a former sergeant in the Royal Irish

Constabulary, and John Roberts, a publican. Having considered the candidates, the guardians elected Magill. The Local Government Board refused to sanction the appointment and instructed the board to hold another election. When the guardians showed no signs of making another appointment, the Local Government Board issued a sealed order requiring them to re-advertise the post and to appoint a fit and proper person as poor rate collector for the district.[62]

The guardians' immediate response to the sealed order was to ask their MP, T.W. Russell, to use his influence to obtain the consent of the Local Government Board to Miss Magill's appointment.[63] There was good reason to believe that Russell's intervention might be effective since he had had joined the government as parliamentary secretary to the English Local Government Board in 1896. The guardians also asked a number of Ulster MPs to raise the matter in the Commons. On 16 July the Clogher guardians once again elected Miss Magill as rate collector and called on the government to amend the local government bill in order to allow women to act as rate collectors. Having removed Miss Magill by sealed order on 22 July, the Local Government Board appointed Robert Cuthbertson as rate collector for the Aughnacloy district on 5 August. The guardians refused to sign the warrants authorising Cuthbertson to collect the rates. After issuing a number of warnings, the Local Government Board finally dissolved the board of guardians on 25 October and appointed Major G.M. Eccles and Edward Saunderson vice-guardians.[64] The Clogher Board of Guardians was restored following fresh elections in January 1899. The new board immediately attempted to continue the campaign. They maintained their belligerent stance until April 1899, when elections were held under the new local government act. On 6 May, the Clogher Rural District Council, whose members also served as poor law guardians, distanced itself from the actions of the previous board and declared its full confidence in Cuthbertson. Under general orders issued by the Local Government Board in April and July 1899, women were declared ineligible to be appointed as poor rate collectors in either rural or urban districts.

The case of Miss Magill attracted considerable media attention in England and Ireland. Public discussion focused on two issues, the rights of women in local government and the freedom of local authorities. The Clogher guardians and their supporters were careful to present themselves as champions of women's rights and opponents of the autocratic power of the Local Government Board. A resolution passed by the guardians on 10 September 1898 condemned the Local Government Board's threat to dissolve the Clogher Board as representing 'an injustice both to the said Ann Eliza Magill and to the Guardians of the Clogher Union and other women who might be found to be fit and proper person to fill such offices in other places'.[65] It is questionable, however, how far the guardians' commitment to women's rights really went.

Women's organisations in England and Ireland worked together to publicise the injustice done to Miss Magill and to lobby MPs for a change in the law. To this end they adopted well-established methods of campaigning, focusing their efforts on the press and on parliament. During the summer of 1898, for example, the Women's Local Government Society (WLGS) 'sent out a statement of the case to the English press; supplied information as to women holding similar posts in England; and called the attention of private correspondents, both English and Irish, to the case; and interviewed many Members of Parliament'.[66] The Magill case was used to draw attention to anomalies in poor law administration in Ireland, and to argue for the right of women to employment. Women, it was pointed out, could act as rate collectors in England and had been doing so without incident. Since Miss Magill had proved her ability to perform the duties of the post, there was no reason not to appoint her to the position.[67] The fact that a woman had recently been appointed as a relieving officer in England, despite the initial objection of the Local Government Board, was held to further undermine the opposition of the Irish Board to Miss Magill. The Oswestry Board of Guardians had appointed Rebecca Price a relieving officer on the death of her husband, having acted as a temporary relieving officer during the last six months of her husband's life. The Local Government Board had objected to the appointment but had subsequently backed down, merely requiring the guardians to review Mrs Price's appointment after twelve months.[68] An article in the *Methodist Times* in August 1898 drew two important lessons from the

Oswestry and Clogher cases. First, that it was 'of the utmost importance to life and liberty that all powers vested in local boards throughout the country should be exercised without fear of undue influence or domination from the central board ... in London'. This was the 'best safeguard against the encroachments of bureaucracy and official tyranny'. And secondly, that the

> importance of such cases to the progress of woman cannot be over-estimated. Everything which tends to the economic independence of woman tends to the elevation of womanhood. Every new field opened to woman's labour gives a greater range of choice in the pursuit of a livelihood, and has the effect of making woman more independent of marriage as a mere provision for the future.

Women, the author suggested, owed a debt of gratitude to the men of Oswestry and Clogher who, 'in espousing the cause of respectable and efficient women in their own localities have advanced the cause of women everywhere'.[69]

The treatment of Miss Magill reinforced the conviction of suffrage campaigners that women would only obtain justice when they had the vote. Writing in the *Westminster Review*, the secretary of the Women's Emancipation Union, Elizabeth Elmy, argued that 'the tendency of permanent officialism is naturally and inevitably towards despotism and towards an overweening estimation of sex privilege'. Such injustice, she concluded, would continue 'until women possess that safeguard of their liberties and that security for human justice which their political enfranchisement can alone insure to them'.[70] In a further article the following February, Elmy claimed that the actions of the Local Government Board had 'been based throughout on mere sex bias ... They have exhibited themselves to the world as antiquated and reactionary opponents of justice to women and pitifully small and mean in their tyranny'. The Clogher guardians on the other hand 'fully deserved the hearty thanks of every woman in the three kingdoms, of every one who desires justice between the sexes, and of every believer in the advantages of good local administration'.[71]

Women's organisations placed considerable stress on the questionable legality of the Irish government's position in attempting to exclude first Magill and then all women from positions as rate collectors. The WLGS made much of the fact that the government's claim that the police could not be called on to execute decrees for the collection of poor rates by process of distress, was based on a misunderstanding of the law.[72] Raising the case in the Commons, William Johnston, who was a member of the Society's executive committee, declared that 'the decision of the Local Government Board was not founded on law', and as a consequence an injustice had been done, 'not only to Miss Magill individually, but to the whole of that large class who would be excluded from public appointment if this decision were to pass unchallenged'.[73] Having obtained counsel's opinion that the General Order of April 1899 declaring women ineligible for the post of rate collector should have been approved by parliament, the WLGS concluded triumphantly that the order 'issued by the Chief-Secretary for Ireland was not in pursuance of any existing law, but entirely autocratic'.[74]

Magill's supporters on the Clogher board of guardians made frequent reference to the wider debate about women's rights. Significantly, however, while guardians referred to the advances made by women in order to justify their position, few declared themselves in favour of those advances. Proposing the appointment of Miss Magill on 11 June 1898, the vice-chair of the board, William Richey, commented that 'as ladies were now eligible for a great many offices hitherto denied them, they might as well take the lead in Clogher as in any other union, and appoint Miss Magill'. Speaking at the same meeting, Colonel Knox Browne declared that while he would vote for Miss Magill, 'he was one of those that believed that women should confine themselves to their own sphere of duties, and he was not an admirer of the new woman, and all that sort of thing'.[75] Even Hugh de Fellenberg Montgomery, a local landlord and Magill's leading champion, disassociated himself from the women's rights campaigners who were taking up the case. Citing Elmy's first article in the *Westminster Review*, Montgomery remarked, that 'the point of view of this article is not mine, but if this Board, consisting of men only, cannot give fair play to Miss Magill, and obtain fair play for her, the argument in this article will be difficult to answer'.[76]

The majority of Irish guardians appear to have regarded the affair with amusement rather than outrage. But many clearly felt threatened by the advances made by women. One member of the Clogher Board who opposed Magill's appointment declared that he was 'hanged if I give my breeches to any woman'.[77] During a discussion of the case at the Carrick-on-Suir Board of Guardians in September 1898, Mr Terry commended the actions of the Clogher guardians and expressed the hope that they would have 'the pluck to go out of office with the distinction on their back that they went out of office in defence of women's rights. (Laughter.) This sort of thing might be good enough a hundred years ago; but times have changed'. It was, he suggested, 'the height of nonsense to say that the Local Government Board will sanction women to hold the office of Poor Law Guardian and not to sanction a woman as a rate-collector. The one orders a certain rate to be paid and why shouldn't the other collect it? There is no difference; they are all women, and if they are to have the control of Irish affairs what is the use of our objecting? We may as well grin and bear it. (Renewed laughter.)' The resolution was carried.[78]

If women's organisations saw the Magill case as demonstrating the continuing injustice done to women and the need for women's suffrage, unionists saw it as demonstrating the hypocrisy of the government's Irish policy. At meeting of the Clogher guardians on 16 July 1898, Montgomery rejected the Local Government Board's assertion that there was no analogy between the appointment of a woman rate collector in England and in Ireland: 'Let them make the analogy. (Hear. hear.) There is a Local Government Bill about to be completed, which many in Ireland think was not at all required; but if we are to have equalisation with the laws on England, then why doesn't the Government equalise this matter of the appointment of ladies to the position to which we again propose to elect Miss Magill. (Hear. hear.)'[79] The Dublin *Evening Telegraph* took up this argument in November 1898. Members of the Irish government had answered objections to the Local Government Act by saying that the aim of the legislation was to assimilate local government in Ireland to that in force in England, thus disregarding 'the peculiarities of our local conditions'. Yet in the Clogher affair 'the Board of Guardians has only been seeking to do what is allowed to be done in England, and the central authority bases its objections to its so doing on the ground of the dissimilarity of the poor-law administration in the two countries'.[80]

Montgomery's primary objective was to embarrass the government. The Magill case provided an ideal means to do this since it combined the issue of women's rights with that of the assimilation of Ireland within the United Kingdom. On both these issues the government could be shown to be have abandoned core Conservative principles. Tory ministers had been making overtures to women's suffrage campaigners, and they were responsible for a local government bill that they knew would result in a massive increase in nationalist representation on local bodies. The potential for embarrassment did not lie with the government alone, however. The Clogher guardians were on potentially shaky ground in adopting a position of open defiance to the Local Government Board since this was a stance more generally adopted by nationalist boards of guardians, and consequently condemned by unionists. The editor and owner of the *Impartial Reporter*, W.C. Trimble, one of the guardians' chief supporters in the press, recognised this from the beginning of the dispute. In July 1898 he confessed in an editorial that there were 'very few cases indeed where we would advocate resistance to the Local Government Board'. At beginning of August he found it necessary to deny that the guardians were adopting the policy of the Land League. This was a 'misconception ... The Land League policy violated the laws of both God and man ... In the case of Miss Magill, it is the Local Government Board who have taken upon themselves to set aside our relations to our neighbour and the law of the land.' Trimble expressed outrage that having consistently ignored the depredations of nationalist boards in the south and west, the Local Government Board had determined to 'pounce on one of the best managed Boards in Ireland – and a Unionist Board, as politics go. Fancy the Unionist Chief Secretary overlooking all the corruption of Nationalist Boards in the South and West and reserving his crushing powers for the well managed Unionist Union for adherence to the law. The situation is too strikingly grotesque!!'[81]

Such comments did little to encourage nationalists to support the Clogher guardians. Addressing a meeting of the Irish National Federation on 9 November 1898, John Dillon, was critical of the Local Government Board's action in dissolving the Clogher Board. In England, he observed, the Local Government

Board carried on its work 'under the chastening influence of the fear of public opinion'. The only opinion the Irish Local Government Board took regard of was 'the opinion of the Castle'. But he was scathing about the calls that had been made in the pages of the Tory press for nationalist MPs to make common cause with unionists in the affair, pointing out that those 'who are so deeply interested in the fate of Clogher Board seem to forget the fact that the same treatment has again and again been dealt out to Nationalist boards without exciting the slightest sympathy in these august breasts'.[82] Nationalist newspapers adopted a similar approach, concentrating their attacks on the autocratic powers of the Local Government Board.[83]

Opposition to the appointment of Miss Magill within the Local Government Board was rooted in fear of the consequences. Such an appointment threatened to open the floodgates to a tidal wave of applications from women that would undermine the very foundations of Irish local government. Women could not be allowed to act as rate-collectors because they could not be expected to distrain for unpaid rates. As Robinson explained to Balfour, collectors in western districts frequently found that 'their only chance of recovery from the small occupiers, when there is a combination against payment, is to go out before sunrise with their bailiffs and lie under the walls of the house and wait to make a seizure before the cattle are driven off the mountains or commons'.[84] This was not something that a woman could be expected to do. Local government inspector R. Kelly put this point to the Clogher guardians on 16 July 1898, observing that a woman 'could not rise at unreasonable hours in the morning and lie about farms waiting for an opportunity to seize'. The Local Government Board, Kelly insisted, had nothing against Miss Magill personally but they objected to the principle of her appointment, for 'if her appointment was confirmed they would have any amount of such applications from the south and west of Ireland'.[85]

No-one suggested that Miss Magill would be required to make dawn raids on ratepayers in Aughnacloy, but the Local Government Board was wary of establishing a precedent at a time when the burden of rates was about to be transferred from owners and occupiers, to occupiers alone. Under the local government bill the payment of rates would, Robinson reminded Balfour, 'fall upon the occupiers, and there will be a much larger number of small amounts to be collected than heretofore. If the rules which the Board have hitherto insisted upon are relaxed, and the collection of the rates is allowed to fall into the hands of women, the financial position of the new County bodies might be seriously affected'.[86] It is difficult to see where the danger really lay. Poor law boards in the south and west were hardly going to appoint women rate collectors en masse. Nevertheless, by stressing the practical problems that Irish rate collectors might encounter, the Local Government Board did persuade some English women to reconsider their support for Magill. The Secretary of the Women's Liberal Unionist Association, Agatha Richardson, judged a written explanation of the Board's position, 'to show conclusively that the office of rate-collector in Ireland cannot be satisfactorily filled by a woman'.[87]

The Local Government Board was anxious to provide local councils with a justification for not appointing women. Explaining why it was necessary to disqualify women from being rate collectors in urban as well as rural districts, Robinson informed Balfour that this would 'enable the majority of councils – who, we have reason to believe, are opposed to giving the collection to women – to refuse to entertain applications from them'.[88] The disqualification sent out a clear message to local officials. When Margaret Milligan applied for the position of polling clerk or interpreter during the 1899 local elections, the Sheriff at Westport informed her that her appointment 'would be against the rules'. This was not in fact the case and the Local Government Board was obliged to notify the Chief Secretary's Office that they were 'not aware of any rule prohibiting women from acting as poll clerks or interpreters at elections. The matter is entirely in the hands of the returning officer'.[89]

Robinson had his own explanation for the actions of the Clogher guardians. The blame, he believed, lay with two people: T.W. Russell and Hugh de Fellenberg Montgomery. One of the Clogher guardians, Thomas Connolly, had written to the Local Government Board in June 1898 claiming that Miss Magill had 'a letter from a member of the Government stating that if she got a majority of the Board to vote for her he would see that the decision of the Local Government Board would be overruled'.[90] It would appear that Russell, who was a strong supporter of women's rights, had assumed that if the Clogher guardians followed the example of the Oswestry board they would achieve a similar result. What he had forgotten was that the Irish Local Government Board possessed the power of dissolution. When it was clear that the Board was prepared to use this power, Russell advised the Clogher guardians to back down, but they refused to do so.[91] Montgomery's motivation was rather different. According to Robinson, he had been determined to pursue the issue, 'because he thinks as the Government have been "coquetting with that abominable women's rights movement" they are bound to be made uncomfortable over Clogher'.[92] Robinson was clearly correct in suspecting that Montgomery's advocacy of Miss Magill was tactical rather than principled. To dismiss Montgomery's actions as mere mischief making, however, was to ignore the substantive issues that the Magill case raised regarding women's rights and opportunities.

The Clogher rates strike

Despite their efforts to disassociate themselves from nationalist boards of guardians that had defied the Local Government Board, the Clogher guardians adopted strikingly similar tactics both before and after their dissolution. They challenged the Local Government Board to dissolve them claiming popular support, and they sought to mobilise local ratepayers behind their campaign. In July 1898, Montgomery had, in effect, called a rates strike. Responding to the Local Government Board's refusal to sanction Magill's appointment, Montgomery had announced that 'should the Local Government Board proceed to make the appointment, I should hesitate, under the circumstances to pay rates to their collector'.[93] Johnston referred to Montgomery's statement in the Commons on 28 July, noting that the supersession of Miss Magill was 'creating more difficulties than could possibly arise from the confirmation of the appointment'.[94]

Enough ratepayers in the Aughnacloy district acted on Montgomery's suggestion to create problems for the Local Government Board appointee, Robert Cuthbertson. He was eventually forced to seize the goods of a number of defaulters, thus bringing about the very situation that the Local Government Board had insisted a woman would be unable to deal with.[95] Local functionaries saw little sign of genuine popular support for Miss Magill. Only five people, all local shopkeepers, attended a meeting held in Aughnacloy on 19 November 1898 to petition the Local Government Board to restore the board of guardians. Acknowledging that the low attendance might have been partly attributable to the fact that the meeting took place at midday on a stormy Thursday, the local constabulary inspector nevertheless concluded that by declining to attend, local residents had shown that 'they take little interest in the matter'.[96] Robinson informed Balfour in March 1899 that the vice-guardians appointed to administer the union were of the opinion that 'the people didn't care two pence about Miss Magill but were only too delighted to take the hint not to pay rates given by Montgomery'.[97] Whatever the reason for the non-payment of rates, the Local Government Board was anxious to bring resistance to an end. In striking contrast to the policy generally adopted in response to a rates strike, whereby the Local Government Board would refuse to restore the guardians until the resistance was broken or at least showing clear signs of weakening, the Board decided to restore the Clogher guardians after just a few months on the condition that they would give their backing to Cuthbertson.[98]

Emboldened by the apparent capitulation of the Local Government Board, the Clogher guardians were in no mood to abandon the fight. At their first meeting on 26 January 1899, the guardians elected Montgomery as chair in place of James Anketell, who had filled the position for over twenty years. Declaring that they had Montgomery to thank for their success in fighting the Local Government Board, H. Treanor proposed that 'the best we can do by him, at the same time showing the Local Government Board that we adhere to our action, is to place him in the chair'.[99] In the following weeks the board passed resolutions calling for an inquiry into the actions of the Local Government Board, and drawing attention to the unsatisfactory state of the rate collection in the Aughnacloy district. The only way to remedy this, the guardians maintained was for the Local Government Board to issue 'a sealed order dispensing with Colonel Cuthbertson's services, cancelling the sealed order of July 22nd 1898 and directing Ann Eliza Magill to complete the collection'.[100] Pointing out that Cuthbertson's difficulties in recovering rates were unsurprising, having regard to the advice given to the ratepayers by the present Chairman of the Board of Guardians', the Local Government Board urged the guardians to adopt a resolution calling on ratepayers to pay their debts, 'as in the opinion of the Board the unprofitable resolution passed by the Guardians at their last meeting as to the reappointment of Miss Magill only places a further obstacle in the way of Mr Cuthbertson completing his collection'.[101]

Support for Montgomery and for Miss Magill melted away following the elections for the new rural district council in April 1899. Having taken their seats, the first act of the 44 district councillors was to elect James Anketell as chair for the ensuing year.[102] Montgomery remained an influential figure, acting as chair of the finance committee for example, but he found little support amongst his colleagues for his attempts to continue the campaign against Cuthbertson. When the rate collector's name was omitted from a list of men to be recommended for employment by the Tyrone County Council, one councillor suspected 'an attempt to revive that farcical comedy known as the "Magill case"'. Commenting that he did not see how Miss Magill's cause had 'been aided by all this undignified wrangling with the Local Government Board', Mr Coote questioned the motives of the men, 'who in this schoolboy fashion disturbed this board for the past twelve months at such serious cost to the ratepayers, keeping alive this piece of nonsense'. A resolution to recommend Cuthbertson was passed overwhelmingly, Montgomery alone dissenting.[103] Robinson welcomed the vote, noting that it placed Montgomery 'in a very unfavourable light'.[104]

While it may seem difficult not to agree with Coote's dismissive description of the Magill affair, its significance should not be underestimated. By treating the Clogher guardians more leniently than nationalist boards of guardians behaving in a similar fashion, the Local Government Board reinforced the impression that nationalist defiance was taken more seriously within government than unionist defiance. The former was assumed to be more dangerous than the latter. The same assumption was to undermine attempts to respond effectively to

Ulster unionist resistance to home rule. Indeed, the actions of the Clogher guardians and the official response to them can be seen as a template for later acts of resistance. In embarking on a course of action that they had previously condemned, and in maintaining that the Local Government Board had forced them into a position where defiance was their only option, Montgomery and his colleagues were foreshadowing Ulster unionist opposition to home rule.

Far from advancing the cause of women, the Magill case reinforced the restrictions on Irish women's employment, at least in the short term. Responses to the case in Ireland were largely determined by political factors that had little direct bearing on women's rights. The Local Government Board was anxious to ensure the successful implementation and operation of the Local Government Act. Facilitating the employment of women was seen as an indulgence they could not afford. Unionists saw an opportunity to draw attention to Conservative policies on Ireland that appeared to be sacrificing the political power of the Irish landed elite to the principle of assimilation. Nationalists were wary of any issue that distracted attention from home rule and, despite some sympathy for Miss Magill, were mistrustful of her supporters. Women's organisations in Britain appear to have had little understanding of the political context in which the Magill case was unfolding. It seems unlikely they would have embraced the Clogher guardians with such enthusiasm had they had read some of their statements regarding the case and the women's issue more generally. In this respect, they may actually have damaged their cause by confirming popular perceptions of women as unable to grasp the true import of major political questions.

Notes

1 For example, women made up 73 per cent of the adult recipients of outdoor relief on 1 January 1892 and 53 per cent of adult workhouse inmates: *Return relating to In-door and Out-door Relief in Ireland*, PP, 1892 (360), lxviii, 995–1002. For more information on women and poor relief in Ireland, see Virginia Crossman, 'Viewing Women, Family and Sexuality through the Prism of the Irish Poor Laws', *Women's History Review*, forthcoming.

2 *Return of all Inspectors now in the service of the Local Government Board...*, PP, 1906 (297), civ, 670–1.

3 *Royal Commission on the Civil Service*, PP, 1914 [Cd.7340], xvi, 204.

4 Maria Luddy, *Women and Philanthropy in Nineteenth-Century Ireland* (Cambridge, Cambridge University Press, 1995), p. 23.

5 Mrs Morgan John O'Connell, 'Poor-Law Administration as it Affects Women and Children in Workhouses', *Journal of the Statistical and Social Inquiry Society of Ireland*, viii (April 1880), 20–1.

6 Isabella Tod, 'The Place of Women in the Administration of the Irish Poor Law', *The Englishwoman's Review*, 15 Nov. 1881, 486–8. In 1896, the Marquess of Londonderry was to note the strong support for women guardians in Ulster: *Hansard 4*, xxxvii, 1449 (2 Mar. 1896).

7 For ladies visiting committees, see Luddy, *Philanthropy*, pp. 199–200.

8 *Report from the Select Committee Appointed to Inquire into the Administration of the Relief of the Poor in Ireland*, PP, 1861 (408), x, 246–7.

9 Ibid., 344.

10 'Report of the Dublin Workhouse Visiting Society', *Journal of the Workhouse Visiting Society*, xxi (Sept. 1862), 708.

11 This was not to change until 1899, when the Local Government Board issued an order directing that a ladies committee should be formed in each union where boarding-out was practiced to take responsibility for the management of the system. Luddy, *Philanthropy*, pp. 200–1. See also Diane Urquhart, *Women in Ulster Politics 1890–1940* (Dublin, Irish Academic Press, 2000), p. 138.

12 *Report from the Select Committee Appointed to Inquire into the Administration of the Relief of the Poor in Ireland*, 72.

13 Cited in Maria Luddy, '"Angels of Mercy": Nuns as Workhouse Nurses, 1861–1898', in Elizabeth Malcolm and Greta Jones (eds), *Medicine, Disease and the State in Ireland, 1650–1940* (Cork, Cork University Press, 1999), p. 105.

14 Ibid., pp. 105–6.

15 *Return of Number of Workhouses in Ireland in which Nuns are engaged as Nurses*, PP, 1873 (246), lv, 865.

16 Fanny Taylor, *Irish Homes and Irish Hearts* (London, Longmans, Green and Co., 1867), p. 136.

17 William H. Hurlbert, *Ireland Under Coercion: The Diary of an American* (Edinburgh, David Douglas, 1889), p. 275.

18 Robinson, *Further Memories*, pp. 232–5. An exception was the dispute that arose in the late 1860s between the Sisters of Mercy working in Limerick workhouse and a local medical officer, Dr O'Sullivan. See, Luddy, 'Angels of Mercy', pp. 111–12.

19 This proposal was incorporated in the Local Government Act of 1898: 61 & 62 Vict., c. 37, sec. 58 (a) ii.

20 Robinson to E.T. O'Dwyer, 14 Nov. 1899, copy in Mercy Archives, Limerick.

21 Robinson to Balfour, 14 June 1899: NA, Balfour Papers, PRO 30/60/15.

22 Taylor, *Irish Homes and Irish Hearts*, p. 190.

23 Robinson to Balfour, 19 Feb. 1899: NA, Balfour Papers, PRO 30/60/15.

24 1 & 2 Vic., c. 56, sec. 19.

25 *Report from the Select Committee on Poor Law Guardians*, PP, 1878 (297) xvii, 501. See also evidence of John Byrne, ibid., 565.

26 Anna Haslam, 'Irishwomen and the Local Government Act', *The Englishwoman's Review*, 15 Oct. 1898, 221.

27 *Report from the Select Committee on Poor Law Guardians*, 571. See also evidence of B. Banks, ibid., 504. The application was subsequently withdrawn pending legal advice.

28 *United Ireland*, 24 June 1882.

29 Emily W. Dickson, 'The Need for Women as Poor Law Guardians', *Dublin Journal of Medical Science*, xcix (Apr. 1895), 309.

30 Ibid., 311.

31 *Hansard 4*, xxxvii, 631 (18 Feb. 1896).

32 Ibid., 629–30

33 Ibid., 631.

34 Ibid., 629. The Marquess of Londonderry moved the second reading of the bill in the house of lords. *Hansard 4*, xxxvii, 1449 (2 Mar. 1896).

35 59 Vict., c. 5.

36 'Suggestions for Intending Lady Guardians', appended to 'Report of the Executive Committee of the Dublin Women's Suffrage and Local Government Association for 1898', *Reports of the Irish Women's Suffrage and Local Government Association from 1896 to 1918* (Dublin, Ormond Printing Co., 1919).

37 'Women Poor Law Guardians in Ireland', *The Englishwoman's Review* (15 Oct. 1896), 257.

38 Women Guardians' Society, 17th Annual Report (1899), p. 9.

39 *United Ireland*, 3, 10 Apr. 1897.

40 Kathryn Gleadle, *British Women in the Nineteenth Century* (Basingstoke, Palgrave, 2001), p. 158. See also Patricia Hollis, *Ladies Elect: Women in English Local Government 1865–1914* (Oxford, Clarendon Press, 1987).

41 Women's Local Government Society, 6th Annual Report, 10 Mar. 1899, p. 8.

42 Anna Haslam, 'Irishwomen and the Local Government Act', *The Englishwoman's Review* (15 Oct. 1898), 223.
43 Cited in Donal A. Murphy, *Blazing Tar Barrels and Standing Orders: North Tipperary's First County and District Councils 1899–1902* (Nenagh, Relay Books, 1999), p. 72.
44 *Tyrone Constitution*, 24 Feb. 1899.
45 *Galway Express*, 18 Mar. 1899, quoted in Mary Clancy, 'The "Western Outpost": Local Government and Women's Suffrage in County Galway 1898–1918', in Gerard Moran and Raymond Gillespie (eds), *Galway: History and Society* (Dublin, Geography Publications, 1996), p. 559.
46 Urquhart, *Women in Ulster Politics*, p. 121. She was not elected.
47 Mrs Maurice Dockrell, 'Irish Women in Local Government', in Countess of Aberdeen (ed.), *Women in Politics: The International Congress of Women, 1899* (London, T. Fisher Unwin, 1900), pp. 87–9.
48 Tod, 'The Place of Women in the Administration of the Irish Poor Law', 489.
49 Urquhart, *Women in Ulster Politics*, p. 127.
50 Clancy, 'The "Western Outpost" …', pp. 559–60.
51 Luddy, *Women and Philanthropy*, p. 53.
52 'List of Women elected under the Local Government Act in 1899', appended to 'Report of the Committee for 1899', *Reports of the Irish Women's Suffrage and Local Government Association*.
53 'Report of the Committee for 1899', ibid., pp. 3–4.
54 Women Guardians' Society, 17th Annual Report (1899), p. 9.
55 Haslam, 'Irishwomen and the Local Government Act', 222.
56 'List of Women elected under the Local Government Act in 1899', *Reports of the Irish Women's Suffrage and Local Government Association*.
57 Urquhart, *Women in Ulster Politics*, pp. 131,132, 133.
58 'Report of the Committee for 1899', *Reports of the Irish Women's Suffrage and Local Government Association*, p. 3.
59 Crossman, *Local Government in Nineteenth-Century Ireland*, pp. 91–7.
60 Pauric Travers, *Settlements and Divisions: Ireland 1870–1922* (Dublin, Helicon, 1988), p. 66.
61 Ann E. Magill to Clogher Board of Guardians, 12 May 1898: Clogher Board of Guardians Minutes (hereafter CBGM), PRONI, BG9/A/41, 189.
62 CBGM: May–July 1898: ibid., 189–237.
63 Resolution of Clogher Board of Guardians, 2 July 1898: ibid., 237.
64 CBGM: ibid., 246, 262, 357.
65 Resolution of Clogher Board of Guardians, 10 Sept. 1898: ibid., 297–8.

66 Women's Local Government Society, 6th Annual Report, 10 Mar. 1899, p. 10.
67 Ibid.
68 *Impartial Reporter and Farmers' Journal*, 1 Sept. 1898.
69 Reprinted in *Impartial Reporter*, 1 Sept. 1898.
70 [Elizabeth Elmy], 'The Part of Women in Local Administration', *Westminster Review*, cl (Sept. 1898), 253, 260.
71 Ibid., cli (Feb. 1899), 164.
72 Women's Local Government Society, 6th Annual Report 10 Mar. 1899, pp. 12–15.
73 *Hansard 4*, lx, 1201, 1203 (30 June 1899).
74 Women's Local Government Society, 7th Annual Report, 19 Mar. 1900, p. 24.
75 *Impartial Reporter*, 16 June 1898.
76 Ibid., 15 Sept. 1898.
77 *Impartial Reporter*, 16 June 1898.
78 Ibid., 29 Sept. 1898.
79 Ibid., 21 July 1898.
80 Ibid., 3 Nov. 1898.
81 Ibid., 6 Oct. 1898. See also 25 Aug. 1898.
82 Ibid., 17 Nov. 1898.
83 *Freeman's Journal*, 24 Sept. 1898.
84 Robinson to Balfour, 6 July 1898: NAI, CSORP, 1898/20157.
85 *Impartial Reporter*, 21 July 1898.
86 Robinson to Balfour, 2 July 1898: NAI, CSORP, 1898/20157.
87 Richardson to Micks, 18 July 1898: ibid.
88 Robinson to Balfour, 5 July 1899: NA, Balfour Papers, PRO30/60/15.
89 Robinson to Harrel, 5 Apr. 1899: NAI, CSORP, 1899/6371.
90 Connolly to Secretary of LGB, 13 June 1898: NAI, CSORP, 1898/20157.
91 Russell to Clerk of the Union, 15 Sept. 1898, printed in *Impartial Reporter*, 22 Sept. 1898. See also CBGM, 17 Sept. 1898: PRONI, BG9/A/41, 304.
92 Robinson to Balfour, 12 Feb 1899: NA, Bafour Papers, PRO 30/60/15.
93 *Impartial Reporter*, 21 July 1898.
94 *Hansard 4*, lxiii, 287–8 (28 July 1898).
95 *Fermanagh Times*, 30 Mar. 1899. See also *Hansard 4*, lxviii, 298–9 (9 Mar. 1899); 959 (16 Mar. 1899).
96 Report by DI W.J. McAuley, 26 Nov. 1898; NAI, CSORP, 1898/20157.
97 Robinson to Balfour, 8 Mar. 1899: NA, Balfour Papers, PRO 30/60/15.

  98 See comments of PLG William Richey, *Fermanagh Times*, 23 Feb. 1899.
  99 *Fermanagh Times*, 26 Jan. 1899.
 100 CBGM, 4 Feb. 1899: PRONI, BG9/A/41, p. 485; 11 Feb. 99, ibid., p. 490.
 101 Thomas Mooney to Clerk of Clogher Union, 17 Feb. 1899: Clogher Board of Guardians In-letters, PRONI, BG9/BC/1.
 102 Clogher Rural District Council Minute Book, 15 Apr. 1899: PRONI, BG9/A/41, 555.
 103 *Fermanagh Times*, 11 May 1899.
 104 Robinson to Balfour, 12 May 1899: NA, Balfour Papers, PRO 30/60/15.

Conclusion

By the end of the nineteenth century, the responsibilities of Irish poor law guardians had expanded to encompass a wide range of welfare services from poor relief and hospital care to social housing. The causes of this expansion are to be found in the social and political developments of the period. Government was encroaching on areas that it had previously avoided and there was a growing recognition that poverty and under-development in Ireland required the active intervention of the state. At the same time, the increasing influence of elected poor law guardians encouraged a more populist approach to poor law administration, most evident in the provision of labourers' cottages and outdoor relief. By the end of the nineteenth century state spending was increasingly coming to be seen as beneficial to all, but in Ireland the developing welfare state became enmeshed in the struggle to establish an independent nation state. Membership of the nation and access to welfare became linked to political identity.

Throughout the nineteenth century, national politics overshadowed the conduct of local affairs. Control of local administration could never be seen as a non-political issue as long as central government was directed from outside the country. Thus the idea that local government represented a potential area of co-operation between different classes, and religions, was always an unrealistic one. Ministers and officials often overlooked this point and as a result they interpreted the refusal of local functionaries to behave in what they deemed to

be an appropriately sober and responsible manner as an indication of their political immaturity. The suspicion with which
central administrators regarded those in the localities was
reflected in the level of central supervision and control. Without
such control it was thought local government bodies would
spend extravagantly and ignore minority interests to the detri-
ment of the community as a whole.

The 'nationalisation' of Irish poor law boards in the south
and west of the country changed the character of poor law
administration in those areas. The consequences of this were
felt not only in the localities, where people expected the boards
to be more responsive to local concerns, but also within the
wider political community. As the only example of representative local government in rural areas, poor law boards were
scrutinised as exemplars of home rule. For if nationalists could
not manage the poor law successfully, how could they hope to
govern the country? Assessments of poor law administration
need to be understood in this context. Opponents of home rule
characterised the management of poor law boards as a combination of inefficiency and oppression. Unionist publications
reported the activities of nationalist guardians under headlines
such as 'Typical Local Administrators', 'How They Legislate',
and 'Home Rule in Kerry'.[1] Advocates of home rule replayed
the equally well-worn theme of landlord cruelty and irrespon-
sibility, and condemned landlord-dominated boards as
self-serving. Visiting Listowel workhouse in County Kerry in
1887, the editor of the *Western Daily Mercury* noted that the
administration of the workhouse was 'now conducted by
Nationalist Guardians to the great advantage of the inmates.
When the ascendancy section controlled its affairs the neglect
was shameful'. He went on to blame the increase in outdoor
relief in the union on 'the despotism of the landlords'. A few
years later, *United Ireland* condemned the action of the chair of
the Roscrea Board of Guardians in refusing to receive a resolution opposing rack-renting, describing this as a 'pretty
specimen... of local self-government, as it is at present understood in Ireland'.[2]

Conscious that nationalist guardians were 'on trial as to their
power to manage their own affairs', nationalist newspapers
worried that poorly run boards reflected badly on their locality

and afforded 'the enemies of the country material for reflecting on the administrative capacity of Irishmen'.[3] Examples of good management received prominent coverage. *The Nation* welcomed the success of the Limerick Board of Guardians in reducing a debt of £6000 to £249 in twelve months, noting that such 'an example of skill in Local Government weighs more than the vapourings and mouthings' of all the critics of the national movement 'packed together'.[4] Poor law guardians were conscious of the media spotlight. William Abraham accepted the nomination for chair of Limerick Union in 1888 in order, he said, to demonstrate to people in England who believed that the Irish desired 'to oppress their Protestant fellow-countrymen', that this was not the case.[5] Nationalist MPs accepted that there were instances of local maladministration but insisted that these were rare. In 1892, John Dillon repudiated the idea that dissolved boards of guardians could be taken as fair examples of popular administration in Ireland, 'because these suppressions arose for the most part not from causes of corruption; they had their origins in the disturbed and distracted state of the country'.[6] MPs were wary of associating themselves too closely with dissolved boards. Thus while they were prepared to condemn the Local Government Board for dissolving the New Ross and Athy boards, for example, they were reluctant publicly to defend the guardians. Calling for the restoration of his erstwhile colleagues on the Athy Board of Guardians in December 1888, Denis Kilbride was careful to state that he did not defend the illegality the guardians' actions, but felt their 'punishment was beyond the gravity of the offence committed'.[7] Whatever its impact in Britain, unionist propaganda fuelled the fears of Irish nationalists that local activists were discrediting the movement, making leading figures such as Dillon and Redmond more determined to concentrate power at the centre and limit local autonomy. William O'Brien recalled that Dillon had opposed the degree of local autonomy enjoyed by branches of the United Irish League, predicting that 'all sorts of clashings and chaotic rebellions on the part of the local governing bodies and the destruction of all national authority would be the inevitable result'. O'Brien claimed that the 'wholesome vigour of local initiative turned out to be the chief secret of the amazing success of the League'.[8] Few of his colleagues agreed with him.

The debate over self-government provided the backdrop for Balfour's crusade against nationalist boards of guardians in the 1890s. As we have seen, one of Balfour's first acts as Chief Secretary was to attempt permanently to dissolve a number of insolvent boards in the west of the country. During his period of office, the number of board dissolutions rose sharply. Between 1880 and 1892, the Local Government Board dissolved 14 boards and issued warnings to another 10 regarding irregular proceedings or violations of the general regulations. Eight of the dissolutions and six of the warnings took place while Balfour was Chief Secretary.[9] Balfour was convinced that nationalist boards were assisting and in some cases directing the Plan of Campaign. He was supported in this belief by the reports of divisional magistrates and constabulary officers. Amongst the reasons given for the proclamation of County Waterford under the Criminal Law and Procedure Act of 1887 was the intimidation allegedly exercised by the National League over the Ely tenants.[10] Defeating the Plan thus required the suppression of the boards most actively involved. Speaking in the Commons in 1888, Maurice Healy observed that there was 'a very prevalent impression in Ireland that this policy of suppressing Irish boards of guardians was simply part of the general policy of "twenty years of resolute Government", which they were promised when the Government came into office'.[11] But this was not the only reason why Balfour engaged in his crusade. He wanted to exploit the propaganda value of dissolutions. Alleged cases of maladministration and oppression by poor law boards provided Balfour with a reason not to extend English local government reform to Ireland in 1888, and to include so many restrictions and safeguards in his Irish reform measure of 1892 as to make it unworkable.

The Local Government Board shared Balfour's concerns about the determination of some boards of guardians to use their powers to promote nationalist campaigns. They were, however, anxious to maintain a sense of perspective. The vast majority of guardians, they believed, were anxious to carry out their duties responsibly. Where boards did pursue an overtly political agenda, this was seen as a symptom rather than a cause of heightened political tension. Most elected guardians, George Morris declared in 1885, were 'thoroughly honest, thoroughly straight'. Irregularities such as the granting of excessive relief to evicted tenants were, he maintained, a product of 'disturbances in the country'.[12] Commenting on the composition of the Athy Board in 1889, H.A. Robinson acknowledged that 'the propertied and educated classes are no longer represented among the elected guardians', but questioned whether it followed that 'intelligence' and 'industry' were no longer represented. 'Nationalist guardians', he observed, 'are intelligent enough according to their lights', and magistrates did 'not have any special claim to be looked upon as representatives of industry'. While nationalist guardians did sometimes act in a way that 'the exigencies of patriotism oblige them to', it was 'nevertheless a fact that they are extremely sensitive about the capabilities of transacting the ordinary poor law business.'[13]

Board officials refuted Balfour's claim that nationalist boards of guardians conducted an oppressive regime. They accepted that guardians might like to do this but argued that the regulatory framework prevented them. Reflecting on local administration in 1892, Morris concluded that had the power of dissolution

> not been placed in the hands of the Local Government Board, the poor law administration would have completely broken down when any strain was imposed upon it; that abuses which the audit was powerless to check would have been carried on, and that when political agitation was rife and the country divided into bitterly hostile sections, the laws would have been made use of by Boards of Guardians for the purpose of oppressing and impoverishing their political opponents.

In the event, however, this had not happened. Having been asked for examples of known cases of oppression by public bodies, Morris replied pointedly that the Board had 'no official record of the proceedings of public bodies other than the Boards of Guardians and we believe that the powers vested in us have enabled us to prevent oppression by them'.[14] Throughout the period of this study, the Board remained confident in its ability to control the boards of guardians without resorting to wholesale dissolutions. As Balfour was well aware, however, this could only be achieved by turning a blind eye to the transgressions of some nationalist guardians. Despite strong pressure from the chief secretary's office, the Board managed to resist demands for a more aggressive approach.

In its anxiety to ensure adherence to poor law regulations, the Local Government Board focused its energies more on preventing boards of guardians from doing things than on encouraging them to improve or develop the services they provided. This was in part a product of the way central-local relations operated throughout the United Kingdom. But concern to protect the rights and interests of private individuals and property holders was even more marked in Ireland, where central suspicion of local authorities was greater than in Britain. The adversarial nature of central-local relations and the politicisation of poor law administration had the effect of marginalising social activists and undermining campaigns for reform. Criticism of the poor law system tended to be interpreted in political terms. Attempts to reform and humanise the system were tainted by nationalist condemnations of it as an alien imposition unsuited to Ireland. At the same time, nationalist guardians, who were often socially conservative, were far from enthusiastic about proposals that threatened to disrupt class or gender relations. Thus despite agreement across religious and political divides over the evils of the general workhouse and the need for more targeted relief, advocates of change were unable to unite behind an agreed programme of reform.

By redefining criteria for relief, nationalist guardians helped to introduce a greater degree of flexibility into the relief system. This meant that some people were able to obtain relief who would not otherwise have done so. Those such as the elderly who were widely regarded as entitled to assistance received a much more sympathetic hearing and generally better treatment than other applicants perceived to be less deserving. In seeking support amongst a wide range of social groups, including sections of the poor, elected guardians contributed to the creation of a broad-based nationalist community, albeit one in which there were different levels of citizenship. Not all sections of the community were encouraged to be active citizens. Groups that had previously been marginalised from political activity, such as labourers and women, were expected to be passive rather than active citizens, following the lead of their male, middle-class colleagues.

The growing influence of the less well off both as electors and as poor law guardians did not lead to the wholesale abandonment of older ideas and practices. As José Harris has recently reminded us, the new English poor law was criticised by contemporaries not because it treated some people harshly, but because it failed to distinguish clearly enough between those people for whom harsh treatment was appropriate and those for whom it was not.[15] Nationalist campaigns were based on commonly held notions about rights, legitimacy and community, and the language in which they were conducted was highly moralistic. In this respect, nationalist ideology had much in common with poor law ideology. Both held, for example, that those who excluded themselves from the community by their actions were liable to punishment. Evicting landlords could expect to be boycotted just as paupers could expect harsh treatment within the workhouse. Nationalist guardians categorised evicted tenants as deserving of relief both on account of their participation in the nationalist campaign, and as victims of landlordism. Paupers proved more difficult to categorise since it remained unclear whether they were victims of the system or a drain upon it. The strength of Irish nationalism lay in its ability to construct a cohesive political community that cut across gender and class boundaries. In theory, membership of the community was open to all those who adopted its beliefs and tenets. However, since its legitimacy rested in part on its claim to moral superiority, some groups were less easily accommodated than others. Any attempt to expand the nationalist community to include the destitute and non-respectable threatened to destroy its cohesiveness by undermining the sense of moral superiority on which it rested.

Introduced as a means of facilitating the assimilation of Ireland into the United Kingdom, the poor law system came to provide Irish nationalists with a forum from which to challenge British rule and to advance the cause of Irish self-government. In England the poor law could be seen to reflect and indeed strengthen national identity through its emphasis on the archetypal English virtues, independence, self-reliance and hard work. In Ireland, poor law principles had the same cultural resonance only in Ulster. Elsewhere, if the poor law promoted a sense a national identity it was through opposition and confrontation. Thus while the poor law did foster independence, it was an independence that was national and political, not personal and economic.

During the struggle for Irish independence, county and district councils drew on the tradition and experience of local autonomy to establish a parallel system of local administration answerable not to the Local Government Board but to the Local Government Ministry of the First Dáil. Condemning the poor law as foreign, degrading and uneconomic, Dáil ministers encouraged councils to close workhouses and amalgamate poor law unions.[16] The process of reorganisation continued in the early years of the Irish Free State. The workhouse system was formally abolished in 1925 when boards of guardians were replaced by boards of health and public assistance empowered to grant outdoor relief to all needy persons. But while the poor were spared the humiliation of the workhouse, they had no right to assistance and in demonstrating their entitlement to relief were required to meet moral as well as financial criteria. In the 1920s as in the 1880s and 1890s the radical impulse in Irish poor law politics was directed more towards rejection of British practices and the saving of ratepayers' money than the creation of a more responsive and humane welfare regime.

Notes

1 *Notes from Ireland*, 19 Nov. 1887, 14 July 1888, 4 Aug. 1888, 24 Aug. 1888.
2 [H. Whitfield], *Mr Balfour's Instruments and Victims being a record of the experiences of coercion and eviction as encountered during a tour in Ireland* (Plymouth, Plymouth Home Rule Education League, n.d.), p. 26; *United Ireland*, 3 May 1890.
3 *Munster News*, 28 Nov. 1888.
4 *The Nation*, 8 Sept. 1888.
5 *Limerick Reporter*, 6 Apr. 1888.
6 *Hansard 4*, iv, 1733–4 (24 May 1892).
7 *Hansard 3*, cccxxxi, 1185 (5 Dec. 1888).
8 O'Brien, *An Olive Branch in Ireland*, p. 106.
9 *Return of Boards of Poor Law Guardians in Ireland Dissolved or Warned by the Local Government Board for Ireland since and inclusive of the year 1880, with a statement of the reasons in each case*, PP, 1892 (298), lxviii, 965–7.
10 Supplemental Report by Captain Slacke, Divisional Magistrate, giving reasons for recommending the proclamation of counties in

the South East Division under the Criminal Law and Procedure (Ireland) Act 1887: NA, Cabinet Papers, CAB 37/18/41.

11 *Hansard 3*, cccxxxi, 1197 (5 December 1888). See also ibid., 1208.

12 *Report from the Select Committee of the House of Lords on the Poor Law Guardians (Ireland) Bill. . .*, PP, 1884–5 (297), x, 340.

13 Observations by H.A. Robinson, 26 Apr. 1889: NAI, CSORP, 1890/7728.

14 Memorandum on administration by Local Governing bodies, 2 Apr. 1892: ibid., 1892/4813.

15 José Harris, 'From Poor Law to Welfare State? A European Perspective', in Winch and O'Brien (eds), *The Political Economy of British Historical Experience*, pp. 431–2.

16 Mary E. Daly, 'Local Government and the First Dáil', in Brian Farrell (ed.), *The Creation of the Dáil* (Dublin, Blackwater Press, 1994), pp. 123–36; Tom Garvin, *1922: The Birth of Irish Democracy* (Dublin, Gill and Macmillan, 1996), pp. 63–91.

Select bibliography

Manuscript sources

Bodleian Library, Oxford
Morley Papers
[Uncatalogued papers of John Morley (Chief Secretary 1886 and 1892–95)]

British Library, London
Althorp Papers
[Papers of 5th Earl Spencer (Lord Lieutenant 1868–74 and 1882–85)]
Balfour Papers
[Papers of Arthur James Balfour (Chief Secretary 1887–91)]

Cork Archives Institute, Cork
Bandon Board of Guardian Records: Labourers Acts Ledger
Macroom Board of Guardians Records: Minute books
Youghal Board of Guardians Records: Minute books, Out-Letters

National Archives, London
Balfour Papers
[Papers of Arthur James Balfour (Chief Secretary 1887–91) and Gerald Balfour (Chief Secretary 1895–1900)]

National Archives of Ireland, Dublin
Chief Secretary's Office Registered Papers
Crime Branch Special Files

National Library of Ireland, Dublin
Belmullet Board of Guardians Minute Books
Swinford Board of Guardians Minute Books
Westport Board of Guardians Minute Books

Public Record Office of Northern Ireland, Belfast
Clogher Board of Guardian Records: Minute books, In-Letters
Enniskillen Board of Guardian Records: Minute books, Out-Letters
Local Government Board Precedent Book

St Vincent's Hospital, Athy, County Kildare
Athy Board of Guardians Minute Books

Scottish Record Office, Edinburgh
Balfour Papers
[Papers of Gerald Balfour (Chief Secretary 1895–1900)]

Trinity College Dublin
Dillon Papers
[Papers of John Dillon MP]

Wexford County Library, Wexford
New Ross Board of Guardians Minute Books

Parliamentary Debates and Papers

Hansard Parliamentary Debates, 3rd and 4th series
Annual Reports of the Commissioners for Administering the Laws for the Relief of the Poor in Ireland
Annual Reports of the Local Government Board for Ireland
Third Report of the Commissioners for Inquiring into the Condition of the Poorer Classes in Ireland, PP, 1836 (43), xxx, 1.
Report from the Select Committee Appointed to Inquire into the Administration of the Relief of the Poor in Ireland, PP, 1861 (408), x, 1.

Civil Service (in Ireland) Enquiry Commission, 1872, PP, 1873 [C.788], xxii, 1.

Reports from Poor Law Inspectors in Ireland... [on] Labourers' Dwellings in that Country, PP, 1873 [C.764], xxii, 615.

Report from the Select Committee on Poor Law Guardians, PP, 1878 (297), xvii, 263.

Poor Law Union and Lunacy Inquiry Commission (Ireland), PP, 1879–80 [C.2239], xxxi, 1.

Report from the Select Committee on Agricultural Labourers (Ireland), PP, 1884 (317), viii, 1 and 1884–85 (32), vii, 559.

Report from the Select Committee of the House of Lords on the Poor Law Guardians (Ireland) Bill, PP, 1884–85 (297), x, 1.

Poor Relief (Ireland) Inquiry Commission, PP, 1887 [C.5043], xxxviii, 1.

Royal Commission on Labour: The Agricultural Labourer: Ireland, PP, 1893–94 [C.6894–xviii], xxxvii, 1.

Report and Special Report from the Select Committee on Housing of the Working Classes Act Amendment Bill, PP, 1906 (376), ix, 1.

Report of the Vice-Regal Commission on Poor Law Reform in Ireland, PP, 1906 [C.3202], li, 1.

Royal Commission on the Civil Service, PP, 1914 [C.7340], xvi, 1.

Newspapers
Belfast Newsletter
Clare Journal
Connaught Telegraph
Cork Constitution
Cork Examiner
Freeman's Journal
Galway Vindicator
Impartial Reporter (Enniskillen)
Ireland's Gazette
Kildare Observer
Leinster Express
Leinster Leader
Limerick Chronicle
Limerick Reporter
Mayo Examiner
Mayo News
Munster News

The Nation
Notes from Ireland
People (Wexford)
The Times
Tyrone Constitution
United Ireland
Wexford Independent

Reference works

Connolly, S.J. (ed.), *The Oxford Companion to Irish History* (Oxford, Oxford University Press, 2nd edn., 2002)
Luddy, Maria, et al., *A Directory of Sources for Women's History in Ireland* (Dublin, Irish Manuscripts Commission, 1999) available at www.nationalarchives.ie/wh/
Mooney, Thomas Aiskew, Compendium of the Irish Poor Law; and General Manual for Poor Law Guardians and Their Officers (Dublin, Alex. Thom and Co., 1887)
Muldoon, John and M'Sweeny, George, *A Guide to Irish Local Government* (Dublin, Eason and Son Ltd, Dublin, 1899)
Thom's Irish Almanac and Official Directory
Walker, B.M. (ed.), *Parliamentary Election Results in Ireland, 1801–1922* (Dublin, Royal Irish Academy, 1978)

Contemporary works

Clancy, J.J., *The 'Castle' System* (Dublin, Irish Press Agency, 1886)
Distress in the West of Ireland, 1898 (Manchester, 1898)
Dickson, Emily Winifred, 'The Need for Women as Poor Law Guardians', *Dublin Journal of Medical Science*, xcix (Apr. 1895), 309–14
[Elmy, Elizabeth], 'The Part of Women in Local Administration', *Westminster Review*, cl (Sept. 1898), 248–60; cli (Feb. 1899), 159–71
Fottrell, George, and Fottrell, J.G., *A Handy Guide to the Labourers (Ireland) Acts, 1883 & 1885* (Dublin, M.H. Gill and Son, 1885)
Fox, J.A., *Reports on the Condition of the Peasantry of the County of Mayo in 1880* (Dublin, Dublin Mansion House Committee, 1881)

Hancock, W. Neilson, 'The Workhouse as a Mode of Relief for Widows and Orphans', *Journal of the Statistical and Social Inquiry Society of Ireland*, i (Apr. 1855), 84–91

Reports of the Irish Women's Suffrage and Local Government Association from 1896 to 1918 (Dublin, Ormond Printing Co., 1919)

Letters from Ireland, 1886, by a special correspondent of *The Times* (London, 1887)

Light on the Local Government Board (NLI, undated pamphlet, reprinted from the *Leader*, 1907).

McGrath, Terence, *Pictures from Ireland* (London, C. Keegan Paul and Co., 1880)

Nicholls, George, *A History of the Irish Poor Law* [1856] Reprints of Economic Classics (New York, Augustus M. Kelley, 1967)

O'Brien, William, *An Olive Branch in Ireland and its History* (London, Macmillan and Co., 1910)

O'Connell, Mrs Morgan John, 'Poor-Law Administration as it Affects Women and Children in Workhouses', *Journal of the Statistical and Social Inquiry Society of Ireland*, viii (Apr. 1880), 20–31

R.J.B., *Ireland As It Is and As It Would Be Under Home Rule: 62 Letters Written by the Special Correspondent of the Birmingham Daily Gazette between March and August, 1893* (Birmingham, Birmingham Daily Gazette, n.d.)

Robinson, Rt Hon Sir Henry A., *Memories: Wise and Otherwise* (New York, Dodd, Mead and Company, 1923)

—— *Further Memories of Irish Life* (London, Herbert Jenkins Ltd, 1924)

Stephens, Laura, 'An Irish Workhouse', *New Ireland Review*, xiii (May 1900), 129–134

Tallon, Daniel, *Distress in the West and South and Ireland, 1898. Report of the Work of the Mansion House Committee* (Dublin, Dollard Printing House, 1898).

Tod, Isabella, M.S., 'Boarding-out of Pauper Children', *Journal of the Statistical and Social Inquiry Society of Ireland*, vii (Aug. 1878) 293–9

—— 'The Place of Women in the Administration of the Irish Poor Law', *The Englishwoman's Review*, ciii (15 Nov. 1881), 481–89

Tuke, J.H., *Irish Distress and its Remedies... A Visit to Donegal and*

Connaught in the Spring of 1880 (London, W. Ridgway, 1880).
[Woodlock, Ellen], 'St Joseph's Industrial Institute with Special Reference to its Intern Class of Workhouse Orphans', *Irish Quarterly Review*, xxxii (Jan. 1859)

Secondary works

Aalen, Frederick H.A., 'The Rehousing of Rural Labourers in Ireland under the Labourers (Ireland) Acts, 1883–1919', *Journal of Historical Geography*, 12, 3 (1986), 287–306
Bellamy, Christine, *Administering Central–Local Relations, 1871–1919: The Local Government Board in its Fiscal and Cultural Context* (Manchester, Manchester University Press, 1988)
Burke, Helen, *The People and the Poor Law in Nineteenth Century Ireland* (Littlehampton, The Women's Education Bureau, 1987)
Brundage, Anthony, *The English Poor Laws, 1700–1930* (Basingstoke, Palgrave, 2002)
Cassell, Ronald D., *Medical Charities, Medical Politics: The Irish Dispensary System and the Poor Law 1836–1872* (Woodbridge, Boydell Press, 1997)
Crossman, Virginia, *Local Government in Nineteenth-Century Ireland* (Belfast, Institute of Irish Studies, 1994)
—— 'The New Ross Workhouse Riot of 1887: Nationalism, Class and the Irish Poor Laws', *Past and Present*, 179 (May 2003), 135–58.
—— '"With the Experience of 1846 and 1847 Before Them": The Politics of Emergency Relief 1879–84', in Gray, Peter (ed.), *Victoria's Ireland? Irishness and Britishness, 1837–1901* (Dublin, Four Courts Press, 2004), pp. 167–82.
—— 'The Charm of Allowing People to Manage their Own Affairs: Political Perspectives on Emergency Relief in Late Nineteenth-century Ireland', in Boyce, D.G. and O'Day, Alan (eds), *Ireland in Transition 1867–1921* (London, Routledge, 2004), pp 193–208
—— 'Viewing Women, Family and Sexuality through the Prism of the Irish Poor Laws', *Women's History Review*, forthcoming.
Cullen, Frank, *Cleansing Rural Dublin: Public Health and Housing Initiatives in the South Dublin Poor Law Union, 1880–1920* (Dublin, Irish Academic Press, 2001)

Daly, Mary E., *The Buffer State: The Historical Roots of the Department of the Environment Institute of Public Administration* (Dublin, Institute of Public Administration, 1997)

—— (ed.), *County and Town: One Hundred Years of Local Government in Ireland* (Dublin, IPA, 2001)

Dickson, David, 'In Search of the Old Irish Poor Law', in Mitchison, Rosalind and Roebuck, Peter (eds), *Economy and Society in Scotland and Ireland 1500–1939* (Edinburgh, John Donald Publishers Ltd., 1988), pp. 149–59

Feingold, William L., 'The Tenants' Movement to Capture the Irish Poor Law Boards, 1877–1886', *Albion*, vii, 3 (1975), 216–31

—— 'Land League Power: The Tralee Poor-Law Election of 1881', in Clark, Samuel and Donnelly, J.S., jr. (eds), *Irish Peasants: Violence and Political Unrest, 1780–1914* (Manchester, Manchester University Press, 1983), pp. 285–310

—*The Revolt of the Tenantry: The Transformation of Local Government in Ireland 1872–1886* (Boston, Mass., Northeastern University Press, 1984)

Fraser, Murray, *John Bull's Other Homes: State Housing and British Policy in Ireland, 1883–1922* (Liverpool, Liverpool University Press, 1996)

Harris, John S., *British Government Inspection: The Local Services and the Central Departments* (London, Stevens and Sons, 1955)

Innes, Joanna, 'The Distinctiveness of the English Poor Laws, 1750–1850', in Winch, Donald and O'Brien, Patrick K. (eds) *The Political Economy of British Historical Experience, 1688–1914* (Oxford, British Academy/Oxford University Press, 2002), pp. 381–408

Kidd, Alan, *State, Society and the Poor in Nineteenth-Century England* (Basingstoke, Macmillan, 1999)

Kinealy, Christine, *This Great Calamity: The Irish Famine 1845–52* (Dublin, Gill and Macmillan, 1994)

King, Steven, *Poverty and Welfare in England 1700–1850: A Regional Perspective* (Manchester, Manchester University Press, 2000)

Legg, Marie-Louise, *Newspapers and Nationalism: The Irish Provincial Press 1850–1892* (Dublin, Four Courts Press, 1999)

Lees, Lynn Hollen, *The Solidarities of Strangers: The English Poor Laws and the People, 1700–1948* (Cambridge, Cambridge University Press, 1998)

Luddy, Maria,*Women and Philanthropy in Nineteenth-Century Ireland* (Cambridge, Cambridge University Press, 1995)

—— '"Angels of Mercy": Nuns as Workhouse Nurses, 1861–1898', in Malcolm, Elizabeth and Jones, Greta (eds), *Medicine, Disease and the State in Ireland, 1650–1940* (Cork, Cork University Press, 1999), pp. 102–17

McKay, Enda, 'The Housing of the Rural Labourer, 1881–1916', *Saothar*, 17 (1992), 27–39

McLoughlin, Dympna, 'Workhouses and Irish Female Paupers, 1840–70', in Luddy and Murphy (eds), *Women Surviving: Studies in Irish Women's History in the Nineteenth and Twentieth Centuries* (Dublin, Poolbeg, 1990), pp. 117–47

Mitchison, Rosalind, 'Permissive Poor Laws: the Irish and Scottish Systems Considered Together', in Connolly, S.J., Houston, R.A. and Morris, R.J. (eds), *Conflict, Identity and Economic Development: Ireland and Scotland, 1600–1939* (Preston, Carnegie Publishing, 1995), pp. 161–71

O'Brien, Gerard, 'The Establishment of Poor-law Unions in Ireland, 1838–43', *Irish Historical Studies*, 23, 90 (November 1982), 97–120

—— 'A Question of Attitude: Responses to the New Poor Law in Ireland and Scotland', in Mitchison, Rosalind, and Roebuck, Peter (eds), *Economy and Society in Scotland and Ireland 1500–1939* (Edinburgh, John Donald Publishers Ltd., 1988), pp 160–70

Ó Gráda, Cormac, *Ireland: A New Economic History 1780–1939* (Oxford, Clarendon Press, 1994)

O'Neill, Timothy P., 'The Food Crisis of the 1890s', in E. Margaret Crawford (ed.), *Famine: The Irish Experience 900–1900. Subsistence Crises and Famines in Ireland* (Edinburgh, John Donald, 1989), pp. 176–97

—— 'Minor Famines and Relief in Galway 1815–1925', in Moran, Gerald (ed.), *Galway: History and Society* (Dublin, Geography Publications, 1996), pp. 445–86

Robins, Joseph, *The Lost Children: A Study of Charity Children in Ireland 1700–1900* (Dublin, Institute of Public Administration, 1980)

Urquhart, Diane, *Women in Ulster Politics 1890–1940* (Dublin, Irish Academic Press, 2000)

Vaughan, W.E., *A New History of Ireland. v. Ireland under the*

Union, I, 1801–70 (Oxford, Clarendon Press, 1989)

—— *Landlords and Tenants in Mid-Victorian Ireland* (Oxford, Clarendon Press, 1994)

—— *A New History of Ireland. vi. Ireland Under the Union, II, 1870–1921* (Oxford, Clarendon Press, 1996)

Index